Software Copyright Law

Fourth Edition

David Bainbridge BSc, LLB, PhD, CEng, MICE, MBCS

Barrister

Butterworths
London, Edinburgh, Dublin
1999

United Kingdom	Butterworths, a Division of Reed Elsevier (UK) Ltd, Halsbury House, 35 Chancery Lane, London WC2A 1EL and 4 Hill Street, Edinburgh EH2 3JZ
Australia	Butterworths, a Division of Reed International Books Australia Pty Ltd, Chatswood, New South Wales
Canada	Butterworths Canada Ltd, Markham, Ontario
Hong Kong	Butterworths Asia (Hong Kong), Hong Kong
India	Butterworths India, New Delhi
Ireland	Butterworth (Ireland) Ltd, Dublin
Malaysia	Malayan Law Journal Sdn Bhd, Kuala Lumpur
New Zealand	Butterworths of New Zealand Ltd, Wellington
Singapore	Butterworths Asia, Singapore
South Africa	Butterworths Publishers (Pty) Ltd, Durban
USA	Lexis Law Publishing, Charlottesville, Virginia

© David Bainbridge (UK) Ltd 1999

A CIP Catalogue record for this book is available from the British Library.

ISBN 0 406 9218 49

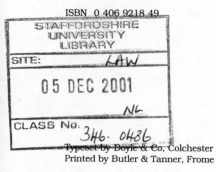
Typeset by Doyle & Co, Colchester
Printed by Butler & Tanner, Frome

Visit us at our website: http://www.butterworths.co.uk

Preface to the fourth edition

My interest in software copyright law arose in the early 1980s at a time when I was involved in the development of computer programs and databases. There were relatively few lawyers specialising in that field and only a handful of academics were interested in what was seen as area of little practical significance. At that time, the main issue was piracy of computer software such as applications software and computer games. This problem was exacerbated by the uncertain state of legal protection afforded to programs. Indeed, the problem of software piracy was itself a new phenomenon which had been fuelled by the development and spread of the personal computer. Before very long, computers, which had been viable proposition only for large and powerful organisations, came within the grasp (and expectation) of most children. Computers proliferated throughout schools small- and medium-sized businesses, and computer technology was incorporated into a wide variety of equipment and machines, ranging from the humble washing machine to complex industrial processes.

After much pressure from the computer industry, the law eventually caught up and the protection of computer programs was put beyond doubt. However, many issues remained to be resolved, such as the scope and extent of that protection; and case law, in the United Kingdom and elsewhere, gradually provided some indication of the boundaries of copyright protection for computer programs. The impact of European Community initiatives also became important and, after much controversy and lobbying, defined the extent to which programs could be decompiled for the purposes of writing 'interoperable' programs.

One of the most fascinating features of computer technology is the way in which it is constantly advancing at breakneck speed. The pace of change is so fast that, at best, the law can only provide solutions to what could be described as 'yesterday's problems'. The protection of computer programs is reasonably settled, though not without a number of unresolved uncertainties. But, more recently, the law has had to address the protection of forms of software other than computer programs. Computer databases provide an important example and developments in the United States cast some doubt as to the scope of copyright protection for such works. To address this problem, and to ensure that databases that were the result of investment were protected even though they might fail to attract copyright protection, further European responses have resulted in more changes to copyright law and the introduction of a new, *sui generis,* database right.

Multimedia articles such as CD-ROM and DVD have the capability of providing ready access to a great many works, all or most of which are likely to be subject to economic and moral rights under copyright law in addition to rights in performances. CD-ROMs can be mass-produced very cheaply and the problem of piracy, on an international scale, raises its head again. Worse still, from the copyright owner's point of view, is the growing use of networks, particularly the Internet, which pose many issues as to the scope of copyright law, its practical effectiveness and jurisdiction. The law is these areas is far from clear and it is likely that copyright will require further modification but this can only be effective if international cooperation on an impressive scale is achieved. As might be expected, the United States is a prime mover in this area but work has also been carried out by the World Intellectual Property Organisation and the European Commission. Further legislative change is to be expected in due course.

Software copyright law is no longer the province of a handful of technically minded lawyers. The consequences of the information revolution have been very significant. It is not unreasonable to claim that this phenomenon is the most important thing to happen since the invention of the printing press, as now the subject matter of this fascinating area of law is no longer restricted simply to computer programs. Any traditional work of copyright, whether it be a photograph, painting, music or film or, indeed, any other form of information can be represented digitally. That being so, computer software is all-embracing. Everything is software now and the law protecting it and constraining its use is of importance to us all. No lawyer can afford to ignore software copyright law, either in terms of providing advice and services to clients or in terms of being a user of computer software. The amount of information of use to lawyers currently available, for example, on the Internet, is very significant and is growing exponentially. Many firms of solicitors have their own Web pages on the Internet. Even if they are only a user of computer software, every lawyer needs to know the extent and nature of the use that he or she can make of computer software without infringing copyright or other legal rights.

Computer and information technology professionals developing, modifying and using computer software need to know about the impact and scope of copyright law as it applies to computer software. A large proportion of the litigation thus far in this field has indicated the difficulties that arise from a lack of understanding of the subject, particularly in the setting of the employment contract. The mobility of skilled software engineers, programmers and analysts is a feature of the software industry and it is all too easy to infringe copyright by making inappropriate use of materials created for another employer. But it is not simply a matter of knowing what not to do. To make full use of copyright law, some measure of proactivity is desirable, if not essential. For example, all sorts of problems are likely to arise if the ownership of copyright in software to be developed by a self-employed consultant or freelance programmer is not dealt with at the outset. Auditing the use of software is another important aspect, as is training and education in the practical implications of software copyright law.

The aim of this book is to provide an accessible description and insight into the practicalities of software copyright law. It is intended to be of practical application rather than being a dry academic study of the subject. Many of the examples in the book are modelled on real-life situations and it is hoped that the book will prove useful to lawyers and computer professionals alike.

The layout of this book has been set out so as to provide the reader with an understanding of the basic principles of copyright law before looking in detail at copyright as it applies to computer software. Following a comprehensive description of copyright law and a look at developments in the United States, aspects such as the scope of copyright protection, literal and non-literal copying and reverse analysis are considered. There are chapters on two issues of particular current concern relating to the protection of databases and copyright in the context of electronic publishing, including multimedia and the Internet. The remainder of the book covers ownership of copyright in computer software and the ways in which it may be exploited, the nature and meaning of computer-generated works, modifications to computer programs by users, and semiconductor protection. The Appendices contain the full text of the European Directives on the legal protection of computer programs and the legal protection of databases. There are also some annotated extracts from the Copyright, Designs and Patents Act 1988, as amended, and the Copyright and Rights in Databases Regulations 1997 and a 'navigator's guide' to the parts of the 1998 Act and the Regulations of particular relevance to computer software.

I wish to thank all those who have contributed, directly or indirectly, to the writing and publication of this book. I have learnt so much from others, whether they be lawyers or computer professionals. In particular, my wife Sylvia deserves special mention for her patience and support. The law as stated in this book is as I understand it to be at 1 August 1999.

David I Bainbridge
August 1999

As a result of the Civil Procedure Rules 1998, which came into force on 26 April 1999, the plaintiff in a legal action is now known as the claimant. Readers should be aware of this if they refer to cases where proceedings commenced on or after that date.

Preface to the first edition

The information technology revolution is proving to be as powerful a catalyst for change as the industrial revolution was around two centuries ago. Working practices, leisure activities and even society itself are steadily being transformed by the introduction and spread of computers and information technology. The first wave of change was heralded by the development of the mainframe computer bringing greater efficiency and the ability to process vast amounts of data; initially, the computer was simply a powerful data processing machine which used specially written computer programs. It was so expensive to buy, operate and maintain that only the largest organisations could contemplate having one and, consequently, the need for legal protection of computer software was not an urgent matter. However, phenomenal improvements in hardware technology changed all that and paved the way for the second wave of the information technology revolution. Before long, computer technology was within the grasp of small businesses and even private individuals. The power of personal computers grew rapidly whilst the cost of acquiring them shrank dramatically. Other technological developments such as the ability to link computers together, locally and remotely, in networks increased the flexibility and usefulness of computers. From a few dozen computers in the mid 1950s, the world population of computers now runs into many millions.

No matter how impressive the hardware technology, computers must have computer software to be of any use.

Computer software is a term which can be taken to include computer programs, databases, computer stored or generated documents and information and, also, the documentation which accompanies or is associated with these items. The massive growth in the numbers of computers around and their power created an almost insatiable hunger for computer software. Alas, much of this newly-created demand was fed by unauthorised copying of available software, often referred to as computer software piracy. The computer software industry, which had grown very quickly to meet the demand for new and better software, soon felt itself threatened by the scale of piracy. Without effective and enforceable legal protection, the incentives to develop new computer software or to invest in this would be lacking and any software which was produced for the marketplace would be highly priced as a result of low sales volumes.

One problem for the software industry was the perceived lack of legal measures to combat unauthorised copying and piracy together with the apparent indifference of legislators to the plight of software producers. There was a period, from the late 1970s to the mid 1980s, when computer software was left to fend for itself and software companies could only try to protect their investment through the contracts they had made with persons and organisations acquiring their products. Eventually, in some cases at a frustratingly pedestrian pace, copyright laws in most of the world's developed countries were examined and, where necessary, extended to protect computer software and the first battle had been won. However, the campaign is far from over and many secondary issues have now raised their heads. The strength and scope of copyright protection for computer software is of such fundamental importance that it requires detailed and careful consideration requiring a fundamental reappraisal of the philosophy and rationale of copyright law. Most people now accept the desirability of protecting computer software from unauthorised copying but there is much disagreement about how far copyright protection should extend and this remains a difficult point.

Copyright law, like other forms of intellectual property law, does not give rise to absolute rights but carefully circumscribes the property in the subject matter of the right. There is a requirement to balance such rights and reconcile them with the position and needs of others such as the general public and even existing and potential competitors. A cardinal principle of copyright law is that it does not support monopolies and, consequently, the independent creation of a similar work does not infringe the right in the first work. Copyright law can be seen in the context of balancing the protection given to creators of works including computer software with the wider interests of society, permitting 'fair' competition. It is in this respect that much still lies to be resolved for computer software, especially as to what may or may not be done by a potential competitor without infringing copyright. For example, can the competitor study and examine computer software with the intention of making use of the ideas contained within it? Can screen displays, program structure and program function be copied and, if so, where does lawful use of another's software end and illegal use start? The special nature of computer software means that answers to these questions require an appreciation of copyright law and a good grasp of computer science and software engineering. We have relatively little judicial guidance on these points and what there is varies in its quality.

The aim of this book is to describe the law relating to copyright protection of computer software, dealing in particular with computer programs and other works created by computer or stored in a computer. The book concentrates on the limits of copyright protection and the boundaries between what is permitted and what is prohibited by copyright law. Interspersed within the text of the book are descriptions and discussions of legal cases and practical examples which are intended to provide food for thought for persons and organisations developing or owning computer software.

The layout of this book is designed to provide the reader with an understanding of the basic principles of copyright law before looking in detail at computer software copyright. Following a comprehensive description of copyright law and computer software and a look at developments in the United States, particular aspects are considered such as the scope of copyright protection, the meaning and permissibility of reverse analysis, the ownership of copyright in computer software and the ways in which it may be exploited, the nature and meaning of computer-generated works, modifications of computer programs by users and semi–conductor protection. Where appropriate, the implications of the European Council Directive on the legal protection of computer programs are discussed. The main United Kingdom legislation concerning computer software copyright is the Copyright, Designs and Patents Act 1988 and throughout the book references are made to this Act. However, to improve the clarity of discourse and to avoid undue complexity resulting from a mass of cross-referencing, specific references to sections and subsections to the Act are omitted. Towards the end of the book is a 'navigator's guide' to the parts of the Act relevant to computer software for those readers who wish to examine the Act's provisions in detail.

This book is intended to be of use to computer professionals, particularly those engaged in the development and commercial exploitation of computer software and those concerned with the extent and limitations of copyright protection for software. It should also prove useful for those who are responsible for acquiring and operating computer software or engaging staff and consultants to develop or modify computer software systems. Persons using computer software to create their own new works will find the chapters on authorship, ownership and computer-generated works to be particularly helpful. Practising lawyers dealing with computer software copyright matters should find the book to be of practical assistance and students of law or computer science investigating this fascinating area of copyright law should be stimulated by the discussion of cases and examples in the text.

I wish to thank all those who have contributed, directly or indirectly, to the writing and publication of this book. In particular, my wife Sylvia deserves special mention for her patience and support. The law as stated in this book is as I understand it to be at 1 March 1992.

David I Bainbridge
March 1992

Contents

Table of legislation

Table of cases

W

List of figures

Chapter 1

Introduction and overview of copyright law

COMPUTER SOFTWARE

The phrase 'computer software' is commonly used to describe computer programs and ancillary materials. It has no precise meaning and has never been defined in United Kingdom legislation, which is just as well because the rapid rate of change, and the introduction of new developments in the field of computer science, would quickly date static legal definitions. Nor is the definition of 'computer program' attempted in any Act of Parliament although some minor definitions exist in statutory instruments, none of which is relevant to copyright law. However, for the purposes of this book, it is important to state what is intended to fall within the meaning of computer software.

A starting point is to consider computer software as a collection of items and materials associated with the development and operation of a computer program, but which does not include computer hardware. Computer hardware comprises the physical, tangible pieces of mechanical and electronic equipment necessary to, or ancillary to, the operation of the software. The following examples should help to elaborate the meanings.

Computer software

- Preparatory design materials, eg flowcharts, diagrams, specifications, form and report layouts, designs for screen displays, etc

- Computer programs (object code and source code) and other executable code
- Software development tools, eg relational database development systems, compilers, report generators, etc
- Information stored on computer media, eg conventional works such as literature, artistic works, music, etc, stored digitally
- Databases and data files
- Computer output, eg sound, print-out, computer file or data, electronic signals
- Screen displays
- Manuals and guides (on paper or stored digitally)
- Programming languages

Computer hardware

- Computers
- Monitors and display devices
- Printers
- Disk drives
- CD-ROM readers
- Modems
- Cabling
- Computer mouse, etc

To this, one proviso must be added. Computer hardware often includes software, especially in the form of programs permanently stored in computers, computer equipment and other devices. Start-up and bootstrap programs (the programs which operate automatically upon switching on a computer, setting it up so that it is then able to operate other computer programs) are often 'hard wired' in a computer, permanently stored in integrated circuits. The same applies to some disk operating system programs. Hard wired programs are still classed as computer software for the purposes of this book. In the United States of America, it has been held that such programs, sometimes referred to as microprograms or microcode, fall within the meaning of 'computer program'. (Unlike the position in the United Kingdom, the United States Copyright Act defines this phrase, being 'a set of statements or instructions to be used directly or indirectly in a computer to bring about a certain result'.) Some commentators decided that these programs (and other information permanently hard-wired in a computer chip) should be called 'firmware'. However, this has no significance apart from distinguishing the form of storage although judges have sometimes, incorrectly, considered the method of storage to be important in the appropriateness of various forms of protection. A computer program does not cease to be a computer program because it is stored in an integrated circuit.

Figure 1.1 shows some of the items falling within the meaning of computer software and how they are connected in a creative sense. The program itself is considered to be in two forms, the source code (the original form of the program written in a computer programming language) and the object code (the program converted into the machine language of the computer's central processing unit).

Figure 1.1 Computer software items

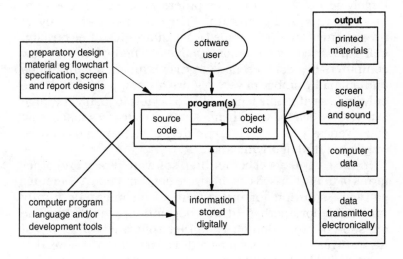

INTELLECTUAL PROPERTY LAW AND COMPUTER SOFTWARE

Intellectual property law is that area of law which is concerned with the protection of ideas, the expression of ideas, invention and commercial goodwill. It includes copyright law, the law of patents, breach of confidence, design law, trade mark law and the law of passing-off. Being concerned with innovation, intellectual property law has needed occasional modification and enlargement so that it could keep pace with technological change and new discoveries. But never has the challenge to law been so great as that provided by computer software. This challenge has not been restricted to intellectual property law, but has been felt in relation to criminal law, the laws of contract and tort, and the law of evidence.

A few years after the development of the programmable computer in the mid-1940s, questions were being asked as to how this new form of creative work, the computer program, should be protected against unauthorised copying. Initially, this was not a serious practical problem and the question was largely academic because computers were very expensive to buy, operate and maintain. They required an army of programmers and consumed vast quantities of electricity, being powered by thermionic valves. There were very few computers in existence, and large government organisations and a small number of very big private companies were the only bodies with sufficient wealth to be able to justify the large expense associated with them. Another factor was that of cost effectiveness which made computers a viable proposition for only a handful of organisations.

In the early days of computing, software piracy and other forms of unauthorised copying were not common. A computer software solution for one organisation might be totally unsuitable for another. It was not until the 1970s that the question of protection for computer software became a real issue. This could be seen as a direct result of the spread of computers, both mainframe and mini-computers, to much greater numbers of users. At that time typical issues were whether computer software should be protected by copyright law, which protects the tangible expression of creative works such as literary, musical and artistic works, or the stronger monopolistic protection afforded by patent law for new inventions. Later, the protection of computer software became a matter of very substantial concern following the computer population explosion brought about by the advent of the personal computer.

The problem of protecting computer software

The pervasiveness of computers has brought many problems relating to the legal protection of computer software. Of course, whether a particular unauthorised use is deemed to be unfair may be a matter of opinion. Many persons and organisations creating computer software consider any use made of their software without permission to be unfair and that all unauthorised use ought to be made illegal. However, intellectual property law, including copyright law, is also concerned with striking a balance between competing interests and with limiting the rights of owners within reasonable bounds and, hence, absolute control and protection is not granted to copyright owners.

At this stage, it is worthwhile considering some of the particular issues of concern to those involved in the development, exploitation and use of computer software.

- What use can an ex-employee make of his previous employer's computer programs and other materials? Is an ex-employee permitted to create a computer program which performs the same function as one he or she had previously written for a previous employer?
- Can a new program be written which performs the same function as an existing program?
- Of all the things which make up computer software, which are protected by copyright law?
- What is the scope of protection? Are items such as screen displays, the structure of programs and files, menu command systems, icons, etc, protected?
- Can reverse analysis be performed on a computer program in order to find out how it works or how it interfaces with other programs or hardware? Can the information thus obtained be used to make a new computer program?

- Are databases and other works stored digitally protected by copyright?
- Are areas of law other than copyright law relevant?
- In practice, how is new software created without infringing rights in existing software which performs the same function?
- What is the position of software on the Internet and who is liable for infringement of copyright of software?

The following example is intended to form a platform or reference point to assist the reader in the consideration of legal issues associated with the protection of computer software described in the book. It involves most of the issues described above and concerns a fictitious person and company, Betty Bliss and Zenith Construction plc. It is adapted from a real life situation. At the end of the book some solutions to Betty's quandary are suggested in the form of advice as to how she can develop a rival computer system without infringing copyright or being liable for breach of other legal duties. The scenario reflects the types of problems that recur so frequently in software development.

Example

Betty Bliss worked for Zenith Construction plc as an estimator responsible for working out the cost of new building projects so that Zenith could submit quotations or bids (tenders) for these projects. A considerable amount of work, skill and experience is required to calculate the cost of constructing a large building such as a new supermarket, theatre, or warehouse, and to decide on other factors such as the risk involved and the desired profit.

Betty became interested in computer programming and took a course at evening classes. She realised that much of the estimating work done at Zenith would lend itself to computerisation and, in her spare time, she wrote some small programs to assist in the calculation of the cost of certain elements of building work, for example, the cost of a brick wall per square metre. She demonstrated her small programs, which were written in the BASIC programming language, to some of the directors of Zenith who were very impressed.

They allowed Betty time off from her estimating duties to convert the programs so that they would operate on the company's microcomputers (which used a different version of BASIC). There was no mention of payment over and above Betty's normal salary and she was pleased to do the work because of her new found interest in computers. The programs were used by other estimators who found them to be very useful and time-saving.

The directors of Zenith were contemplating acquiring a computer system to deal with the whole estimate for building projects. They evaluated the few available systems but found them lacking in one or more respects. Therefore, they asked Betty if she could write a prototype system to explore the possibility of producing a system 'in-house'. Betty agreed to try and, in a few months, developed a working prototype which was tested successfully to work out the cost of a small building project. It was written in BASIC. The system used computer files, a database of work items (WORK ITEM FILE) and the resources required, a separate database of resources (RESOURCE FILE) and a database containing the quantities of items (QUANTITIES FILE) which form the building. It was intended that the estimators using the system would go through the QUANTITIES FILE, assigning appropriate work items from the WORK ITEM FILE, making any modifications deemed necessary. Sometimes, if no appropriate item existed in the WORK ITEM FILE, the estimator would have to build up a new item using the RESOURCE FILE. In this way, the whole estimate of cost was built up. A major advantage of the system over the manual methods was that several new and useful reports were now available.

The directors and estimators were, on the whole, impressed by the system. The directors decided to sanction the development of a complete system and they asked Betty to liaise with the Computer Department which converted the program to run on a network of computers allowing multiple file access for concurrent use. The full system was written in COBOL and comprised 75 programs and the databases. It was a menu-driven system. Suggestions for additions to the databases and improvements to the system were dealt with by a committee which included Betty. Those suggestions which were approved were incorporated in the COBOL programs. During the two years that it took to develop the full COBOL system, Betty was given some substantial salary increases. Her original written contract of employment was not modified expressly.

Realising that there was a demand in the building industry for an effective estimating system, Betty decided to leave Zenith and set up a small software company. She engaged a COBOL programmer, recently graduated from University, to carry out the programming work involved in developing a complete estimating system, and to improve the small programs originally written by Betty. However, Betty is unsure what use she can make of the ideas and materials she had access to at Zenith. She has retained her original BASIC programs on disk. She has parts of the specification for the COBOL system such as screen layouts, flowcharts and file structures. She also has a print-out of the WORK ITEM and RESOURCE databases which contain some thousands of records. Betty also has an object code version of the COBOL programs but she does not have a source code version nor a printed listing of the COBOL programs.

Betty may be tempted to make as much use as possible of the materials she has retained. Copyright issues concern the ownership of her early BASIC programs, whether and to what extent the databases are protected by copyright, whether the object code programs can be decompiled to find useful information concerning the methods employed and interfaces of the COBOL programs. Other copyright issues relate to the 'non-literal' elements of the COBOL programs such as the general structure of the programs, the menu command system, screen displays and file structures. The law of breach of confidence must also be taken into account, particularly in respect of the techniques used and the contents of the databases. We will return to Betty towards the end of Chapter 12.

Why protect computer software?

That computer software should be protected from being copied or otherwise used without permission is not an unchallengeable axiom, and it is important to consider the reasons why software should be protected by the law. If software is developed for use by only one person or by a very restricted class of persons, the need for legal protection may be largely irrelevant. Perhaps the software is useful only to the person who wrote or commissioned it and it would not be of interest to others. For example, if an angling club has a computer program which helps in the organisation of fishing matches based on the club's rules which are unlike those of any other angling club, there would be little point in other clubs copying the program. There is no market for the program. In other cases, it may be possible to keep details of the software secret. However, most software does have a market value and others will find it useful and be anxious to acquire a copy of it. The owner of the software will face two problems; first, some potential users will want to copy the software without payment (or acquire a single-user licence and then copy the programs rather than paying for a multiple-user licence). The second problem is that competitors will wish to examine the software closely so that they can make competing products. In both of these cases, the owner's economic interests are at risk and this gives a clue to some important justifications for copyright law (and some other forms of intellectual property law such as patent law and the law of designs).

Justifications for the legal protection of computer software

The following justifications for the legal protection of computer software may be put forward.

- Economic reasons: a person who has expended time and effort in creating computer software should be given the opportunity to reap an economic reward; this will encourage people to be creative. Investment will also be stimulated by the promise of legal protection bearing in mind that investment in the development of computer software can be substantial and, even with strong legal protection, resulting profit is not assured. The increase in creative work and investment will have the effect of benefiting society by increasing and stimulating employment, technical development, commercial growth and wealth.

• Moral reasons: a person who has created computer software (as with any other creative work) has a paternal (or maternal) bond with the software. It is his or hers and, morally, belongs to that person. It is an item of property that the person has brought into existence. He or she should, therefore, be able to prevent other persons exploiting the software without permission, and be able to control its subsequent use.

• By acknowledging the economic and moral rights in software and thus encouraging creativity, innovation and investment, the total store of human knowledge is enriched. By limiting the legal protection in time and in scope, knowledge is disseminated and made available to the public at large. Some might argue that the person creating the work in question, whether it be computer software or music or poetry, etc, should own legal rights in the work in perpetuity (the work owes its very existence to that person). However, the law has a ingrained dislike of perpetual ownership which caused problems in previous times by allowing landowners to tie up parcels of land for long periods of time. Because land is finite, this led to a shortage, especially at the time of the industrial revolution. However, unlike land, the totality of innovative ideas is not finite.

There are some arguments against giving legal protection to creative works and inventions, for example because it stifles competition and allows the owner of the work or invention to charge exorbitant prices and to make a profit out of proportion to the investment and risks undertaken. Those who make such claims suggest that the owner still has certain advantages in the absence of legal protection. The owner is able to get his or her product into the market place before any competitors. The owner has the advantage of a 'lead-time', the time taken to set up the necessary manufacturing capability and to produce and distribute products. This lead-time could, in terms of computer hardware, be several months and, during this period, the originator will be able to charge a premium. However, for computer software, the lead-time can be very small and significant numbers of copies of computer programs and accompanying documentation could be mass-produced in a matter of days.

If the software is placed on the Internet, the lead-time is, in effect, zero. In any case, the lead-time argument fails to address the costs associated with research and development (including market research and testing). These costs can account for a considerable proportion of the final price of the product concerned and this is so in the computer industry. The costs are also high in the pharmaceuticals industry where a new drug can cost millions of pounds to develop and test yet be produced for a few pence per pill. The final price must reflect these indirect costs and, without legal protection, a competitor would easily be able to undercut the original developer of the drug. All incentive to develop new drugs would disappear overnight, and the same is largely true in terms of computer software. The large scale of computer software piracy which occurred in the early to mid-1980s was a good example of this and may have contributed to the failure of a number of software companies and the relatively high prices then asked for legitimate software.

On the whole, it is clear that effective legal protection is in everyone's best interests, provided that it is not too strong. Protection should be such as to provide for a fair return on investment, and in terms of the effort associated with the development of new software products and the enhancement of existing software. Protection should not be so strong as to stifle competition (in the past, competition has been a great stimulus to the rate of improvement in the quality, power and availability of computer software). A software company which markets poor quality software should not be able to succeed because it has monopoly control of its market. Having said this, it lies to determine the most appropriate form of legal protection for computer software.

Form of protection for computer software

Two contrasting forms of intellectual property rights which could be used to protect computer software are patent law and copyright law. Other forms of protection might be relevant, for example, the law of contract, design law, the law of breach of confidence and trade mark law. Design law includes two forms of rights, one which is similar in nature to patent law (registered designs) whilst the other is more akin to copyright (the design right). Design law will be discussed in Chapter 11 because a modified form of the design right is used to give protection to semiconductor products. Figure 1.2 indicates the potential forms of legal protection of computer software (especially computer programs), the width of the linking arrows gives a general measure of the relative frequency of each form of protection. Copyright will protect all but the most trivial computer programs. Patent law can protect software inventions providing the software produces or has the potential to produce a 'further technical effect' and design law may provide indirect protection of programs stored on integrated circuits.

Figure 1.2 Forms of legal protection for computer programs

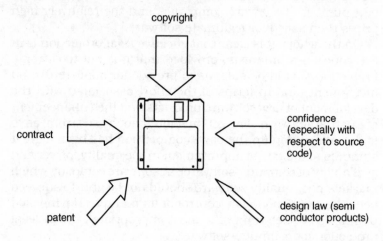

The law of breach of confidence frequently works as a supplement to other rights, it is an ally both to copyright law and, in the early stages, to patent law. It is, therefore, most appropriate to consider and contrast patent law and copyright law. During the 1970s, there was a considerable debate as to which of these two forms of protection was the most appropriate for computer software. In some quarters, the debate still rages on!

Patents are granted for inventions which are new, involve an inventive step, and are capable of industrial application. A patent gives its proprietor (owner) a monopoly to work the invention for a period of time up to a maximum of 20 years. Patents are the oldest and strongest form of intellectual property as we know it today and, consequently, strict formalities have to be complied with. There is a rigorous examination procedure where the scope of the patent claims is tested, and searches are made for anticipation of the invention by others. The application for a patent will be thoroughly examined for compliance with the legislative requirements. Often, a patent will be valid in a number of countries depending on which were selected by the proprietor during the application process. The European Patent Convention and the Patent Co-operation Treaty exist to facilitate obtaining patents in a number of countries. Obtaining a patent is an expensive and lengthy process and the more countries involved, the greater the cost, but this has to be balanced against the strength of protection thus gained. Because of the strong protection afforded by patent law, there are several controls on the abuse of the monopoly arising from statute law, common law and European Community and United Kingdom competition law.

In contrast, copyright law does not give rise to monopolies. At least, in principle, it should not do so. However, where the information comprised in the copyright work is available only to the copyright owner, a monopoly might arise. This was so in *RTE & ITP v EC Commission* [1995] FSR 530 where it was held that refusal to make available in advance details of television programme schedules was an abuse of a dominant trading position under Article 82 of the EC Treaty (the Treaty of Rome 1957). Nevertheless, this is the exception rather than the rule and, in most cases, the information on which a copyright work is based may be independently acquired by others. An example is a database containing names and addresses of practising solicitors.

A general, though not entirely precise maxim, is that copyright law does not protect ideas, but it does protect the expression of ideas. Thus, copyright law will not protect a generalised idea for a story but it will give remedies against persons who copy from a book of the story without permission. Copyright law does not prevent the *independent* creation of a new work which is similar to a pre-existing work. In this way, copyright law protects the skill and judgment which goes into the creation of a work, including most elements of computer software, without locking away the basic ideas underlying the work. In terms of a computer program which performs a particular function, others will be permitted to create their own programs to perform the same function as long as they do so without copying the original program or certain features of that original program. Indeed, the second program will have its own copyright protection. Copyright protects the computer program without protecting the idea of writing a computer program to fulfil a particular function. (The law of confidence can protect the idea if the function performed is secret; see later in this chapter.)

Of these two forms of protection, patent and copyright, the leading industrial countries of the world agreed upon the latter as being most appropriate for computer software and, in particular, computer programs. Some commentators had argued for a short-term patent protection for a maximum period of up to seven years, but it was generally felt that copyright secured the best compromise between protection and competition. This was reinforced by suggestions that computer programs were probably already protected by copyright as literary works and the world has chosen the copyright path to protection. Notwithstanding this and the fact that computer programs and other items of computer software are generally excluded from patents, it is possible to obtain a patent for an invention which includes a programmed computer if there is a technical effect and the application is directed towards the technical effect rather than the computer program. Section 1(2) of the Patents Act 1977 states that a computer program, *inter alia*, is not patentable 'as such'.

Section 1 of the Patents Act 1977 is based on Article 52 of the European Patent Convention (one of the main purposes of the 1977 Act was to bring United Kingdom patent law in line with that under the Convention which extends to all the Member States of the European Community in addition to some other European countries). As the exclusion on computer programs (and other excluded matter including mathematical methods, discoveries, schemes, rules or methods for performing mental acts and the presentation of information) is stated to apply only in as much as the application for the patent relates to that thing 'as such', there is scope for patenting computer programs. However, the invention claimed must go beyond simply claiming a computer program on its own.

Case

Vicom Systems Inc's Patent Application [1987] 2 EPOR 74

An application to the European Patent Office concerned an invention related to digital image processing carried out under the control of a programmed computer. Because the claim was directed towards the technical process it was not regarded as relating to a computer program as such. It was the process for which the protection of patent law was sought. Consequently, the application was allowed to proceed. It was said that it made no difference whether the image being processed was that of a physical entity or an image stored as an electronic signal.

Because the United Kingdom Patents Act 1977 is equivalent in most respects to the European Patent Convention (one of the aims of the Convention was to harmonise patent law in Member States) this case represents good law here and has been approved of and applied by the courts in the United Kingdom.

Case law before the European Patent Office's Boards of Appeals indicates that there must be some 'further technical effect' for the software invention to be patentable in principle. This does not include electronic currents generated in the computer during the operation of the computer. In *Computer*

Program Product II/IBM, 4 February 1999, the Board of Appeal confirmed that a software invention may be patentable if the further technical effects themselves have a technical character or where they cause the software to solve a technical problem.

This is potentially quite wide but it must be remembered that the other requirements for the grant of a patent must be fulfilled, being that the invention is new, involves an inventive step and is capable of industrial application. A great many software items will not be patentable for lack of novelty or because they are not inventive. For example, if a computer programmer decides to automate a simple manual task, if this would have been obvious to skilled programmers at the time, it will not be patentable. It may be that other programmers had considered the possibility and decided it was not worthwhile.

Outside Europe, patents may be more readily obtained for software inventions, for example, in the United States of America and Japan. Indeed, the Agreement on the Trade-Related Aspects of Intellectual Property Rights (TRIPS Agreement); administered by the World Trade Organisation, appears to allow software patents as Article 27(1) of the Agreement states that '. . . patents shall be available for any inventions, whether products or processes, *in all fields of technology* provided they are new, involve an inventive step and are capable of industrial application' (emphasis added). The Agreement has no express limitation on the patenting of computer programs 'as such'.

Where a software invention does produce the desired further technical effect or method, it is possible to claim that effect or method, the programmed computer which produces it and, as a result of the *IBM* case mentioned above, a 'computer program product' (for example, a computer program stored on an integrated circuit) which has the potential to produce the effect or method when run on a computer.

Often, the question of obtaining a patent will not be relevant as the operation of a computer program will have no significant further technical effect. The same applies as regards other items of software such as databases from which information is simply retrieved and displayed. It is unlikely that a programmed computer which operates a conventional printer will be deemed to have a technical effect for patent law purposes. An application to obtain a patent on a method of calculating square roots by means of a computer program stored in a read-only memory (ROM) chip was rejected by the Court of Appeal as being unpatentable; *Re Gale's Patent Application* [1991] RPC 305. The effect was entirely software based and the fact that the program was stored on an integrated circuit did not alter this finding.

Other things apart from computer programs are expressly excluded from the grant of a patent and can reduce the possibility of obtaining a patent for a software product. For example, the presentation of information as such is excluded, as is a scheme, rule or method for performing a mental act. This latter exclusion potentially is very wide-ranging as the following case shows.

Case

Fujitsu Ltd's Application [1997] RPC 610

Fujitsu applied to patent a method and apparatus to be used for modelling the synthetic structure of inorganic chemical compounds. The operator used a programmed computer to manipulate a visual representation of two crystal structures allowing them to be combined to produce a new 'designer' chemical. A patent for the invention had previously been granted in Japan.

At first instance ([1996] RPC 511), it was held in the Patents Court that the application was for a method of performing a mental act. Although a programmed computer could be patentable by virtue of the process it carried out, it was necessary to consider the nature of the process itself and, if all that entailed was the performance of one of the excluded activities, the invention was not patentable. Here, the programmed computer simply enabled the operator to exercise mental skill and assessment. As such it was in substance a scheme or method of performing a mental act. The Court of Appeal confirmed that, to be patentable, there had to be a technical contribution. This was so even in the presence of excluded matter such as a computer program. However, determining what was and what was not a technical contribution was not an easy task and depended on the facts of each case. In the present case, the application was for a computer program as such. The invention used a conventional computer to do what was previously done using physical models made from plastic. The only technical advance was that using a computer enabled the result to be displayed more quickly and this is just the sort of advantage that is obtained by the application of a computer program. The Court of Appeal also said that the application related to a method of performing a mental act as such.

Patents remain available for technical effects which are not themselves excluded and which may be produced by the operation of a programmed computer, but it is the effect which is protected by patent law rather than the program itself which remains within the province of copyright law. However, copying the program and putting it to use probably will infringe the patent also by replicating the technical effect. Nevertheless, copyright law is the main vehicle for the protection of computer programs and other items of computer software. In only a handful of cases will a patent be a possibility and, even here, expert advice should be sought, as the patent specification and claims must be drawn up very carefully. This book concentrates on copyright law with references to the law of breach of confidence where relevant, as this sometimes provides protection. In a number of cases involving alleged copyright infringement there will also be a claim for breach of confidence. This is common in cases involving ex-employee computer programmers who have created 'similar' computer programs for subsequent employers. Before proceeding to the next chapter where copyright law as it applies to computer software is described, a brief overview is given of the basic principles of copyright law in general terms followed by the fundamentals of the law of breach of confidence together with a brief note on the law of contract.

COPYRIGHT LAW

Copyright law has a long history going back to Tudor England. Originally, copyright law was concerned with printed materials such as books, and the need for protection from unauthorised copying grew with the invention and development of moveable type and the printing press. Initially, copyright law was used to control printing and as a form of censorship. Something could be published only if registered with the Stationers' Company, and copyright law was enforced through the infamous Court of Star Chamber. After the Tudor monarchs, official support for copyright law waxed and waned. However, in response to the dire straights in which authors and publishers often found themselves as a result of the large-scale copying of their works without permission (including Jonathan Swift's _Gulliver's Travels_), the first Copyright Act was passed in 1709: the Statute of Anne. Since that time, copyright law has spread throughout the world and has been developed to include many things other than works of literature within its scope, for example artistic works, sound recordings, films and, more recently, computer programs. The Copyright Act of 1911 was the model for copyright law throughout the British Empire and Commonwealth and is one reason why copyright law in many of the common law countries is similar to United Kingdom copyright law. The current legislation is contained in the Copyright, Designs and Patents Act 1988, the copyright provisions of which came into force on 1 August 1989. Unless otherwise indicated, statutory references in this book are to this Act as amended.

The subject matter of copyright, the thing protected, is called a work. The following are, by section 1(1), works for the purposes of copyright:

- original literary, dramatic, musical or artistic works,
- sound recordings, films, broadcasts or cable programmes, and
- typographical arrangements of published editions.

The person creating a work of copyright is known as the author. Certain qualification requirements must be satisfied for copyright to subsist (exist) in a work based on either the author or the country of first publication. (In practice, because of reciprocal arrangements for protection by way of international conventions, lack of qualification will rarely be an issue.) Most works will be protected, at least to some extent, in the United Kingdom, irrespective of the nationality of the author or the country of first publication. Copyright in the United Kingdom and in a number of other countries is free from formalities. The lack of formalities is a result of the membership of the Berne Copyright Convention. Protection is automatic and begins at the moment of the creation of the work.

In this book, the first category of copyright works is of most interest. These are the original works of copyright, viz, literary, dramatic, musical or artistic works. Computer programs are classified as literary works, and by section 3(1), a computer program *is* a literary work. Preparatory design material for a computer program is also a literary work. Since 1 January 1998, databases are expressly within the category of literary works, although prior to this most databases would have been compilations. Now compilations are defined as excluding databases. The 1988 Act also recognises, by section 9, that literary, dramatic, musical or artistic works may be generated by a computer. Strictly speaking, there is nothing to prevent the other forms of works being created by computer but, if this is the case, there is no need for special rules as regards the identity of the author.

The second category of works, in particular sound recordings and films, is of some interest for the purposes of this book, particularly as such works may be recorded digitally and be comprised in a software product. For example, a multimedia CD-ROM may contain a considerable amount of music and other sounds as well as film clips and other works such as photographs and textual works. Cable programmes are also relevant as operating an Internet 'Web site' may be regarded as providing a cable programme service.

In respect of the first category of copyright works, the word 'original' has been given a generous meaning by the courts and is not a requirement that the work be new or unique in any way, merely that the work has originated from the author (that is, the author has not copied another work, it is his or her own work) and that it is the result of a minimum of skill or judgment.

Duration

Copyright lasts for a relatively long time compared to other forms of intellectual property. For literary, dramatic, musical and artistic works, by section 12(2), copyright lasts for 70 years from the end of the calendar year during which the author dies. The period has been increased from 50 years after the death of the author as a result of the Duration of Copyright and Rights in Performances Regulations 1995 which implemented the EC Directive on the term of copyright. If the work is the result of the work of more than one author and the contribution of each is not separately identifiable, the 70 years does not begin to run until the end of the calendar year during which the last surviving author dies. For computer-generated literary, dramatic, musical or artistic works, the period is less, being 50 years from the end of the calendar year during which the work was created.

The duration of copyright in films has been increased by the Regulations and is now 70 years from the end of the calendar year during which the last of the following individuals dies: the principal director, the author of the screenplay, the author of the dialogue or the composer of music specially written for the film. For sound recordings, broadcasts and cable programmes, the term of copyright is unchanged being based on 50 years from the end of the calendar year during which the recording was released (provided it was released within 50 years of its recording), the broadcast made or the cable programme included in a cable programme service. The copyright in a typographical arrangement lasts for 25 years from the end of the year of publication. The Regulations also give rise to revived copyright where the copyright had expired in the United Kingdom but the work was still in copyright elsewhere within the European Economic Area (the Member States of the EC plus Iceland, Norway and Liechtenstein). In Germany, the period of protection was already life plus 70 years. Therefore, many works in which the United Kingdom copyright expired within the last fifteen years or so had their copyright revived in the United Kingdom.

The extension of copyright to life plus 70 years and the possibility of revived copyright is of little consequence to those involved in writing and exploiting computer programs. However, these provisions are very important for those digitising older works. For example, a publisher developing a multimedia product incorporating old film clips and old music and photographs must take special care to determine whether each of the works included are in copyright. Fortunately, the Regulations on duration of copyright do have special transitional provisions and savings in respect of extended and revived copyright. For example, with respect to revived copyright, licences are available as of right provided the person entitled to give permission to carry out the relevant act has been informed of the proposed use of the work. A royalty will be agreed or, failing agreement, will be determined by the Copyright Tribunal.

Ownership

A copyright is a form of property and as such must have an owner. The basic rule is given in section 11 and is that the author of a work is the first owner of the copyright subsisting in it, unless he or she is an employee and the work is created in the course of employment. In this case, the employer is the first owner of the copyright, subject to agreement to the contrary. Other exceptions concern Crown and parliamentary copyright and works created for certain international organisations (for example, the United Nations). It must be stressed that a person commissioning the creation of a work does not automatically own the copyright in the work. Provision should be made at the outset for arrangements as to the ownership and section 91 of the Act provides for prospective ownership of copyright; that is, ownership of copyright in a work yet to be created and for dealing with that 'future copyright'. The point about ownership of commissioned works is particularly important in the computer industry due to the large numbers of freelance workers and self-employed consultants.

Copyright can be assigned, that is, the ownership of the copyright can be transferred to a new owner. An assignment may be partial or may be limited in terms of duration or geographical scope. However, to be effective at law, by section 90, an assignment must be in writing and signed by or on behalf of the person making the assignment. Alternatively, the copyright owner may grant licences in respect of the software. In terms of copyright law, a licence is a permission, usually contractual, to do something which would otherwise infringe copyright. For example, a licence might permit a person who has acquired software under a licence agreement to use the software for his or her own purposes on a single computer. A licence may be exclusive or non-exclusive and may be partial or restricted in scope. An exclusive licence is one in which the person acquiring the software under the licence has the exclusive right to perform certain acts in relation to the software such as using it or making copies of it. The mere use of software almost certainly will involve an act restricted by the copyright. Under an exclusive licence, the copyright owner cannot perform the acts falling within the scope of the licence agreement.

An exclusive licence is almost as good as an assignment and in practice there is little to choose between them. From the point of view of the person acquiring the software, an assignment is preferable because it can override third party interests, whereas a licence can be vulnerable to a subsequent assignment taken without knowledge of the licence, although this is unlikely in practice. Section 92 requires an exclusive licence to be in writing, signed by or on behalf of the copyright owner. Of course, if the software is to be distributed to several users, this must be done by way of non-exclusive licences. The licensor is paid a licence fee or royalties as appropriate. An exclusive licensee can sue for infringement of copyright just as the owner can, although leave of the court is required for the licensee to proceed on his or her own without joining the copyright owner in the court action, either as co-plaintiff or defendant.

Where difficulties occur because a work has been commissioned without any express agreement as to the ownership of the copyright, the courts have been willing to use the concept of beneficial ownership. This allows the person or organisation commissioning the work to continue to use the work for the intended purposes.

Example

Sagacious Software Ltd, a company developing and writing expert systems, commissions Oliver, a self-employed computer programmer, to write a computer program to produce various attractive screen displays to be used at a computer trade exhibition. Oliver is paid £2,500 for the work. The program attracts a lot of attention at the exhibition and brings a lot of potential customers to their stand. Because the program is so well received, Sagacious Software decide to use parts of the program in a demonstration of their expert systems to be supplied on diskette to selected businesses as part of Sagacious Software's continuing marketing strategy. When Oliver hears of this, he writes informing Sagacious Software that he owns the copyright in the program and screen displays and that he only gave permission for their use at the original exhibition. Oliver states that he now requires an additional fee of £3,000 to assign the copyright to Sagacious Software and that if they do not agree, he will seek an injunction to prevent further use of the whole or part of the program and the screen displays without his permission.

It is possible that a judge would infer from the circumstances that the original intention was to transfer the ownership of the copyright. The judge would confirm the grant of beneficial ownership to Sagacious Software, a solution which would allow the company to continue to use the program. The copyright would then have two owners, Oliver would be the legal owner of the copyright and Sagacious Software would be the beneficial owner. Sagacious would be able to sue if someone else copied the program or screen displays but would be unable to obtain a permanent injunction or damages unless Oliver was joined as a co-plaintiff. An alternative approach to the problem would be to imply a licence in favour of Sagacious permitting the continued use of the program and/or screen displays for marketing purposes.

The concept of beneficial ownership is appropriate where the circumstances suggest that the presumed intention of the parties was that ownership in the copyright would be transferred. Where this is not so, there may still be a sufficient inference to suggest that an implied licence is apposite. The court might imply a term into the agreement to the effect that the person commissioning the work has the copyright owner's permission to continue using it or exploiting it and that, because of the supposed permission, the continued use or exploitation will not infringe the copyright (regardless of the fact that the copyright owner now does not wish to give such permission without further payment).

As a great deal of software is not individually written for a particular client but is licensed to many users, it is unsafe to rely on the courts granting beneficial ownership. The Court of Appeal pointed out in *Saphena Computing v Allied Collection Agencies* [1995] FSR 616 that the fact that much software was licensed ran counter to any presumption that beneficial ownership was appropriate. It is far better to deal with ownership of copyright at the outset and provide for it in a proper manner.

Moral rights

In line with the requirements of the Berne Copyright Convention (of which the United Kingdom is a member), sections 77 to 89 of the Copyright, Designs and Patents Act 1988 provide for moral rights for authors. These are rights belonging to the author of a work no matter who the owner of the copyright is. These rights recognise that the author has a creative bond with the work which gives him or her a right to a certain degree of control as regards the subsequent use of the work. In normal circumstances, these moral rights will not be onerous as far as the exploitation of the work is concerned. The moral rights apply only to literary, dramatic, musical, artistic works and films and are as follows.

- A 'paternity right': a right to be identified as the author of a work (or as the director of a film).
- An 'integrity right': a right not to have a work subjected to a derogatory treatment, being a treatment which is

prejudicial to the honour or reputation of the author/director.

- Additionally, any person has a right not to have a work falsely attributed to him or her.

(There is also a right to privacy in relation to certain commissioned photographs and films.)

Unfortunately for computer professionals, neither the paternity right nor the integrity right apply in relation to computer programs even though they are literary works. The moral rights do, however, apply to flowcharts, specifications, information other than computer programs stored on computer media (for example, a database or an image in digital form) and most computer output unless it is 'computer-generated'. It is difficult to say whether moral rights apply to user interfaces such as menu command systems or windows environments as these items may be deemed to be a part of a computer program. It should be noted that there are other exceptions to moral rights. For example, employees do not have moral rights in respect of things done by or with the authority of the owner when the employer is the first owner of the copyright. Also, any author can waive his or her moral rights and the right to be identified must be asserted. However, the false attribution right applies to all forms of works and could apply where a sub-standard computer program was falsely claimed to have been written by an eminent, respected and famous computer programmer.

Rights granted to the owner by copyright law

Copyright law operates by granting the owner of the copyright the exclusive right to do certain acts in relation to the work. These acts are sometimes referred to as the acts restricted by copyright. The owner of the copyright subsisting in a work has, by section 16, the exclusive right to:

- copy the work,
- issue copies to the public,
- rent or lend the work to the public (as from 1 December 1996),

- perform, show or play the work in public,
- broadcast the work or include it in a cable programme,
- make an adaptation of the work,
- do any of the above in relation to an adaptation.

Infringement of copyright

Copyright is infringed by any person who performs (or authorises the performance of) any of the above acts without the licence (permission) of the copyright owner; section 16(2). Sections 17 to 21 of the Act further elaborate on the meaning and scope of the exclusive rights. For example, making a copy of a work includes making copies which are transient or incidental to some other use of the work. Thus, loading a copy of a work into a computer's volatile memory will infringe the copyright unless the owner has given permission for this.

For infringement to be made out, the act must be done to a substantial part of the work, but this is measured qualitatively and not quantitatively. For example, to copy a few bars of a song which includes the main melody will infringe copyright even though the part taken may be only a small percentage of the entire work.

Infringement is delineated by the scope of the restricted acts and the defences to infringement and, therefore, the creation of a similar work does not infringe if it is created independently without copying the original work. However (and significantly), the burden of proof may shift where a causal connection exists, and there is an objective similarity between the works, for example in the case of an ex-employee responsible for the creation of two competing programs for different employers. It also appears that copyright can be infringed subconsciously.

Additionally, there are other forms of infringement described as 'secondary infringements', some of which also give rise to criminal penalties. These secondary infringements are mainly concerned with 'dealing' with infringing copies. For example, selling, exposing for sale or importing infringing copies. Secondary infringement also extends to dealing with articles to be used for making infringing copies, for example, a master CD-ROM from which duplicates may be made.

Remedies for copyright infringement

A wide range of civil remedies are available for infringement of copyright and are as follows:

- damages,
- injunctions,
- account of profits,
- additional damages (punitive), and
- delivery up.

Damages are not available if the defendant did not know and had no reason to believe that copyright subsisted in the work (illustrating the importance of attaching a prominent copyright notice to copies of the work). Damages should reflect the loss to the plaintiff resulting from the infringement and may be calculated on how much the plaintiff would have received by way of a licence fee or in royalties had the infringer obtained the plaintiff's permission to carry out the acts which constituted the infringement.

Injunctions are useful to prevent the continuing or future infringement of copyright, for example by a computer software pirate or a video pirate. Interim injunctions (previously known as 'interlocutory injunctions') are common. They are granted pending a full trial. They are appropriate if the damage to the copyright owner's interests in the period up to a full trial would be substantial and a later award of damages would not fully compensate for the harm done. A court will also take into account the harm done to the alleged infringer in a 'balance of convenience' in deciding whether or not to grant an interim injunction. A number of early software copyright cases in the United Kingdom were interim hearings.

An account of profits is an alternative to damages and might be worthwhile claiming if the infringer has made a profit substantially greater than the plaintiff's loss, although proving the precise profit flowing from an infringement will be difficult.

Additional damages are discretionary and must take into account the flagrancy of the infringement and the benefit accruing to the defendant. They cannot be claimed alongside an account of profits but may be claimed together with ordinary damages. Additional damages might be awarded where normal damages would be inappropriate such as where the copyright owner had no intention of licensing others to use his or her computer software and the infringer deliberately copied and published the work in this knowledge. For example, the software may have been confidential and for private or personal use only and it has been deliberately distributed against the owner's wishes.

A problem which often confronts a copyright owner is obtaining hard evidence of the alleged infringement. For example, the owner of the copyright in a computer game might suspect that someone has pirate copies of the game on his or her premises but there is a danger that these will be destroyed when that person finds out that he or she is to be sued for copyright infringement. For this reason, the common law has developed a weapon called the search order (previously known as the 'Anton Piller Order', from the name of the case in which it first evolved), sometimes referred to as the law's nuclear deterrent. The copyright owner can apply for a search order which allows him or her, accompanied by a solicitor, access to the premises of the alleged infringer to inspect and copy or remove evidence. The purpose of the order is to preserve evidence, not to put the alleged infringer out of business by taking everything and cleaning out the premises. Any abuse of the order will result in damages being awarded to the defendant. In the case of both search orders and interim injunctions, it must be remembered that, at the time of the order or injunction, the alleged infringement of copyright has not been proved. Of course, the applicant will have to convince the judge that he or she has a strong case, usually referred to as having a *prima facie* case, particularly in the case of an application for a search order.

Case

Series 5 Software Ltd v Clarke [1996] FSR 273

The plaintiff company developed and licensed software used in printing and publishing. Its main product was QC2000 software for use in print shops. The defendants had worked briefly for the plaintiff but claimed they were owed salary payments. In order to encourage the plaintiff to pay up, the defendants took computer software, back-up tapes and client lists belonging to the plaintiff. The defendants had also set up in competition with the plaintiff. The plaintiff had obtained an order for delivery up of its materials but now claimed that the defendants had not handed over everything they had taken. The plaintiff also asked for an injunction to prevent the defendants contacting the plaintiff's customers or using or disclosing trade secrets relating to the software.

The injunctions were refused. First, the plaintiff's case was weak. Second, as the plaintiff had other competitors, allowing the defendants to continue in their venture would not seriously affect the status quo. The judge continued the order for delivery up even though the defendants claimed to no longer have any of the plaintiff's materials in their possession. He did point out, however, that if they were not telling the truth as to this fact, they would be in contempt of court.

Penalties for the criminal offences depend on the form of dealing. Some of the offences are triable either way (that is, in either a magistrates' court – summary trial – or the Crown Court – trial on indictment), others are triable summarily only (that is, triable in a magistrates' court only). The maximum penalty for conviction on indictment is two years' imprisonment and/or a fine. The maximum penalty for summary conviction is six months' imprisonment and/or a fine not exceeding £5,000. Criminal proceedings for copyright infringement are not common but there have been a number of successful convictions and software pirates are likely to be imprisoned and/or fined heavily. The courts now take these offences much more seriously than in the past. Other forms of criminal law may also be relevant such as trade descriptions law, forgery and the deception offences.

Defences and exceptions to copyright infringement

Doing a restricted act in relation to a substantial part of a work of copyright without the permission of the copyright owner infringes that copyright. However, to strike a balance between competing interests and to limit the strength of copyright protection, the law contains various defences and exceptions to infringement. In the case of an alleged infringement, first considerations must concern whether the work is protected by copyright and whether the act complained of is, indeed, an act restricted by the copyright. If it is clear that the work is protected by copyright and the act concerned is a restricted act, the defendant might claim that the act does not relate to a substantial part of the work. The consent of the copyright owner itself may be an issue, for consent need not be express but can be implied. For example, the copyright owner may have acquiesced in the infringement and the court might consider this to be a form of implied consent or, alternatively, it could refuse to enforce the copyright on the basis of estoppel. By allowing the infringement to occur, the copyright owner will be estopped from enforcing his copyright. In some situations, a common law defence of public interest will be appropriate, for example, where a computer program has been written to assist computer hackers and fraudsters and someone has made a copy of it to send to the appropriate authorities in order to alert them to the danger.

The Copyright, Designs and Patents Act 1988 provides for some specific exceptions to copyright infringement collectively known as the 'permitted acts'. These are acts which can be done without requiring the permission of the copyright owner and without infringing the copyright in the work in question. The permitted acts can be classified as follows:

- fair dealing,
- educational purposes,
- library and archive use,
- use associated with public administration,
- certain acts carried out by lawful users of computer programs, and
- a great many other miscellaneous exceptions.

The specific permitted acts relating to computer programs are obviously significant. These allow lawful users to make back-up copies of computer programs, to decompile computer programs in limited circumstances and to copy and adapt computer programs in ways consistent with lawful use. These acts are described in some detail in the relevant parts of the book.

The fair dealing provisions are important in terms of acts other than decompilation of computer programs and also have some importance as regard other forms of computer software such as preparatory design material and databases. Of special significance is fair dealing for the purposes of research or private study. Figure 1.3 shows a flowchart with the defences and exceptions to copyright infringement set out in a logical sequence to be used to check whether there is a defence to or justification for an act that would otherwise constitute an infringement of copyright.

Figure 1.3 Defences and exceptions to copyright infringement

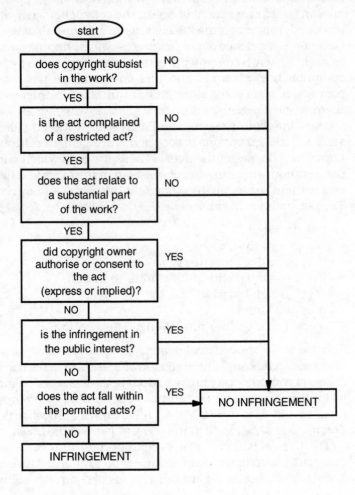

In addition, by virtue of the United Kingdom's membership of the European Community and depending on the circumstances, a 'Euro-defence' may be applicable. The EC Treaty contains provisions promoting the free movement of goods or services and controlling restrictive trading agreements and abuses of monopoly situations. An example of a situation where European Community law might be relevant is where a copyright owner grants licensees in a number of Member States but places onerous terms in the licence agreements used in one Member State. For example, a licence agreement may attempt to prevent a licensee in Germany exporting copies of the copyright work to France. Or the licence may include a term which attempts to control the licensee's ability to deal with other suppliers. The owner of the copyright in an operating system might refuse to license it to certain persons or organisations or license it subject to the licensee acquiring applications software in addition. A copyright owner trying to maintain price differentials in different Member States could fall victim to parallel importing, which is where someone lawfully buys copies of the work in a country where they are sold cheaply and then exports the copies to another country where the price is higher and is able to undercut the copyright owner or the owner's licensee. The European Court of Justice can refuse to enforce intellectual property rights where the exercise of those rights is affecting or likely to affect trade between Member States. European Community competition law is anything but straightforward and specialist advice should be sought by a copyright owner who wishes to exploit his work outside the United Kingdom. It must be said that this area of law affects patents and trade marks much more than it does copyright law. However, as copyright law becomes further harmonised, European Community competition law is having more impact even in this field. It is particularly important where software contains information which is not available from any other source.

International copyright conventions

There are two international conventions, the Berne Copyright Convention and the Universal Copyright Convention. Most of the developed countries in the world belong to at least one of these and some, such as the United Kingdom, belong to both. The purpose of the Conventions is to lay down minimum requirements, to stimulate harmonisation and to encourage reciprocal protection between Member States. Until recently, the European Community had relatively little effect on United Kingdom domestic copyright law but this is now changing. We have already seen the Directives on the legal protection of computer programs, the term of copyright, rental and lending rights and the legal protection of databases implemented in the United Kingdom. These Directives, together with their implementing legislation, are discussed in this book as appropriate. The texts of the Directives on the legal protection of computer programs and databases are reproduced in full in Appendices 1 and 2 to this book.

THE LAW OF BREACH OF CONFIDENCE

This introductory chapter would not be complete without a brief description of the law of breach of confidence because this area of law often is involved where there is an alleged infringement of copyright. Confidence is especially important in cases concerning ex-employees, freelance staff or consultants. Frequently, an action for infringement of copyright will be coupled with a claim that there has been a breach of confidence. Confidence is also relevant in that it can provide protection in the early stages in the development of a work of copyright in general and computer software in particular. Confidence may also be important where the program or its function is secret and it is used internally by the organisation for which the program was created.

The same goes for data that are stored on computer media. The data may represent all manner of things such as a list of customers, a musical work, an image or a list of co-ordinates describing the shape of an article.

Initially, when there are only a few basic ideas and little, if anything, has been written down, the law of confidence can give protection by providing remedies against someone who has, or is about to divulge that confidential information, or make some other unauthorised use of it. The law of confidence can and does protect ideas, whereas copyright law gives protection only when there is something which has been recorded or stored in some tangible way. Even if the work is well developed, the law of confidence can still give protection. For example, a computer program developed and used 'in-house' will be protected by confidence and copyright. It is only when something is available to the public, or a particular section of the public, that the law of confidence ceases to give protection, leaving copyright law alone with which to join battle with infringers.

The law of breach of confidence derives entirely from case law and is rooted in the branch of law known as equity. Although of earlier origins, its significance was recognised by the Court of Chancery in the early to middle part of the nineteenth century. The law of confidence is important in the computer industry especially in terms of 'trade secrets' and its impact on employees, and freelance workers. This area of law is not, however, limited to protecting information which is particularly special or unique in some way, such as ideas for a completely new operating system or storage medium, but it also protects rather more mundane information such as lists of customers and suppliers; the sort of information which is useful in the everyday running of a business and which is commonly in software form.

The law of confidence is particularly effective in protecting trade secrets, a term described in *Lansing Linde Ltd v Kerr* [1991] 1 WLR 251, which involved a director of a fork-lift truck company who, in breach of a covenant in restraint of trade, went to work for a rival firm and divulged confidential information within twelve months of leaving. Lord Justice Staughton said of trade secrets that the term '. . . can thus include not only secret formulae for the manufacture of products but also, in an appropriate case, the names of customers and the goods which they buy'. Thus, databases of customers, clients and suppliers, their credit-worthiness, buying preferences and other such information can be subject to the law of confidence.

The following types of information may be protected by the law of confidence:

- personal secrets and information,
- secrets relating to the government of the country,
- trade secrets, and
- business information of commercial value.

The second type of information may also be covered by the Official Secrets Act 1989 (which replaced the notoriously wide section 2 of the Official Secrets Act 1911).

Obligations imposed by the law of confidence are independent of contract so they will apply to preliminary negotiations, for example, where a business organisation and software company are negotiating with a view to the latter writing some computer software. If the negotiations break down and no contract is executed, the law of confidence can be used to prevent either from making use of information and ideas derived from the other. In many cases, this will be so whether or not there is an express mention that the negotiations are in confidence. The courts may imply obligations of confidence in such circumstances. If there is a contract between the parties, the basic protection provided by the law of confidence may be strengthened or modified by express terms in the contract. This is common in contracts for writing software, employment contracts and service contracts.

There are three basic requirements for an action in breach of confidence.

1. The information must have the necessary quality of confidence about it.
2. The information must have been imparted in circumstances importing an obligation of confidence.
3. There must be an unauthorised use of that information to the detriment of the party communicating it.

The Achilles' heel of the law of confidence is that there is nothing to prevent third parties who have acquired the information innocently, unaware of its confidential nature, from using it themselves or divulging it to others. However, the person responsible for the original breach may still be liable and any third parties may be liable if the circumstances are such that they ought to have realised that the information was confidential. They will not escape liability simply by closing their eyes to the truth.

The remedies available for a breach of confidence include injunctions, damages, accounts of profits and destruction orders. Injunctions are very important especially to prevent an anticipated breach of confidence and it is essential that a person who believes that someone is about to compromise a confidence takes immediate action and applies for an anticipatory (*quia timet*) injunction.

Assessment of damages for breach of confidence may be made in one of two ways. Lord Denning MR has identified two formulae which might be used to determine the *quantum* of damages.

1. If there is nothing very special about the information, and it could have been obtained by employing a competent consultant, then the value (for the purpose of damages) is the fee that consultant would charge.
2. If the information is something special involving an inventive step, then the value is the price a willing buyer would pay for it.

An example of a situation where the former method of calculating damages might be appropriate is where the information relates to the design of a database of customers using a fourth-generation language. The latter approach might be used if the information is concerned with the design of a new method of controlling an industrial process using a programmed computer.

The main defence to an action for breach of confidence is that of public interest which is similar to the equivalent defence for infringement of copyright. In terms of computer software, this defence may be suitable if the information concerns computer software to facilitate fraud, hacking or piracy.

CONTRACT LAW

Finally, brief mention must be made of contract law because a contract may provide express remedies for infringement of copyright by treating the infringement also as a breach of contract. Typically, licence agreements for computer software make reference to copyright, including ownership aspects, permitted use of the software, and whether the software can be transferred to another person. Questions of maintenance and modification also may be addressed by the licence agreement. Copyright law may be strengthened, extended or otherwise modified by such contractual terms and it is important that parties to an assignment or licence agreement clearly think through the implications in terms of copyright law. For example, it may be that the courts will be able to imply a term to the effect that the person acquiring computer software can decompile any programs included in the software for the purpose of maintaining or modifying the software. However, an express contractual term to the contrary would probably override the court's ability to imply such terms into the licence agreement unless the term is void either by virtue of the appropriate permitted acts under copyright law (see sections 50A and 50B of the Act and also section 296A) or on the basis of non-derogation from grant. This latter principle is discussed in detail in Chapter 10 and may be used to prevent a copyright owner forcing a licensee or other person lawfully having a copy of the relevant work to deal exclusively with the owner for the purpose of future maintenance or repair. The obligation of confidence, where it exists, also may be modified by contract law.

Software houses have, in the past, considered their licence agreements to be the most important form of protection for their software. Contract law certainly remains an important aspect even though computer programs are unquestionably protected by copyright law. Some licences contain terms to the effect that making copies of software, in excess to that permitted by the licence agreement and/or allowing copies to fall into the hands of third parties, will entitle the licensor to terminate the agreement and take possession of all copies of the programs and documentation. This is usually expressed as being without prejudice to other legal remedies the licensor may wish to pursue, such as an action for infringement of copyright. A contractual duty to take precautions against unauthorised copying by others can be imposed by a licence agreement, giving the licensor remedies in a situation where the licensee has either infringed copyright or authorised or allowed another to do so. (Authorising another person to infringe copyright is itself an infringement of copyright.)

The law of contract applies to licences and assignments of copyright. Apart from the express terms in a contract, the law will sometimes imply other terms into the contract. These terms may be implied by statute or by common law. In a contract for the writing of software, terms will be implied by sections 12 to 14 of the Supply of Goods and Services Act 1982 such as a duty to exercise reasonable care and skill in writing the software. The law also controls terms by which one party attempts to exclude or limit his or her liability under the contract, for example, by virtue of the Unfair Contract Terms Act 1977. Detailed consideration of the contractual implications of acquiring computer software is outside the scope of this book, but the reader should be aware that contract law and, indeed, the law of confidence are relevant to the development, exploitation and use of computer software. Chapter 8 does contain some further material on licensing and assignment of copyright.

Chapter 2

Copyright law and computers

INTRODUCTION

At one time, a significant factor in the legal view of copyright in computer software was the question of tangibility. Object code versions of computer programs stored on magnetic disks or in integrated circuits have caused particular difficulties. Traditionally, the law has distinguished between tangible and intangible property. Whilst judges have been quite happy to make this distinction when dealing with more conventional items (for example, a share in a company is intangible property as, indeed, is copyright; land and personal goods such as a car, desk or washing machine are tangible property), computer software has proved something of a riddle. For example, the Criminal Damage Act 1971 makes it an offence to deliberately or recklessly destroy or damage property but 'property' is defined as meaning property of a tangible nature. One court decided that a computer program stored on magnetic media was not tangible property.

Case

Cox v Riley (1986) 83 Cr App R 54

A vengeful employee erased several programs from magnetic cards used in his employer's computerised saw which was used for cutting out timber sections for window frames. The employee was charged with criminal damage and he argued that he could not be guilty of the offence because the computer programs that he had deliberately erased were not tangible property within the meaning of the Criminal Damage Act 1971.

It was held that although the computer programs stored on magnetic cards were not tangible property, the magnetic cards themselves had been damaged by the defendant's actions. Before the programs were erased, the cards were useful and now they were practically worthless and it would take a considerable amount of work to re-program the disks, restoring them to their previous condition.

The reasoning behind the judgment was criticised as it failed to take account of the magnetic pulses which represent the program and which, although invisible to the naked eye, do nevertheless exist. The magnetic pulses could be deemed to be tangible. In a later case, *R v Whiteley* (1991) Cr App R 381, the Court of Appeal said that it did not matter if the damage itself was not tangible providing tangible property had been damaged. Now, the deliberate erasure or modification of computer programs or data is now covered by the Computer Misuse Act 1990 which puts the matter beyond doubt as far as problems of intangibility are concerned. The *Cox v Riley* case is interesting because it highlights the difficulties some judges have in deciding how to categorise computer programs and data stored 'invisibly' and this was particularly so before amendments made to copyright law. Before considering present copyright law as it applies to computer software, it is useful to look briefly at the history of computer software copyright law as this helps to explain the mechanisms used in the current legislation and the nature of case law pertaining to software copyright.

SOFTWARE COPYRIGHT LAW – HISTORY

Although computer technology had been around for a few years at the time of its enactment, the Copyright Act 1956 made no mention of computers or computer programs. One explanation is that unauthorised copying was not perceived to be a problem either at that time or in the near future. In the early 1950s, few people foresaw the incredible rate of development and widespread use of computers and the then president of IBM suggested that total world demand for computers would be unlikely to exceed a few dozen! Despite the omission of computer programs from the 1956 Act, some academic writers considered that they were protected as literary works, especially if they were written down or printed on paper. This was not particularly controversial because copyright law had developed in a pragmatic nature as witnessed by Mr Justice Peterson's statement in 1916 that '. . . what is worth copying is *prima facie* worth protecting.'

Tables, compilations, books of telegraphic codes and football coupons all came within the family of literary works. However, even if it was accepted that source code programs listed on paper were protected by copyright, this did little to assuage concern regarding computer programs in object code form especially if they were stored invisibly. It was generally accepted, uncontroversially, that preparatory materials such as specifications and flowcharts were protected by copyright, independently of computer programs, as being literary and artistic works respectively. Until recently, very little consideration was given to the copyright position of computer databases, user interfaces, screen displays and other works stored or transmitted digitally. Printed output was generally considered to be either a literary or artistic work according to its nature, although doubts as to the identity of the author of computer output had been expressed.

A committee, known as the Whitford Committee after its chairman Mr Justice Whitford, an eminent intellectual property judge of the High Court, was set up to examine copyright law generally and its report was published in 1977, at a time when the problems of unauthorised copying of computer programs were at last beginning to cause significant unease within the computer software industry. Not surprisingly, the committee found that copyright law was unsatisfactory as regards computer programs and works produced by or with the aid of a programmed computer, and recommendations were made to improve copyright law accordingly. A later Green Paper, published in 1981, reiterated these recommendations although with some modifications.

Even though it was now clear that copyright law was unsatisfactory in its protection of computer software generally, and computer programs in particular, it remained unchanged and during the first few years of the 1980s the problem of computer software piracy snowballed. This was partly due to the perceived ineffectiveness of copyright law and partly as a result of inexpensive computer power in the form of the personal computer. The exponential growth in the computer population was accompanied by a parallel growth in applications software and, very quickly, the ease with which computer programs and accompanying documentation could be copied became a major issue for the computer industry. Not surprisingly, the United States of America was the first country to enact specific legislation directed towards the copyright protection of computer programs, the Computer Software Copyright Act 1980.

In the United Kingdom, the loss attributable to computer software piracy was estimated in 1984 by the Federation Against Software Theft (FAST) at some £150 million. A more recent estimate of the cost of unauthorised use of software in the United Kingdom is £540 million; *Computing*, 2 August 1996, at p 4. On the whole, the computer software industry was nervous about taking legal action in case a judge ruled that computer programs were not protected by copyright. Some software companies firmly believed that the law of contract provided the most certain and enforceable way of preventing unauthorised copying. For example, a licensee who permitted the software to be copied would be in breach of the licence agreement with the software owner, allowing the latter to sue for breach of contract. Terms were often draconian, giving the software owner the right to terminate the licence agreement forthwith and recover any copies of the programs and documentation in the possession of the licensee even if the licensee had not knowingly allowed or authorised the copying.

Even though there were serious doubts about the strength and scope of computer software copyright, on the whole, in the few cases coming before the United Kingdom courts in the early 1980s, judges seemed sympathetic towards the software owner. Judicial sympathy was not, however, sufficient, especially as none of the cases went forward to a full trial; they were all interlocutory hearings. An interlocutory hearing is one at which an interim judgment is pronounced pending the full trial. For example, if a software owner could show that it was probable that an alleged software pirate was copying his software, a judge might be prepared to grant an interlocutory (interim) injunction preventing the alleged pirate from continuing to sell the software in question until a full trial of the issues. One problem with interim hearings is that legal rights are not usually considered in detail, it being a matter of whether the plaintiff can convince a judge that there is at least a serious issue to be tried. Another factor to be taken into account in deciding whether to grant an interim injunction is the 'balance of convenience'; the relative harm to the parties resulting from the grant or refusal of an injunction.

Case

Sega Enterprises Ltd v Richards [1983] FSR 73

The plaintiff had a computer game called 'FROGGER' which became very popular and which involved trying to move a frog across a busy motorway without it being squashed flat by a passing car or lorry. The defendant produced a similar program and offered this, installed on circuit boards, as a replacement for boards in games machines. The plaintiff applied for an interlocutory injunction on the basis of infringement of copyright in the computer program and in the screen displays for his game. Although the defendant admitted that his program was based on the plaintiff's program, he claimed that he had done much work on the program and that, in any case, United Kingdom copyright law did not protect computer programs.

The judge, Mr Justice Goulding, was of the opinion that copyright subsisted in the assembly code version of the program (the source code) and that the object code was either a reproduction of or an adaptation of the assembly code version and, as a result, the object code was also protected by copyright.

However, this case and others like it at the time did not put the matter beyond doubt. The status of interlocutory hearings is not high and, in almost every case, the judge made it clear that the views expressed as to the copyright protection of computer programs were tentative only, and the issue would have to be tried in full for the rights of the parties to be determined conclusively. The computer software industry remained concerned and sceptical and its anxieties were realised in 1984 when, in Australia, the Apple Computer Corporation sued an importer of 'clones' of the Apple II personal computer. Appropriately enough the clones were called 'WOMBATS'. At first, the defendant claimed that he had not copied the Apple chips but this was easily disproved by Apple as the defendant's chips contained within their code the names of the Apple programmers. The defendant then admitted copying but claimed the programs were not works of copyright.

At the trial at first instance the judge agreed and held that literary copyright did not subsist in the computer programs in question, the object code programs in the ROM chips in the Apple II computer. The decision made waves which rippled the world over, especially in the United Kingdom because of similarities between Australian and United Kingdom copyright law. In fact the Australian judge placed great emphasis on the old English case of *Hollinrake v Truswell* [1894] 3 Ch 420 in which it was said that a literary work is one intended to 'afford either information and instruction, or pleasure, in the form of literary enjoyment'. It was difficult to see how an object code version of a computer program, installed on ROM chips, fell within this definition. The plaintiff in the Apple case appealed to the Federal Court of Australia and the appeal was successful, it being held that computer programs, even in object code form, were protected by copyright as literary works; *Apple Computer Inc v Computer Edge Pty Ltd* [1984] FSR 481. A well argued dissenting judgment claiming that an adaptation of a literary work should be capable of being seen or heard, still left doubts so the Australian Parliament acted with admirable swiftness and passed the Australian Copyright Amendment Act 1984 within a couple of weeks of the appeal judgment confirming that computer programs were protected by copyright, whatever their form.

In other countries, there was also substantial doubt, some considering that their existing copyright law extended to computer programs as literary works whilst others made amendments to their domestic laws to take computer programs on board. The international trend was to effect protection for computer programs by means of copyright law and, more particularly, to consider computer programs to be literary works. The Berne Copyright Convention defines literary and artistic works in terms of productions in the literary, scientific and artistic domain.

The United Kingdom government, although sympathetic to the question of computer software copyright, did not immediately follow Australia's lead. In the United States of America, the main issue was the scope of the protection offered by copyright but, in the United Kingdom, doubts about whether copyright could subsist in a computer program whatever its form increased. Eventually, after many vociferous outbursts by or on behalf of the computer industry, amending legislation was passed in the United Kingdom but only by way of a Private Member's Bill introduced by William Powell MP. The Bill had the support of the government and became the Copyright (Computer Software) Amendment Act 1985 which made it quite clear that computer programs were protected by copyright law as literary works. At the time it was enacted, this legislation was seen as being a temporary measure and did not directly deal with some of the copyright issues related to computer technology, such as the ownership of works produced by or with the aid of a programmed computer. A large-scale review of copyright and design law was contemplated and a White Paper, *Intellectual Property and Innovation*, was published in 1986, describing the intended changes. Subsequently, the Copyright Act 1956 and the 1985 amendment were repealed and replaced by the Copyright, Designs and Patents Act 1988. The copyright provisions of this important and wide-ranging Act came into force on 1 August 1989. Pre-existing computer programs are protected in accordance with the 1988 Act although there is some doubt about the position of computer-generated works created prior to the commencement date of Part I of the 1988 Act dealing with copyright.

THE COPYRIGHT, DESIGNS AND PATENTS ACT 1988 AS IT APPLIES TO COMPUTER SOFTWARE

General

An important effect of the Act is that doubts about copyright protection associated with different forms of storage of computer programs and other copyright works are, to all intents and purposes, eliminated. Computer programs and other works are protected irrespective of the way they are stored. Definitions in the Act are generally very wide and should cover all forms of storage now known or likely to be devised in the foreseeable future. By section 3(2), to be protected by copyright, an original literary, dramatic or musical work must be recorded in writing or otherwise. 'Writing' is defined in section 178 as including 'any form of notation or code, whether by hand or otherwise and regardless of the method by which, or medium in or on which, it is recorded'. This should cover all forms of computer storage and applies both to computer programs and to literary works other than computer programs. It also applies to the other 'original' works of copyright. Therefore, word processed documents are protected as are databases and data representing music and graphical works. It should also be noted that the definition is not a restrictive one and something falling outside the specificity of the definition still may be considered to be recorded in writing.

The meaning of the word 'recorded' will usually not be troublesome, for example, if a computer program or file is stored on magnetic media or hard wired into the computer. Where difficulties might arise is where the only form of existence of the work is in the volatile memory of a computer, in other words, the computer's random access memory (RAM). Of course, once the work is stored on a disk or printed out on paper, it will be recorded for copyright purposes. It may be that some permanency greater than volatile memory is required. However, in a case on the previous legislation, the Copyright Act 1956, it was decided that displaying a work on a screen was reproducing the work in a material form.

Case

Bookmakers Afternoon Greyhound Services Ltd v Wilf Gilbert (Staffs) Ltd [1994] FSR 723

The plaintiff organised afternoon greyhound races and a third party broadcaster included details of these races and dividends in its racing service to betting shops. The information was included with the plaintiff's consent which later claimed to be entitled to payment from individual betting shops. The defendant refused to pay.

It was held that copyright subsisted in the lists of greyhounds in races and that, by displaying these lists on its display monitors, the defendant was reproducing the lists in a material form and, to that extent, infringing copyright. Note that under the 1988 Act, copying in relation to a literary, dramatic, musical or artistic work means reproducing the work in any material form; section 17(2). This includes storing the work in any medium by electronic means.

Previous case law suggested that a work which existed only in a computer's volatile memory was not recorded or stored. So it was held in *R v Gold* [1988] 2 WLR 984, a case on computer hacking where the accused were charged with making a false instrument under section 1 of the Forgery and Counterfeiting Act 1981, the 'false instrument' being the password and customer identification number (belonging to the Duke of Edinburgh). The false instrument must be recorded or stored for the purposes of that Act and the House of Lords held that this was not so as these were held transiently only whilst being checked for validity.

Taking the above cases together, and bearing in mind only the first is a copyright case, it would seem that there is some doubt as to whether a work which exists only in the volatile memory of a computer (RAM) is *recorded* for the purpose of copyright subsistence. However, taking a work in which copyright subsists and loading it into a computer's volatile memory is *reproducing in a material form* and will infringe copyright if done without the authorisation of the copyright owner. This is reinforced by section 17(6) which confirms that copying includes making transient copies.

Computer programs

Subsistence of copyright in computer programs

Computer programs, for copyright purposes, are literary works. They are protected by copyright law in the United Kingdom if they are original and have been recorded, in writing or otherwise, and the program qualifies by reason of the identity of the author (programmer) or the country of first publication. Protection may also be available for a computer program because of the reciprocity provided for by either of the international copyright Conventions. The qualification requirements, contained in sections 153 to 156, are fairly complex but will be satisfied if the author is a British citizen or is domiciled or resident in the United Kingdom. They extend to other countries, for example British Dependent Territories, and there are also provisions for incorporated bodies such as limited companies to be the author of a work of copyright (this might be important in terms of computer-generated works). Also, if a computer program is first published in the United Kingdom, or other country to which the provisions have been extended, it will qualify, irrespective of the nationality or place of residence of the author.

The Copyright (Application to Other Countries) Order 1993, as amended, extends the qualification provisions to nationals and bodies in numerous other countries and in respect of works first published in other countries. This is primarily a result of the United Kingdom's membership of the Berne Copyright Convention. In practice, therefore, qualification for copyright protection will seldom be an issue.

A computer program will be original if the programmer has written it himself or herself, without copying, and it is the result of a minimum of skill or judgment. It would seem, therefore, that even very small computer programs will be protected by copyright. Most computer programs, however small, are the result of the application of skill and judgment and will, consequently, be protected by copyright. However, there is a *de minimis* rule in copyright (trivial, insignificant or very small works are not protected) and the following examples written in the BASIC programming language may help to show where the boundary might lie.

Example A
```
10   PRINT "Hello!"
```

Example B
```
10   INPUT"What is your name ",N$
20   PRINT"Hello ";N$
30   END
```

Example C
```
10   ' routine to accept name and add to file
15   OPEN "A",#1,"NAMEFILE"
20   CLS
30   PRINT"Enter your name – as prompted"
40   PRINT"First name(s) followed by lastname"
50   PRINT
60   INPUT"What is/are your first name(s) ",FN$
70   INPUT"What is your last name ",LN$
80   PRINT#1,FN$,LN$
90   PRINT"Name written to file"
95   CLOSE#1
100  END
```

It is extremely unlikely that either example A or B will qualify for copyright protection. It is submitted that example C is approaching the borderline of protectability. There is some skill now involved, for example in deciding the form and sequence of the entry of first and last names, clearing the screen to make things simpler for the user and writing the information to a computer file. However, it could still be argued that the program is, to a great extent, dictated by the relatively simple function it performs. If more skill were expended, for example, by checking the input, allowing the user to modify his or her entry, then the routine should come closer to being protectable.

Protectability may depend on the programming language used. A very simple statement in BASIC or COBOL, for example, multiplying two numbers together might be very much more difficult to program in assembly language or machine language and require a much greater degree of skill. The two following examples written in different languages show a routine which performs the same operation of adding together two integer numbers. The first is in Z-80 assembly language and also shows the equivalent machine code in hexadecimal. The second example is written in FORTRAN.

Example Z-80 assembly language program

program code	machine code equivalent
ld b, 0	06 00
ld a, (loc#1)	3A F4 7B
ld d, a	57
ld a, (loc#2)	3A F5 7B
add a, d	82
ld c, a	4F
jr nc out	30 01
inc b	04
out: ret	C9

The above program takes two integer numbers stored in memory locations loc#1 and loc#2. The numbers may not be greater than 255.

Example FORTRAN program

```
C    THIS PROGRAM ADDS TO INTEGER NUMBERS
C    DENOTED BY VARIABLES I and J
     I = 12
     J = 37
     K = I + J
     WRITE (5,100) K
100  FORMAT (I6)
     STOP
     END
```

The two short programs above are not exactly the same, for example the FORTRAN program can handle numbers in excess of 255 and also negative integers. By using different variable names, such as A, B and C, the FORTRAN program will be able to deal with floating point arithmetic, a task which would be considerably more complex in assembly language.

An assembly language program is, by definition, more difficult to write than an equivalent high level language program to perform the same task. One of the main reasons for developing high level languages was to simplify the process of programming a computer. Does this mean that an assembly language program will be protected by copyright whereas a program written in FORTRAN or COBOL to perform the same function is not protected if it happens to be small? It would certainly seem to be a possibility and, in each case, it is a matter of considering the amount of skill and judgment expended on the writing of the program in the particular language chosen.

To some extent, this may be influenced by how much work has been expended in generating the original design for the program. Formulating the idea may require considerable thought yet, once this stage has been reached, wiring the program is relatively simple. In *Microsense Systems Ltd v Control Systems Technology Ltd* (unreported) 17 June 1991, the judge was prepared to take into account the skill and labour used in devising the operational aspects of a traffic signal controller into account in determining whether the list of mnemonics which were used to program the controller was a work of copyright. Of course, if the preparatory work has been recorded in some form it would qualify as a work of copyright in its own right.

What is the position in relation to a computer program, the form and content of which is predetermined by the function it has to perform? In other words, the program's expression is dictated by the idea, no alternatives are feasible. This situation has been considered at length in the United States in terms of computer programs as discussed in Chapter 3. Although there are no English cases directly on this point involving computer software, there are some old cases where the appropriate principles have been discussed.

Case

Kenrick & Co v Lawrence & Co (1890) 25 QBD 99

> The plaintiff commissioned an artist to draw a representation of a hand holding a pencil and making a mark in the shape

of a cross on a ballot paper. The plaintiff's idea was that this would show illiterate people how to cast a vote. Over a million copies of a card with the drawing on it were sold in five years. The defendant produced a similar card although the hand was in a slightly different position and the end of a sleeve could be seen.

It was held that copyright law did not protect the subject of the drawing (that is, the concept of a hand holding a pen making a cross on a ballot paper). Only an exact representation would infringe copyright. This was because there was no other way of representing the idea and there can be no copyright in an idea otherwise this would lead to a monopoly. This was a case where the expression was dictated by the idea and the decision is as relevant today as it ever was. It is notable that the judge considered that an exact reproduction would infringe. However, if the expression was truly dictated by the idea, even an exact copy should not infringe.

It would seem, therefore, that copyright protection will be denied for a computer program, the expression of which is dictated by the program's function. This will not be so in most cases of application programs because there will usually be several alternative forms of expression. However, this does bring into question the protectability of programs making up a computer's operating system and the instruction set of the central processor. The latter form of program is sometimes referred to as a microprogram or microcode. It could be argued that such programs or program statements are a defining element of the computer and, as such, are dictated by the computer's architecture and design philosophy and concepts.

Denying protection for computer operating system programs and microcode would be unfortunate because of the considerable skill used in their creation. This fact is a distinguishing feature which might help to overcome difficult precedents such as *Kenrick v Lawrence* because, in that case, once the idea had been formulated, the work and skill involved in giving expression to the idea was significantly less than in the case of a microcode program.

The relative importance of a part of a work may be a useful test as to whether that part, taken in isolation, represents a substantial part of the work as a whole. This may be extremely important in determining whether the copyright subsisting in a work has been infringed. In terms of computer programs, every command and expression, even punctuation marks may be critical to the operation of a program. A misspelling or omission of a semicolon may cause the program to halt or 'crash' or produce inaccurate or misaligned output. Apart from non-executable remark lines inserted for the programmer's convenience, it could be said that every single line, command and expression in a computer program is of vital importance. It is, however, unlikely that importance in this sense is not sufficient, *per se*, to justify a finding that a very small part of a program is a substantial part of the program as a whole, as the case below indicates.

Case

Cantor Fitzgerald International v Tradition (UK) Ltd (1999) Times, 19 May

The plaintiffs were brokers and brought an action for infringement of copyright in computer programs which were part of a bond-broking system. It had been argued that a part of a program might be substantial for copyright purposes if the program would not work without it or if it was used a great deal during the operation of the program.

The judge pointed out that a computer program must contain no errors of syntax and no semantic errors. Substantiality was not to be determined by whether the program would work without the code in question or by looking at the amount of use made of that code. If a sub-routine is used frequently during the operation of a computer program that reason alone does not mean it is a substantial part of the program. What is important is looking at the skill and labour which went into writing the program code in question, judged against the program or programs comprising a software system when viewed as a whole.

The defendant admitted that 2,952 lines of source code from the plaintiff's programs (totalling around 77,000 lines) had been copied and the defendant's expert witness identified another 1,964 lines the origin of which was questionable. Most of the program modules were individually compiled (converted from source code into object code) and linked together into a small number of programs, each of which could have been compiled from a single source code file. The judge also accepted that the overall structure of a computer system or program could be protected in its own right if it is the result of sufficient skill, labour and judgment [see the section on 'Look and feel' in Chapter 4].

The judge allowed in part the plaintiff's claim for copyright infringement and breach of confidence.

One difficulty remains. When judging copyright subsistence of a part of a computer program, should the emphasis be placed on the skill and judgment expended on the part in question viewed against the program as a whole or should that part be looked at in isolation to see whether sufficient skill and judgment has been used in its creation? Imagine a particular sub-routine or module has been written which is the result of an amount of skill and judgment. Perhaps it performs a number of complex mathematical transformations based on an algorithm developed by the programmer. The sub-routine is incorporated into a computer program or suite of programs. Two possibilities exist.

- To determine whether the sub-routine is a substantial part of the program or suite of programs ('system'), the skill and judgment used in writing the sub-routine is judged against the entire system. The more complex and extensive the system, the less likely the sub-routine will be deemed to be a substantial part of it.
- The sub-routine should be considered on its own and the question then becomes whether the skill and judgment expended in its creation is sufficient to endow copyright on it as a work in its own right.

The judge in the above case seems to prefer the first approach and this is satisfactory in most cases. However, where a distinct part of a system such as a module or specific sub-routine is concerned, both approaches should be taken and, even if the part fails under the first test, it may still be deemed to be a work of copyright distinct and separate from the system as a whole. Support for such an approach may be obtained by looking at computer program systems as compilations of programs and/or modules.

Computer programs as compilations

By section 3(1) of the Act, literary works include compilations. The Copyright, Designs and Patents Act 1988 does not define the word 'compilation' (although, databases are specifically excluded) but it is reasonable to take a dictionary definition meaning a collection of materials to make a work. Case law confirms this approach and, in *Ladbroke (Football) Ltd v William Hill (Football) Ltd* [1964] 1 All ER 465, it was held that a fixed odds football coupon comprising sixteen lists of matches to which different wagers were appended was a compilation for copyright purposes.

Many computer programs are, in reality, a collection or suite of numerous individual programs. Apart from any copyright subsisting in the individual programs, there may be an additional copyright in the suite of programs as a compilation.

Case

Ibcos Computers Ltd v Barclays Mercantile Highland Finance Ltd [1994] FSR 275

The plaintiff marketed a general accounts package for agricultural dealers which contained a suite of some 335 programs together with 171 record layout files and 46 screen layout files.

Copyright was held to subsist in the individual programs and in the entire software package as a compilation. In a previous case, *Total Information Processing Systems v Daman* [1992] FSR 171, it was suggested that the mere linking of several programs did not constitute a compilation for copyright purposes. The judge in the present case, whilst not disputing that this was so on the facts of that case, said that this was not a general rule. He said that if there was sufficient skill and judgment in selecting and arranging the individual programs in the compilation then, apart from and in addition to any copyright subsisting in the individual programs, the whole suite of programs, being a compilation, could be a work of copyright. (This case is discussed later in this chapter in terms of infringement.)

Treating suites of computer programs as compilations is not unreasonable and to some extent this reflects the moves to protect the look and feel of computer programs, including their overall structure; see Chapter 3. In many cases, once the modular structure of a suite of programs has been decided, writing the individual programs will be a relatively mundane task.

Preparatory design material

Written specifications, flowcharts and drawings showing layouts for screens were all protected by copyright provided they were original in the copyright sense. As a result of the Copyright (Computer Programs) Regulations 1992 which implemented the European Council Directive of 14 May 1991 on the legal protection of computer programs (OJ L122, 17.5.91, p 42, the text of which is reproduced in Appendix 1), such materials are protected as a new species of literary work. There is a slight difference in the wording used in the Copyright, Designs and Patents Act 1988 as amended which states that literary works include, *inter alia*, a computer program *and* preparatory design material for a computer program. The Directive states that computer programs shall include their preparatory design material. In practice, this difference in wording should not be significant. It is arguable that specifically extending copyright to preparatory design material was unnecessary and such materials already were protected in their own right as literary or artistic works as appropriate.

Infringement

Infringement of copyright may occur, by section 16, through copying, the first issue of copies to the public, rental or lending to the public (as from 1 December 1996), public performance or showing, broadcasting or inclusion in a cable programme, making an adaptation or doing any of the previously described acts in relation to an adaptation. These acts are shown diagrammatically in Figure 2.1.

Figure 2.1 Infringement of copyright in a computer program

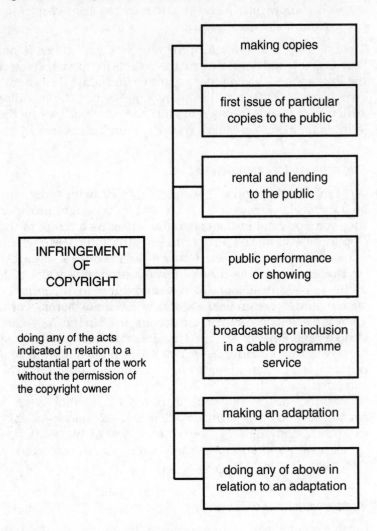

Before looking at each of these acts (the so-called 'restricted acts'), it should be noted that, for infringement, the act must relate to a substantial part of the work concerned and that the question of substantiality is determined primarily by reference to the quality of the part taken and not its quantity in proportion with the entire work. In other words, is the part taken an important part? A sub-routine in a computer program may be a small part of a computer program proportionately and yet be an important part in terms of functionality. Certainly, the taking of less than ten per cent of a program will usually be deemed to be substantial for copyright purposes if that part is important to the operation of the program bearing in mind *Cantor Fitzgerald International v Tradition (UK) Ltd* (1999) Times, 19 May, mentioned earlier.

Case

Hawkes & Sons (London) Ltd v Paramount Film Service Ltd [1934] Ch 593

> A newsreel film contained 28 bars comprising the main melody of the well-known march 'Colonel Bogey'. This portion lasted only 20 seconds whereas the full march lasted for some four minutes. Although a small part in terms of quantity, the newsreel was held to infringe the copyright in the music. It was said that what is substantial is a matter of fact, and value as well as quantity must be considered. An alternative test is to consider whether the copyright owner's economic interests are likely to be harmed by the unauthorised copying.

This approach has been confirmed in a number of cases subsequently and, in one such case, *Spectravest Inc v Aperknit Ltd* [1988] FSR 161, Mr Justice Millett said that in determining whether the defendant had taken a substantial part of the plaintiff's work, attention must be directed primarily to the part which is alleged to have been reproduced and not to those parts that have not. Basically, if the part taken is significant, regardless of its actual size, copying it without the permission of the copyright owner will constitute an infringement of copyright. However, in view of the decision in *Cantor Fitzgerald International v Tradition (UK) Ltd*, to this a *caveat* must be added and relative importance or significance alone does not automatically mean that the part is substantial for copyright purposes. The key is whether and to what extent skill and judgment has been expended in creating the part concerned.

Sometimes, a computer program will be written in separate modules rather than being contained in a single executable file. One program module may 'chain' to another and so on. A program to perform a particular function might be comprised of a single module or it may be broken down into several modules. There may be technical reasons for this, for example ease of maintenance, computer memory limitations, speed of operation, etc. It is possible that this could affect copyright protection by changing the measure of substantiality. Can a computer program be more effectively protected by copyright simply by arranging the program in a number of small modules, bearing in mind that the overall collection of modules may have a separate copyright? Each module may be considered to be a separate program for copyright purposes and, if so, substantiality will be measured by the module and not by the entire set of modules which together make up the whole program. Certainly, if substantiality were a matter of quantity, this would have this effect but, as we are more concerned with quality, the outcome of such action is unpredictable. It is difficult to say whether a judge would be likely to decide by reference to the single module or the set of modules. There can, however, be no doubt that each module will qualify for copyright protection assuming it is the result of a minimum of skill or judgment. Obviously, care must be taken not to break down a program deliberately into numerous tiny modules otherwise, if judged separately, few of these might individually cross the *de minimis* threshold. Even so, however, the selection and arrangement of the modules may be protected by copyright as a compilation.

Presumptions

Before looking at the restricted acts in more detail, some thought should be given to the burden of proof in an action for infringement of copyright. As a general rule, it is the plaintiff that bears the burden of proof. It is he or she who has to prove that the work is a work of copyright, that he or she is the owner (or exclusive licensee) and that the defendant has performed a restricted act in relation to a substantial part of the work without the owner's licence. Of course, some of these elements may be admitted by a defendant. A defendant who tries to run a line of defence which is hopeless and without merit may expect to be punished in costs. Also, where there is a causal link such as where the same person was involved in the creation of both works, the burden of proof may 'shift' to the defendant who may have to prove that his or her work is not a copy of the plaintiff's work.

In order to expedite court proceedings, the law sometimes raises presumptions such that a particular fact is presumed true unless the other party proves otherwise. There are a number of examples in relation to copyright law. Thus, where a name purporting to be that of the author of an original literary, dramatic, musical or artistic work appears on copies of the work as published or on the work when it was made, under section 104(2) of the Copyright, Designs and Patents Act 1988, that person is presumed to be the author and to have made the work in circumstances such that he or she would have been the first owner of the copyright. If the author sues now for infringement of the work, the defendant would have to adduce evidence to prove that the plaintiff was not the author or, for example, had made the work in the course of employment and had no right to bring the action.

The above presumption will apply also to computer programs, preparatory design material for computer programs, databases and other literary, dramatic, musical and artistic works stored in digital form. There are some further specific presumptions relating to copies of computer programs which have been issued to the public in electronic form in section 105(3). Where such copies bear a statement that:

- a named person was the owner of the copyright in the program at the date of issue of the program, or
- the program was first published in a specified country, or
- copies of the program were first issued to the public in electronic form in a specified year,

that statement shall be admissible as evidence of those facts and presumed correct until the contrary is proved.

This shows the benefit of placing an appropriate statement on copies of computer programs issued to the public (and also on the work when made) as without convincing evidence to the contrary, a defendant will be hard put to overturn the presumption. The value of such presumptions was seen in the case below.

Case

Microsoft Corpn v Electro-Wide Ltd [1997] FSR 580

In an action for summary judgment, Microsoft claimed that the defendant had sold unlicensed copies of its DOS and Windows software. The defendant sought to question Microsoft's ownership of copyright in the software. Microsoft claimed the benefit of the presumptions in section 105(3) but the defendant asked for particulars of Microsoft's ownership of copyright, including details of authors, their nationality, their employment status with Microsoft and the country of first publication. The defendant accepted that the presumptions shifted the burden of proof but argued that ownership was still an issue and the defendant was entitled to discovery (disclosure of documents).

Whilst accepting that discovery of all relevant documents may be forced in a full trial it was not appropriate for summary judgment in this case as there was nothing to support the submission that the defendant had a real or *bona fide* defence on such issues as covered by the presumptions. Basically, the defendant was hoping that the process of discovery would unearth some unknown defect in Microsoft's ownership of copyright. Mr Justice Laddie said that there was not a reasonable probability of the defendant having a *bona fide* defence on such grounds being no more than '. . . an unfounded and Micawberish hope that something will turn up'. He granted Microsoft summary judgment including injunctions, an order for delivery up and an inquiry as to damages including consideration of whether additional damages would be appropriate. Of course, if the case went to full trial and a defendant was able to force discovery of what must be very extensive documentation showing ownership of copyright, this would considerably extend the length of the trial and increase costs and, if the defendant lost on this issue, he or she would most likely have to pay those increased costs.

Copying

For literary, dramatic, musical or artistic works, copying is defined by section 17(1) as reproducing the work in any material form including storing the work in any medium by electronic means. The word 'electronic' is very widely defined by section 178 of the Act and should apply to all known forms of computer technology. Therefore, copying a computer program (or any other work falling in the above categories), or a substantial part thereof, from one magnetic disk to another is, if done without the permission of the copyright owner and in the absence of a defence, an infringement of copyright.

Sometimes, copying involves an intermediate stage and is not direct but this is still controlled as section 16(3) states that copyright can be infringed indirectly. The following examples demonstrate this principle.

- Copying a three-dimensional article, made in accordance with a drawing, infringes the artistic copyright in the drawing even though the person making the copy of the article has not had sight of the drawing. (However, it is no longer an infringement of the copyright in a drawing to copy an article subject to the design right represented in that drawing unless the article itself is an artistic work. Section 51 suppresses the protection of designs through their drawings or other design documents.)
- A person creating a work after listening to a verbal description of the original work may infringe copyright.
- An artist making an oil painting using and based on a photograph of an original oil painting infringes the copyright in the painting and the photograph (unless the artist owns the copyright in the original painting and photograph or has the permission of the copyright owners).

Theoretically, the principle of indirect copying could be very far reaching. For example, Figure 2.2 shows a person who writes a new computer program. That person does not have access to the source code of a computer program but studies the program in use and makes a careful note of the screen displays and their sequence and, in this way, determines the function and structure of the original computer program. It is, at least, arguable that the new computer program will infringe the copyright in the first program because it is an indirect copy of it, providing more is taken than ideas and principles alone.

Figure 2.2 Indirect copying of a computer program

original
computer
program

programmer studies
program in use
(does not see the
program code)

writes

new
computer
program

It is immaterial if intervening acts themselves infringe copyright; section 16(3). If Alan carefully studies a computer program in operation, making a mental note of the detailed sequences of operations and structure, this will not infringe copyright assuming the program is a licensed copy and Alan is either the licensee or has the licensee's permission to use the program within the scope of the licence agreement. If Alan then gives a verbal description of the sequence and structure of the program to Bertha this does not infringe the copyright either. However, if Bertha then writes a computer program in accordance with the description there may be an infringement of copyright provided the sequence and structure are deemed to represent a substantial part of the program. The last act infringes even though the first two did not. Alan could also be liable as he may be deemed to have authorised the infringement by Bertha.

The question arises of what the position is if a person copying a program makes considerable alterations and does not copy literally, line by line. A programmer might decide to make some use of the listing of an existing computer program when he or she is writing a new program. There may be some copying although it is not direct copying, line for line, instruction by instruction. The activity can be referred to as non-literal copying. It is possible that other restricted acts might apply such as *making an adaptation* if the first program is converted in the process but this will not always be the case. In the following example, a programmer uses a print-out of an existing computer program to assist in the writing of another program to perform the same function as the first program.

Example

> Jeremy was employed at Advance Marketing Associates (AMA) and, whilst he was employed there, he had access to AMA's computer program classifying clients and their needs. When he left AMA, Jeremy took with him a printed listing of the program which was written in COBOL. Jeremy uses the print-out to determine how the existing program works, what it does and its structure and flow. From this information Jeremy writes his computer program, using the BASIC programming language, to carry out the same function. The programs look different but some variable names, labels and formulae are the same or are similar.
>
> Jeremy has, in effect, taken the ideas from the original program and has not made a literal copy of the program code. Nevertheless, and ignoring the question of how Jeremy obtained the print-out in the first place, he may still be liable for infringing the copyright in AMA's program as copyright law in the United Kingdom has previously recognised the possibility of non-literal copying in a handful of cases and including an important computer software case. Jeremy might argue that he has not copied a substantial part of the expression of AMA's program but AMA will probably feel aggrieved at this use of their computer program to develop another program which might be used by its competitors. There may also be issues of breach of confidence and breach of Jeremy's contract of employment.

Non-literal copying is examined further in the following Chapters 3 and 4 in the context of both United States and

United Kingdom law. It is an area of some importance which is testing the efficacy of copyright law in the context of computer software. Reconciling copyright law's dislike of monopolies with strong and effective protection will not always be easy. However, where copying is an issue, there must be a causal connection between the original work and the creator of the second work who must have had access to the first work (directly or indirectly) and has used his or her knowledge of the first work in creating the second one. The independent creation of a similar work is not copying, however defined. Quite often the causal link will be satisfied because the creator of the second item of software was originally employed by the owner of the copyright in the first piece of software. Two items of similar computer software created by a programmer who left one company to work either for another or himself or herself is a familiar scenario. The required connection can also exist because of a passing familiarity with the first work and the courts have, in the past, seemed prepared to envisage the concept of subconscious copying. However, if the creator of the second work has never seen or heard of the first work, there can be no infringement by copying.

Where the same person has been responsible for the creation of two programs, perhaps for separate employers, the burden of proof can shift so that the defendant has to prove that his program is not a copy of the plaintiff's program instead of the plaintiff having to prove that the defendant copied the plaintiff's program. However, in the past there has been a tendency for judges to insist on at least some evidence to suggest copying to be adduced by the plaintiff.

Case

Thrustcode Ltd v W W Computing Ltd [1983] FSR 502

The plaintiff employed the defendant to write a computer program to be used to control manufacturing processes. Eventually, the relationship between the parties soured and the defendant developed his own program which he admitted was based on the program he had written for the plaintiff. The plaintiff sought an interlocutory injunction to prevent the defendant using or distributing his program on the basis that it infringed the literary copyright in the plaintiff's program.

The Vice-Chancellor, Sir Robert Megarry, proceeded on the basis that copyright subsisted in the plaintiff's program (a point that, at the time, was not entirely free from doubt as discussed earlier in this chapter). However, he said that the plaintiff had failed to adduce sufficient evidence of copying and refused to grant the injunction requested. He said that the plaintiff should have submitted print-outs of the two programs to show similarity. In general terms, the judge suggested that evidence of someone watching one computer being programmed and then programming a rival computer in a similar way would be useful. (Demonstrating, perhaps, a lack of understanding by some judges of the way programs are written.) One very sensible thing the judge did remark upon was that the crucial issue was what the programs are, not merely what they do or can do.

The owner of a computer program can take steps to make it easier to prove copying should someone copy the program later and introduce numerous alterations in an effort to disguise the origin of the program. Mistakes common to both programs can raise an inference of copying. The same applies to similar redundant code found in both programs.

Case

Ibcos Computers Ltd v Barclays Mercantile Highland Finance Ltd
[1994] FSR 275

Mr Poole had worked on the plaintiff's accounts package for agricultural dealers and later developed a competing package for the defendant.

The judge held that there had been disk to disk copying of the plaintiff's program, being heavily influenced by the presence of identical mistakes in the REMARK lines in some of the programs and the presence of the same redundant lines of code in both suites of programs.

A remark line is a label or other note inserted by the programmer and which is not executed by the computer. When compiling a source code program into object code, remark lines are ignored and do not appear in the object code. The purpose of remark lines is to help the programmer understand the program and the function of the various parts of the program, making it easier to modify the source code program in the future.

Having established copying had taken place, the judge then had to determine whether the parts copied represented a substantial part of the plaintiff's programs. In the event the judge held that 28 of the defendant's programs infringed the plaintiff's copyright in addition to an infringement of the structure of the plaintiff's entire package as a compilation. The judge also held that there had been a breach of confidence by Mr Poole in respect of the source code of the plaintiff's programs. However, a claim based on a covenant in restraint of trade failed, such covenants being narrowly construed by judges.

Copying by digitising

All forms of work may be stored in digital form separately or in a computer database. For example, data representing sounds or music may be stored in a computer file which, when accessed by an appropriate computer program, will be used to determine the actual sounds and notes produced. It matters not whether the information is recorded on magnetic media or compact disk, CD-ROM or any other form of storage. The fact that the definition of writing in the Act includes code means that the recording does not have to be instantly recognisable as the work it represents, and that a process involving conversion into a different form does not defeat copyright protection. Subject to the case below in which a judge said that a copy of an artistic work must look like the original work, converting existing and conventional works into digital form will be making a copy of them.

Case

Anacon Corpn Ltd v Environmental Research Technology Ltd
[1994] FSR 659

The plaintiff made an electronic dust meter and claimed to have a copyright in a computer program, engineering drawing of the hardware and a circuit diagram all of which were associated with the meter. The judge, Mr Justice Jacob, was satisfied that there had been a clear infringement of the copyright in the computer program and the engineering drawing. However, the issue was more difficult as regards the circuit diagram. The defendant had used this to create the circuit board upon which electronic components were laid out and, in doing so, created a 'net list' from the circuit diagram (a list of components with details of their interconnections).

It was held the circuit diagram was a literary work being, by section 3(1) of the 1988 Act, any work, other than a dramatic or musical work, which is written, spoken or sung and includes a table and compilation, etc. Writing is defined in section 178 as including any form of notation or code. The fact that the circuit diagram contained information (some of which was in writing, for example, indicating the rating of the components) which was written down and could be read by somebody indicated that it was a literary work. The net list produced by the defendant was, therefore, a reproduction of the information which was the literary work contained in the circuit diagram.

The diagram was also an artistic work but there was no infringement on this count because, according to the judge, the circuit board did not look like an artistic work and the visual significance of an artistic work is what matters. Whilst this was true to some extent under the previous legislation, the Copyright Act 1956, this no longer holds true because section 17(2) of the 1988 Act specifically states that copying in relation to a literary, dramatic, musical or artistic work means reproducing the work in any material form which includes storing the work in any medium by electronic means. Mr Justice Jacob failed to mention that latter proviso to section 17(2) and, whilst his logic about engineering drawings being literary works also because they are intended to be read is impeccable, the suggestion that a copy of an artistic work must look like an artistic work cannot be right. Otherwise, it would contradict the very words of the section – a work stored by electronic means has no visual significance unless retrieved and displayed on a computer screen or printed out.

The danger of what Mr Justice Jacob said about the visual significance of artistic works is that converting an artistic work into digital form would not infringe copyright. Thus, a person could digitise a work in the United Kingdom and from there make and distribute copies electronically, either by exporting disks containing the digital representation or by transmitting over the telecommunications system, say by making the work available on the Internet. Of course, anyone who converted the work back into its visual form would infringe copyright (the fact that intermediate acts do not infringe does not break the chain as far as infringement is concerned). However, according to the above logic, the person responsible for digitising and distributing the work in that form would escape unless deemed to be authorising infringement. Thankfully, this scenario is incorrect because, by digitising the work, the person responsible is 'storing the work in any medium by electronic means' which is within the meaning of copying. Making further copies in digital form is also caught.

Issue of copies to the public

The issue to the public of copies of a work by putting into circulation copies which have not previously been put into circulation infringes copyright and is defined in section 18. This act applies to all forms of works of copyright. However, the subsequent distribution, sale, hiring or loan or importation of copies lawfully put into circulation does not infringe with the exception of the rental of computer programs, films and sound recordings which is treated as equivalent to issuing copies to the public. Unless a licence agreement permits rental, the licensee must not rent out copies of computer programs to the public. Specific rental and lending rights have recently been granted to copyright owners (see later).

In effect, once a copyright owner has allowed copies of his computer software to be issued to the public, he or she cannot subsequently use the public issue right to control further dealings in those particular copies. This might be important where a computer software company operates in several countries and has different pricing structures for those countries. If a software company sells copies of its software to the public in the United Kingdom for £250 and also sells copies to the French public but at a different price (say the equivalent of £150), another company might buy up copies in France and import them into the United Kingdom with the intention of selling the copies to the public there for £200, undercutting the software company with its own copies of the software. The company cannot prevent this by relying on the public issue right. If it attempted to prevent the possibility of this happening by the inclusion of terms in the licence agreements purporting to prevent the subsequent transfer of the software, these will be struck out by the European Court of Justice if it considers the terms to be restrictive and likely to affect trade between Member States of the European Community.

Rental or lending to the public

As from 1 December 1996, renting or lending to the public a copy of a literary, dramatic or musical work, most forms of artistic works, films or sound recordings is a restricted act and will infringe copyright unless authorised by the copyright owner. This is without prejudice to the pre-existing rule as to rental of computer programs, sound recordings and films being deemed to be within the restricted act of issuing copies to the public.

New section 18A of the Copyright, Designs and Patents Act 1988 contains the detail. The new restricted act is wider than the previous and continuing 'rental right' in that it applies to a greater number of types of works and lending also is covered. Now, for example, renting a copy of a database of representations of modern works of art to the public is a restricted act.

Both rental and lending are defined on the basis that a copy of the work (which includes the original) is made available for use on terms that it will or may be returned. Unlike lending, rental is for direct or indirect economic or commercial advantage. Lending under the Public Lending Right Act 1979 does not infringe.

There are provisions for transfer of the rental right in the case of works included in films or sound recordings. These could be relevant in terms of works included in multimedia encyclopaedia. The author of a work in which rental right subsists has, upon transfer of his or her right, a right to an equitable remuneration.

These rental and lending rights result from compliance with a European Community Directive on rental right and lending right and on certain rights related to copyright in the field of intellectual property (OJ L346, 27.11.92, p 61). These and other changes were implemented by the Copyright and Related Rights Regulations 1966.

Public performance or showing

Although unlikely, it is possible for this right to be invoked in terms of computer software. For example, a computer game might be projected onto a large screen in a restaurant or similar establishment to keep the customers entertained. Strictly speaking this will infringe the copyright in the computer software unless the copyright owner's permission was obtained; section 19 of the Act. The word 'public' in the context of public performance has, in the past, been very widely interpreted, even a performance of music in a factory to the employees whilst they worked has been held to be a public performance. Blanket licences for such performances are available for music (from the Performing Right Society) but not for computer software *per se*. Anyone contemplating the display of a computer program or the output of a computer program (for example, screen displays) to a number of persons simultaneously needs to be careful on this point and check whether a licence is available.

Broadcasting or inclusion in a cable programme

Quite simply, the difference between a broadcast and a cable programme is that the first is something which is transmitted via the airwaves (the 'ether') whilst the latter is transmitted by means of cables or wires. Both involve the transmission of visual images, sounds or other information. It is possible to broadcast the screen display of a computer program which should not create any problems (although it is possible that the screen display itself may enjoy a copyright independent of that in the computer program) but what is of more concern to owners of the copyright in computer programs is the transmission of them so that they may be received by others and copied. Section 20 of the Act makes this an infringement. Additionally, transmitting a computer program in this way will involve the act of making an adaptation, as the program will have to be converted into another language or code in order that it can be transmitted.

Making an adaptation

Making an adaptation of a literary, dramatic or musical work infringes the copyright subsisting in the work if done without the permission of the copyright owner by section 21, unless it falls within the defences to copyright infringement. In terms of literary works, making an adaptation includes making a translation of the work and for computer programs a translation includes a version of the program which has been converted into or out of a computer language or code (whether or not a different language or code). Making an arrangement or altered version of a computer program is also within the meaning of adaptation. Therefore, the acts of making a compiled version of a source code computer program and disassembling an object code program are restricted by copyright. The act of making an adaptation would seem also to extend to the situation where a programmer converts a program from one language to another manually, being an arrangement or altered version or, alternatively, a translation. It should be noted that the definition of translation for computer programs is not exhaustive and other forms of conversion may fall within its meaning. The scope of the restricted act of making an adaptation is important in the context of reverse analysis and decompilation and is discussed in more depth in Chapter 5.

Doing any of the restricted acts in relation to an adaptation

Once an adaptation of a computer program has been made, for example a source code program has been compiled into object code, a person who does any of the restricted acts in relation to the object code version of the program also infringes copyright. Thus, even making an adaptation of an adaptation infringes copyright.

Example

> Gregory owns the copyright in a source code program written in the BASIC programming language. He uses the program in interpreted mode and has never compiled it into object code. One day, Gregory lends a copy of the program to Harriet who, unknown to Gregory, uses a BASIC compiler to produce a compiled object code version of the program. Harriet returns the source code to Gregory and then she makes several copies of the object code which she gives to Sam who sells them to the public.
>
> Harriet has infringed Gregory's copyright in two ways, first by making an adaptation when she compiled the source code version and, second, by making copies of the adaptation. Sam has also infringed copyright by issuing the copies to the public. Sam will be liable even if he did not know that the copies were infringing copies although his knowledge will affect the remedies available to Gregory should he sue for copyright infringement. Both Harriet and Sam might have committed criminal offences in addition to their civil wrongs, depending on the circumstances, particularly if they knew or had reason to believe that they were dealing with infringing copies.

Programming languages

Computer programming languages are not protected by copyright law. Indeed, the Directive on the legal protection of computer programs (OJ L122, 17.5.91, p 42) states in its recitals that ideas and principles underlying any element of a computer program are not protected by copyright and that to the extent that logic, algorithms and programming languages comprise ideas and principles, those ideas and principles are not protected under the Directive. A computer program written in a particular programming language, using the commands, instructions and syntax of the language, will itself be subject to copyright protection. The persons responsible for the conception and development of the programming language cannot interfere with the rights in any programs written using the language. The only time when a programming language cannot be freely used in this way is if it is secret, perhaps for a company's own internal use only (or still under development before being ready for public release) and, if this is so, there may be legal protection afforded by the law of breach of confidence.

Whilst a computer programming language is not protected by copyright, the programs used to interpret or compile programs written using the language certainly will be. Also protected will be books and manuals describing the language, its use and syntax although this copyright cannot be used to prevent the use of the ideas contained within the documents. The same basic principles apply to natural human languages like English and French as they do to computer languages. Nobody has ever suggested that natural languages could be subject to copyright protection, even if deliberately created, such as the human language Esperanto. The language is simply the tool by which ideas are expressed and, using a particular language whether natural or computer, there are many ways in which a particular idea can be expressed.

Case

Hollinrake v Truswell [1894] 3 Ch 420

This involved a claim to literary copyright in a book containing a sleeve pattern intended for use in dressmaking. (It was a representation of a lady's arm with a scale for measuring marked upon it.)

It was held that the sleeve pattern was not protected by copyright. It was, in essence, a technique to be applied in dressmaking. The description of an art may be subject to copyright protection but, having been published, the art itself is given to the public and enters the public domain.

A method of using a particular computer programming language can be equated to an art. ('Art' is not used by the judge in the above case in the artistic sense but in a technical and scientific sense. For example, a method of making integrated circuits is an art.) A manual describing a computer programming language is more than likely to have examples of how the language may be used to create certain effects or perform certain operations. These will usually be in the form of small routines and, generally, on their own each will be too trivial for copyright protection. By publishing this information, the developers of the language have, in effect, given them to the public at large. The same must apply, even more so, to the commands, instructions and syntax of the language. Of course, it must be reiterated that the manuals and other documentation in addition to interpreter and compiler programs will all be protected by copyright. In the United States of America, the same result would be achieved simply by classifying the language as an unprotectable idea.

The instruction set for a particular microprocessor will, likewise, not be afforded copyright protection. Because an instruction set is a major defining element in terms of the functionality of a microprocessor, it can be equated to an idea. Others should be free to use the instruction set to develop programs to be used in conjunction with the microprocessor. However, the fact that a considerable amount of skill has been expended in devising the instruction set might influence a judge in the application of copyright principles.

Case

Microsense Systems Ltd v Control Systems Technology Ltd
(unreported) 17 July 1991, Chancery Division

> The plaintiff made traffic control systems including a pelican crossing controller. The operation of the controllers was programmed using a list of mnemonics which were also used to monitor the controllers. The defendant's controllers contained 49 of the plaintiff's mnemonics. The defendant argued, *inter alia*, that standardisation was an important feature required by purchasers of pelican crossing controllers, otherwise confusion could ensue resulting in dangerous traffic conditions if the controller had been wrongly programmed.
> This was an interlocutory hearing, so no final decision had

to be taken on whether the list of mnemonics was protected by copyright but the judge, Mr Justice Aldous, considered that there was an arguable case that copyright subsisted in the list of mnemonics. He took into account the skill and labour expended on the work of devising the functions and operations of the controller to ascertain whether the list of mnemonics was an original work. An interlocutory injunction was denied to the plaintiff because the defendant agreed to pay a royalty of two per cent of the net sale price of each controller into a joint bank account which would be paid over to the plaintiff as damages should it be successful at a full trial.

It is not clear what the position is in relation to microcode or microprograms representing an instruction set. In essence they are computer programs and, as such, will be subject to copyright. Certainly, in the United States, whilst recognising the possibility of protection for microprograms representing an instruction set, the idea/expression merger doctrine, discussed in the following chapter, has compromised the copyright protection of such programs. Furthermore, in *Mitel Inc v Iqtel Inc* 896 F Supp 1050 (D Colo 1995), the District Court of Colorado held that an instruction set used to program telephone call controllers was not a work of copyright, being merely a procedure, process, system and method of operation. Whether this decision is of wider application is not clear but the court did go on to say that even if the instruction set was a work of copyright, the defendant would be able to rely on the fair use defence. However, the silicon chips containing microprograms and instruction sets will have protection as semiconductor products; see Chapter 11.

Computer-generated works

The Copyright, Designs and Patents Act 1988 contains provisions dealing with 'computer-generated works'. By section 178, these are literary, dramatic, musical or artistic works which are created in circumstances such that there is no human author. Works which are produced using a programmed computer, as a tool, such as a word processed document or a table of accounts created using a spreadsheet program are NOT computer-generated works, and the normal rules of copyright such as subsistence, duration and authorship will apply. For example, a person writing a report using a word processor will be the author of that report, which is a literary work. It is not an easy matter to imagine a computer-generated work, but it would be one in which the direct (or even indirect) human contribution, in a creative sense, was slight or trivial. Because a computer-generated work is not created by a human, there are special rules for determining authorship (and, hence, ownership) and duration of copyright. The author of a computer-generated work is, by section 9(3), the person by whom the arrangements necessary for the creation of the work are undertaken and, by section 12(7), the copyright lasts for 50 years from the end of the calendar year during which the work was created. Computer-generated works are discussed further in Chapter 9.

Other works stored in a computer

The fact that all manner of works may be created with the aid of a programmed computer and/or stored in a computer has already been alluded to. The Copyright, Designs and Patents Act 1988 takes account of this in the wide definition of 'writing'. Apart from copyright works, representations of other forms of creative works may be stored in a computer. A design includes aspects of the shape or configuration of an article and might concern a new design to be applied to cutlery, a new shape for a car wing, an ornament, a new shape for a computer mouse or a new design for the external appearance of a printer. Rights in new designs are provided for by two forms of design protection, one is by registration under the Registered Designs Act 1949 (intended primarily for aesthetic designs) and the other is by the design right under Part III of the Copyright, Designs and Patents Act 1988, intended primarily for functional objects but also applying to many aesthetic designs. With the design right, the design may be recorded in a design document which is defined by section 51(2) as being any record of a design and includes data stored in a computer. Computer-generated designs are also anticipated and provided for by the 1988 Act. Indeed, computer-generated computer programs are a possibility under the Act.

Devices to circumvent copy protection

Some computer programs are made available with a form of copy-protection intended to prevent unauthorised copies of the program being made. Copy-protection can be effected by scrambling the code representing the program, or by some other form of encryption. Other methods involved the use of dongles, hardware devices which are plugged into a port in the computer before the program can run. However, human nature being what it is, computer programs which were specifically designed to overcome copy-protection, enabling copies to be made, were soon available. In Australia, one enterprising individual even started selling dongles for a few dollars to be used with a well known computer-aided drawing system. The programs could be easily copied but needed the presence of the dongle so that only one copy of the program could be used at any given time.

Devices and computer programs for making copies of copy-protected computer programs (or, indeed, any form of copyright work which is in an electronic form and which is copy-protected) are now controlled by section 296 of the Copyright, Designs and Patents Act 1988, which provides that the making, importation, sale or hire (or the offering, exposure or advertising for sale or hire) of devices or means specifically designed or adapted to circumvent copy-protection of works issued to the public in electronic form is to be treated as an infringement of copyright. This provision has been extended to cover possession of such devices or means in the course of a business. Also covered is publishing information to enable or assist the circumvention of copy-protection, for example, by publishing the listing of a computer program which has been written for the purpose of overcoming a particular form of copy-protection. The device, means or information must be directed to the form of copy-protection employed by the copyright owner. In addition to devices and means intended to prevent or restrict copying, 'copy-protection' also includes those methods intended to impair the quality of copies.

Some equipment can be used either for making legitimate copies of computer programs or other works stored in a computer, for example, computer disk drives. Although a computer disk drive may also be used to make unauthorised copies it will not fall within the scope of the above provisions because it is not *specifically designed to overcome copy-protection.*

Chapter 3

The look and feel of computer programs

INTRODUCTION

In this chapter, we are concerned primarily with developments in the United States in relation to the copyright protection of computer programs and ancillary works such as screen displays and computer files. There is no doubt that the United States of America is at the leading edge of litigation in these matters and, because it has a common law system owing its origins to English law, developments there are of considerable interest in the United Kingdom. Cases from the United States courts involving software copyright have been cited in argument in English cases and have been approved of and partially applied by an English judge in the important case of *Richardson v Flanders* which is discussed in Chapter 4. The body of American precedent obviously is not binding on the courts in the United Kingdom but, because of the reasons given above, it can be said to be of strong persuasive authority in appropriate circumstances, bearing in mind there are some differences between United States and United Kingdom copyright law. Many issues in the area of software copyright have been argued and considered in the United States courts. Of course, the same points can be made in respect of other common law countries such as Australia, Malaysia and New Zealand but the United States wins in terms of the volume of cases and depth of judicial consideration and the fact that the courts there are frequently the first to consider particular problems associated with software copyright.

The United States Copyright Act of 1976 protects original works of authorship fixed in any tangible medium of expression and the US Congress considered that this included computer programs which were protected as a species of literary work. There was no difficulty in terms of source code printed out on paper but, as usual, object code stored in invisible form posed problems.

Case

Data Cash Systems Inc v J S & A Group 480 F Supp 1063 (ND Ill 1979)

The defendant copied the plaintiff's ROM chip which contained a program for a computer chess game.

The court held that the program was not protected by copyright because it was not in a form in which it could be seen and read with the naked eye.

However, later cases overruled this decision and confirmed that even object code was protected under the 1976 Act. An example is the case of *Apple Computer Inc v Franklin Computer Corpn* 714 F 2d 1240 (3rd Cir 1983) in which the defendant could not deny copying the Apple operating system stored in ROM chips and magnetic media because the name of the Apple programmer was found embedded in the defendant's programs. (Apple also found this trick of hiding their programmer's names in the operating system programs very useful in Australia where unauthorised clones of Apple computers were being sold.) To put the protection of computer programs beyond doubt, irrespective of their nature and mode of storage, the United States enacted an amendment to the 1976 Copyright Act, the Computer Software Copyright Act 1980. One important feature of the 1980 Act is that it defines a computer program for copyright purposes (something from which the United Kingdom legislators have demurred) as 'a set of statements or instructions to be used directly or indirectly in a computer to bring about a certain result'.

In addition to describing developments in the United States, the implications for United Kingdom law and recent developments will be discussed in this chapter. However, two things should be noted. First, apart from many differences in the detail of copyright law, there is a difference in emphasis between the United States and the United Kingdom, although the resulting effect is broadly similar. Copyright law, in the United States, does not protect ideas. What it does protect is the expression of an idea. This principle is deeply ingrained as we shall see. The same can be said for the United Kingdom but this is not explicit in the legislation. We can imply such a rule from the Copyright, Designs and Patents Act 1988 which requires that a work must be 'recorded in writing or otherwise' to attract copyright protection and there have been a number of respected judicial statements to the effect that ideas alone are not protected. This different emphasis has resulted in the United States courts developing sophisticated tests for distinguishing idea from expression and this is a feature lacking, to a large extent, in United Kingdom law. The second point is that the influence on United Kingdom copyright law of the European Community is now being felt and this is moving the United Kingdom closer to the European model of copyright and, arguably, away from United States copyright law. However, the influence of the United States is still important and the EC Directive on the legal protection of computer programs denies copyright protection to ideas and principles as does the Copyright Treaty of the World Intellectual Property Organisation (WIPO – a United Nations organisation based in Geneva) which was adopted on 20 December 1996.

The GATT Agreement on Trade Related Aspects of Intellectual Property Rights (the TRIPS Agreement) specifically denies copyright protection to ideas, procedures, methods of operation or mathematical concepts: Article 9(2).

THE IDEA/EXPRESSION DISTINCTION

Copyright law does not protect ideas. This is a fundamental rule in United States copyright law, whether we are talking of computer programs, works of literature, drawings or music. If the idea is expressed in some tangible form, then it is that expression which is protected and which may not be copied but the idea itself may be used freely by others (subject to trade secret law). However, the mere fact that something is written down does not necessarily mean that it is fully protected by copyright.

Case

Baker v Selden (1880) 101 US 99 (Supreme Court)

> The action concerned the copyright in a book which had been written describing a new system of bookkeeping which included example ledgers, ruled and analysed according to the system.
>
> It was held that the copyright in the book did not extend to the system of bookkeeping described in the book. The description of an art in a book does not confer upon the author an exclusive right to the art itself. The idea/expression distinction so important nowadays in software copyright cases in the United States owes its origin to this seminal case.

This case concerned what could be described as a manual spreadsheet and is of direct relevance today in the context of electronic spreadsheets. Indeed, the case has been cited to great effect in many software copyright actions in the United States and must rank there as one of the most significant leading cases in copyright law. The decision in *Baker v Selden* can be explained by saying that a person copying the pages of the book would infringe copyright but a person who ruled up pages in accordance with the system without directly copying from the book's pages would not infringe copyright. Similarly, the concept of a computer spreadsheet with the facility to produce simple charts from the data entered into the spreadsheet is not protected by copyright. That is *idea* only. However, if a person developing a spreadsheet program copies certain features of an existing spreadsheet program, that would infringe copyright because *expression* has been copied. The logic behind this rule is that if copyright were extended to ideas, it would give the first in the field a monopoly which would last for a considerable period of time (generally, the life of the author plus 50 years or life plus 70 years in Europe) and this would have undesirable effects on competition and innovation. The phenomenal growth and development of the computer industry and the pace of improvement in computer software has been achieved only because copyright law has managed, albeit imperfectly, to strike a reasonable balance between competing interests. Whether it will continue to do so is a moot point.

To a significant extent, in the United States, the idea/ expression dichotomy circumscribes the strengths and limits of copyright protection. To be able to determine whether a particular aspect of a computer program (or any other work for that matter) is protected by copyright, it is essential to be able to distinguish between idea and expression in real cases. This has not proved easy in practice, and the simplicity of the basic statement that copyright protects the expression and not the idea, belies the fact that the application of the principle is unsatisfactory and unpredictable. It is further complicated by the fact that, sometimes, expression can be abstract and idea can relate to a tangible element of a work. It is desirable that the law should be certain and predictable so that persons and organisations can order their affairs accordingly, with a good knowledge of the likely legal outcome of their actions. However, because of the difficulty in identifying in advance what is idea and what is expression, software authors often are uncertain as to what they can and cannot do in relation to other computer programs. The following example gives some idea of the dilemma facing software authors. We will return to it towards the end of the chapter and propose some possible solutions.

Example

> Jakesoft Inc, a software company, wishes to extend its range of software products by developing and marketing a word processing system to run on popular personal computers. To make its system attractive to potential customers, Jakesoft wants to use a command system and basic screen display similar to the leading package, WORDWRAP, so that users of that system can easily transfer to Jakesoft's

new word processing system. Jakesoft also wants to design its software in such a way that it can import charts produced by the market-leading spreadsheet system, LILY A-B-C.

Jakesoft is uncertain about whether they can copy the menu command system and basic screen display from WORDWRAP and whether it can inspect the program code of LILY A-B-C and details of files produced by that system (perhaps using a 'hex dump') to determine the interface details relating to charts produced using LILY A-B-C. Jakesoft does not intend to copy any of the actual code of either program when writing its own system. Effectively what is important here is whether menu command systems and interface details are protected as expression.

LIMITS OF EXPRESSION AND PROGRAM STRUCTURE

If something is deemed to be expression, such as a printed listing of a computer program which is not commonplace, then making a direct copy of the listing will infringe the copyright subsisting in the program just as will making a copy of the program on a magnetic disk or on other storage media. The same applies to the object code version of the program, even if it is contained within a silicon chip. This form of copying is known as literal copying. The copy is the same as the original. No changes have been made in the process of copying, apart from minor changes (such as removal of copyright notices!).

Copying as described above, if done without the permission of the copyright owner, is clearly unlawful. However, not all copying is so straightforward, and substantial changes could be made so that the copy does not, at first sight, look like the original. If the original is a source code program, the 'copy' may have been written in a different computer programming language so a line for line comparison of the programs will not be conclusive. Such copying is referred to as non-literal copying. Making use of an existing program by inspecting it to determine the flow and structure of the program will facilitate the writing of another program, intended to perform the same function, in a different computer programming language. Some persons, particularly the owner of the copyright in the first program, will consider this method of writing a 'new' computer program to be unfair. Others may regard the activity to be fair and in the wider public interest. However, it can be argued that the person writing the second program has made unfair use of the first program; he has used it as a short-cut in the process of writing his own. The question is whether such use is unlawful.

The United States courts have dealt with this question by considering the distinction between idea and expression and extending the expression of a computer program to include its structure and the sequence of operations performed by the program. By doing so, non-literal copying potentially becomes an infringement of copyright, and protection can reach elements of a program which are not directly expressed but are at one level of abstraction from the immediate tangible form of the computer program. Now, not just the code of a program is protected but its whole 'look and feel' is also protected by copyright.

Case

Whelan Associates Inc v Jaslow Dental Laboratory Inc [1987] FSR 1

> After attempting to write a computer program on a personal computer to handle the administration of dental laboratories, J appointed a company to write the program for an IBM computer. The program was written in the EDL programming language and was called 'Dentalab'. The plaintiff acquired rights in the Dentalab program. After about two years, realising that Dentalab would not run on microcomputers used by many dental laboratories, J began to write a program called 'Dentcom' in the BASIC programming language, later employing a programmer to complete the program. At trial at first instance it was held that the Dentcom program infringed the copyright in the Dentalab program because its structure and organisation were substantially similar. On appeal, the United States Court of Appeals (3rd circuit) had to decide whether there had been infringement of the copyright in the program written in EDL. This was not an easy question to answer

because listings of the programs, being written in different programming languages, at first sight, looked very different. Any literal similarity was lacking. The fundamental task of the court was to distinguish between idea and expression in relation to computer programs, and develop a test which could be used in future. An objective test of substantial similarity, known as the Arnstein test, was rejected by the court as being not useful and potentially misleading where the subject matter was particularly complex such as in the case of computer programs.

It was held that, in relation to a computer program designed to carry out a mundane task, anything which was essential to the task was idea whilst anything which was not essential and could have been written in different ways was expression. If these latter parts were copied, then the copyright would be infringed because the expression had been copied. If the programmer had no option but to write a part of the program the way he did because the task to be achieved dictated its form and content then that part was idea and not protected by copyright. Similarly, the purpose of a utilitarian program was idea, and the structure of the program, if there were several different possible structures which could have been adopted, was expression. Consequently, not just the actual program code but the structure of a computer program can be protected by copyright if, because of similar structure, the 'look and feel' of the programs are similar.

Two points must be made about this case. First, there must have been copying of some sort. If the second program had been written independently, there would be no copyright infringement. An independently created computer program cannot infringe the copyright subsisting in another program no matter how similar the programs are. The second point is that the court was trying to lay the foundations of a test which could be used to determine whether the parts copied where idea or expression. Essentially the case is about evidential law, not substantive law. The *Whelan* case has come under scrutiny in subsequent cases in the United States and has been criticised in the later case of *Computer Associates v Altai*, discussed later. In one case involving computer programs written to assist in the marketing of cotton, it was said that the structure of the original program was idea and not expression because the application itself dictated the structure of the program. The program's application was to assist in the marketing of cotton and this, by its very nature, could only be expressed in computer programs exhibiting a substantially similar structure. It left no room for alternative structures. Other cases have concerned screen displays and whether their arrangement and sequence is a manifestation of the computer program's structure.

The look and feel argument as applied in *Whelan* is flawed because, contrary to the views of the court in the cotton marketing program case mentioned above, even the simplest function can be performed using different algorithms. It depends on how sophisticated and user-friendly the program is intended to be. Two programs used to perform the same simple function could have vastly differing structures and, therefore, the hypothesis that a program's application will dictate the structure of the program is a false one.

Example (see Figures 3.1 and 3.2)

Consider a simple program to add information to a database. The information is very simple, it comprises a surname only. The two flowcharts in Figures 3.1 and 3.2 show alternative ways in which this function could be achieved. In the first flowchart, each name is entered one at a time and then added to the database. The user is asked if he or she wishes to enter another name. In the second example, the screen is cleared and then a template is displayed on the screen permitting the user to enter several names at a time. When the template is completed, a separate routine is called up to check whether a name already exists and allows appropriate action to be taken. Before the names are added to the database another check is made to see if the first name is 'END' which is the signal to terminate the program. Several other variations are possible and yet it is harder to think of anything much simpler than this and lacking in scope for individual treatment.

Figure 3.1 Flowchart No 1

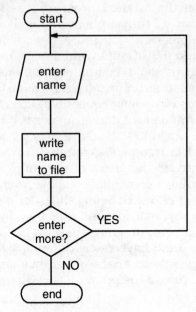

Figure 3.2 Flowchart No 2

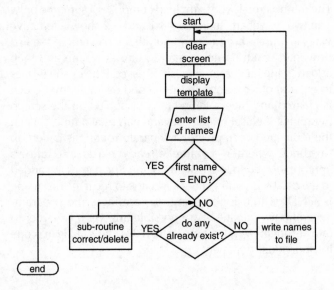

In terms of the 'look and feel' test, the conclusion to be drawn is that if a programmer takes a little care to see that the structure is different he will not infringe copyright if he uses another computer program language when developing his own. In the unlikely event that the structure (or even the actual code) is dictated by the program's function, the programmer may be able to copy those elements directly. It may be possible to draw from the experience and skill of other programmers, providing other things are not done which might infringe copyright, for example, copying a screen display. It may be difficult to sympathise with the defendant in *Whelan* because he had used the plaintiff's program in order to take a short cut in developing his own program but, perhaps, if he had taken a little more care to make structural changes, he would have avoided liability. On the other hand, there is a danger that protecting program structure could discourage computer programmers from using ideas for programs developed during their previous employment for fear of being sued for copyright infringement. Yet, there is a great deal of work expended in developing computer programs before the actual program code is written. Much of this work is concerned with deciding the structure and flow of the program and there is a strong argument for protecting this. In *Whelan*, the court recognised that the actual coding process is a relatively small part of the work involved in creating a program, and that a large portion of the expense and difficulty is attributable to the development of the program structure and logic; that is, its algorithm.

THE LOOK AND FEEL TEST REFINED

The *Whelan* case attracted a great deal of criticism even though it has been used as the basis of many decisions on non-literal copying. One point to bear in mind is that this case was directed, primarily, at the scope of protection available for program structure. Many other elements of a program or associated with a program can be copied without copying the actual program code. Examples are menu systems, user interfaces, database structures and codes, input and output formats and methods of entering and modifying input text. The following case developed the look and feel test in such a way that it would be more readily applicable to all forms of non-literal elements.

Case

Computer Associates Inc v Altai Inc (1992) 23 USPQ 2d 1241

The defendant company produced a program for job scheduling, controlling the order of processing different tasks on a computer. The program was called Oscar and it had a common interface component which made it compatible with different operating systems. This interface had been written by an ex-employee of the plaintiff company which had a similar program with a similar interface, known as Adapter. When the plaintiff complained of copyright infringement, the defendant employed different programmers to re-write the interface. The defendant agreed to pay damages of US $364,444 in respect of its first version of Oscar but the plaintiff now claimed that the new version of Oscar still infringed its copyright. It was held that the new version of Oscar did not infringe the plaintiff's program. This was confirmed by the Court of Appeals which took the opportunity to lay down a more sophisticated test for non-literal copying than that expressed in *Whelan* which was criticised for taking insufficient account of the technicalities of computer programming.

The new test involves three stages. The first stage is *abstraction* by which the non-literal elements of the program are determined by a process like reverse engineering, tracing back the programmer's steps in the process of writing the program. This operation results in the identification of the non-literal elements (structure and other features) of varying degrees of detail.

The second stage is one of *filtration*, filtering out the elements that are not protected by copyright. These will be those features that are unprotectable ideas, dictated by considerations of efficiency, dictated by external factors or taken from the public domain. After these elements are removed the remainder is the program's 'golden nugget'.

The final stage involves a *comparison* of the two programs, a determination of whether the defendant had copied a substantial part of the protected expression of the plaintiff's program.

This test is shown diagramatically in Figure 3.3. Of course, it is intended to be applied to non-literal copying but can be criticised on two grounds. First, it will be difficult to apply in practice, as the judge in the case freely acknowledged saying that further case law would make the test more certain and predictable in its application. The second criticism is that it seems artificial in the extreme to break up a program into many constituent parts and to consider those parts separately. Surely, it should be a matter of considering the whole of the two programs and deciding first of all whether there has been copying and, second, whether the defendant's program contains a part or parts of the plaintiff's program which can be described as substantial in terms of the plaintiff's whole program. However, the above case represents the current approach to non-literal copying in the United States. Another point is that although *Whelan* was heavily criticised, the status of the courts in both cases was the same and the *Computer Associates* case can be described simply as a refinement of 'look and feel' rather than a rejection of it.

Figure 3.3 A test for non-literal infringement

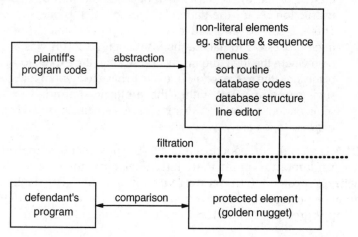

THE IDEA/EXPRESSION MERGER DOCTRINE

There may be occasions when it is impossible to separate idea from expression because of constraints which severely limit the ways in which the ideas contained in a computer program can be expressed. If this is the situation then there is no infringement of copyright even if the expression is copied. This is because the expression is inexorably determined by the idea; the two can be said to have merged. The *Whelan* case suggests that this is so although, in that case, there was no such constraint. We have to turn to a case concerning microprocessors to see the application of the merger doctrine.

Case

NEC Corpn v Intel Corpn (1989) 10 USPQ 2d

> NEC made a set of microprocessors to compete with those made by Intel. The NEC chips contained similar programs, referred to as microcode, dealing with the same instruction set for the microprocessors. (Actually, the NEC chips had an extended version of the Intel microcode and were capable of operating at a faster speed.) NEC had discovered the Intel microcode by reverse analysis, that is, by disassembling the code.
>
> It was held that, generally, microcode is protected by copyright but, in this case, the code was dictated by the instruction set for the particular type of microprocessor. There were no alternative ways of programming the microprocessors to handle the instruction set. This was a case where the idea (the instruction set) and the expression of the idea (the microcode) were said to have merged. (Note: such cases may fall within the protection afforded to semiconductor products. In this case, the architecture of the chip, its topography, was different.)

This is all well and good but it leaves the designer of something as fundamental as an instruction set for a microprocessor without protection under normal copyright law. The designer may be protected, in the United States, by the Semiconductor Chip Protection Act of 1984 or, in the United Kingdom, as a result of the Design Right (Semiconductor Regulations) 1989 (see Chapter 11). Other areas of law may afford some protection against copying, such as patent law or the law of confidence (trade secrets).

One way of looking at the idea/expression merger doctrine is to view it as an evidential test. (The same claim can be made for the look and feel test.) Copyright infringement is determined by considering the acts alleged to have been committed by the defendant. An important example of those acts is copying. If two works are very similar this can mean one of four things.

1. The defendant has copied the plaintiff's work. Several alternative forms of expression were possible.
2. The defendant has copied the plaintiff's work. The function was such that it dictated the form of the expression.
3. The defendant created his work independently. Although works to perform the same function could have been expressed in a number of different ways, the similarity between the works of the defendant and the plaintiff has occurred by chance.
4. The defendant has created his work independently, the similarity is unavoidable because of constraints upon the expression of the work.

Looking at these situations in terms of evidential potency, in the first case there is no merger of idea and expression and the fact of similarity will raise a very strong presumption of copying. The same cannot be said for the second case, indeed, the deliberate act of copying would seem not to be an infringement of copyright in the United States because the plaintiff's work was idea and not expression. In the fourth example, there can be no presumption of copying and there is plainly no infringement of copyright. In the third case, the defendant is unfortunate in that a presumption of copying could be raised, requiring him to prove that he did not copy. Perhaps, in the United States, the courts' attention has been focused on attempting to find workable tests for infringement of copyright and sophisticated ways of distinguishing between idea and expression such that they have lost sight of the basic question – did the defendant copy the plaintiff's work, as expressed?

In essence, the idea/expression merger doctrine is simply a restatement of the basic principle in *Whelan*. A software company sued for infringement of software copyright, where there is evidence of copying or at least a strong presumption to that effect, is likely to raise the argument that, although parts of the plaintiff's program were copied, only those parts which were dictated by the software's function were copied. Those parts ought not to be protected by copyright because the idea and the expression have merged. The question for the courts in the United States is whether those parts are indeed unprotected for such a reason and the merger doctrine provides a crude test which is, in practice, difficult to apply. The use of a test of this nature also brings into question the ability of judges without training in computer technology to apply and resolve it consistently and fairly. Or, indeed, to understand it in the first place.

IDEA/EXPRESSION AND SCREEN DISPLAYS

There have been several cases in the United States about the alleged copying of screen displays. Two possibilities exist. First, that copying the screen display infringes the copyright in the underlying program. There may be difficulties concerning the question as to whether the part of the program generating the screen display represents a substantial part of the computer program as a whole. The second possibility is that the screen display is a work of copyright independent of the computer program generating it. The first approach has been rejected on the basis that program code generating a particular screen display can be written in many different ways. Even if the same programming language is used, the code may be different.

Example

A screen display is to be written by two programmers, Rosie and Arnold. The screen display will contain text only. Both programmers are given a sheet containing a handwritten representation of what the display should look like. They are then told to write a sub-routine to produce the display using the BASIC programming language. Rosie's routine contains a list of PRINT statements, with all the text embedded within the routine. On the other hand, Arnold decided to store all the text in a sequential file and his routine consists of a set of commands to read the file and print it to the screen. The two routines look entirely different. Neither is there any structural similarity because Rosie's routine is a list of statements performed in sequence whereas Arnold's uses an iterative loop which is executed until the end of the file in which he has stored the text is reached.

The fact that the program code generating the screen displays can be written in several different ways does not alter the fact that the displays are identical. Therefore, this suggests that regard should be had to the screen display as an independent work, and this is the approach which has been adopted in the United States. Indeed, the look and feel test has been applied to screen displays as works of copyright on their own, irrespective of the underlying program.

Case

Digital Communications Associates v Softklone Distributing Corp
659 F Supp 449 (ND Ga 1987)

The plaintiff designed a screen display for a communications program called Crosstalk XVI. The display showed a list of commands and the user could select one by entering the first two letters of the required command. The first two letters of each command were highlighted and in block capitals. The defendant developed a communications system called Mirror which had a similar screen display.

The court afforded protection to the screen display and differentiated between idea and expression by regarding the idea of a screen display as being the concept of the screen, whereas the means used to communicate the screen's manner of operation, that is, the arrangement of commands, the highlighting and capitalisation, were all part of the expression of the screen display.

In an earlier case involving screen displays, *Broderbund Software v Unison World* 648 F Supp 1127 (ND Cal 1986), the court held that the screen displays were protected through the copyright in the program. This approach was rejected in the *Digital Communications* case. However, an important point in the *Broderbund* case was that the court held that, as there were several means in which the screens could have been structured, sequenced and arranged, the actual way selected by the plaintiff was copyrightable expression.

In the *Broderbund* case, the defendant argued that there was no other way to structure the screens or design the input formats and that, therefore, these elements were idea and not expression. In other words, the function dictated these elements of the system. This argument was quickly overcome by the plaintiff who produced another competing program which performed a similar function (to design greetings cards, signs, banners and posters) but which had screen displays and screen sequences which were very different. This demonstrates the importance of such evidence in cases involving idea and expression. A defendant will attempt to show that the part copied was idea because there was no scope for alternative implementations, whilst the plaintiff will try to find other products which perform the same function but do so in different ways.

Some screen displays are very distinctive. If they are generated by an applications program a rival can take steps to avoid copying them. However, in some cases, especially where a display, or general format for a display, is concerned with a user interface or general methodology for user interfaces, this can present rivals with problems. The Apple Mac and the Windows environment are good examples of this. They have sometimes been referred to as 'WIMP' environments, standing for 'windows, icons, menus, pointers (eg mouse)'. A windows environment is one in which the screen can be divided up into different areas, often overlapping, so that several files or applications can be viewed at once. Icons are small symbols displayed on the screen representing various actions or devices. For example, a tiny picture of a dustbin may be used to signify that the user may select this to erase a computer file; a picture of a filing cabinet may be used so that the user can select this to open a new file, etc. Rather than typing in a command, the user may move the cursor over an icon and select the function or device it represents by 'clicking' on it using the mouse or other pointing device. A pull-down menu is a menu of commands from which the user can select, which is not normally displayed but which can be called up by the user, usually by clicking on the heading for the menu. An item on the menu can then be selected by moving the cursor to it and clicking the mouse button. A typical windows environment screen display is shown in Figure 3.4.

Figure 3.4 WIMPS environment screen display

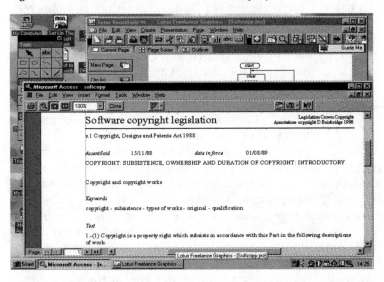

User interfaces raise two issues. The interface may be protected by copyright as a separate work or it may be protected through the medium of the screen display. Protection of the interface itself is considered later. As far as the screen display itself is concerned, there is a tendency for screen displays for application programs written for WIMP environments to look similar. However, there have been rumblings and threats in the United States concerning the alleged copying of such displays. Two important questions have been raised:

1. Is the concept of a WIMPS environment protected by copyright through its screen display?
2. Are the icons protected independently as works of copyright?

On the basis of an initial consideration, the first question must be answered in the negative because the environment must be idea not expression. It is a concept, and anyone wishing to make use of that concept will probably end up with a screen display which looks like the existing ones to a large extent. There are also very good policy reasons why copyright protection should not be extended to the concept. It is desirable that a degree of standardisation is achieved amongst software packages in terms of their user interface, that is, the system employed to display commands, functions and activities to users and to allow those users to make selections and enter data. Such an approach lies at the heart of a user-friendly computer system. Indeed, the Apple Mac is an extremely good example of this. However, the reasoning in the *Lotus* cases discussed later cast some doubt on the copyright protection of user interfaces.

The answer to the second question is probably also in the negative. Attempts by Apple to prevent the use of similar icons (and indeed the concept of a windows environment) by Microsoft have come to nothing. Any drawing (whether displayed on a computer screen or otherwise) is potentially a work of copyright. But icons are usually fairly simplistic, rudimentary outlines with little detail and are too trivial to attract copyright protection. They fail to reach the minimum threshold. The answer might be different if the icon is the result of some skill and judgment and is more detailed, even if it is on a small scale. Alternatively, many icons have become commonplace in the industry and used by numerous software companies, a factor which will weaken or destroy copyright protection.

Of course, copyright infringement requires that some use is made by the infringer of the copyright work, such as making copies of it. There must be a link between the protected work and the infringing work. If a programmer decides to design some new icons for a new application program and he or she does this independently, without looking at other software packages, then there can be no infringement of copyright even though the new icons may look similar to those in other packages. The simplicity of icons generally and the objective of designing them so that their purpose is apparent merely by looking at them will result in many similarities in icons for different packages. If a dozen programmers were asked to design independently some icons to represent a number of different functions, such as opening a file, saving a file, running a spell-checker, etc, the chances are that many of the resulting icons would look similar. There are parallels here to the United Kingdom case of *Kenrick v Lawrence*, discussed in Chapter 2. In that case, the fact that most artists asked to draw a simple diagram showing persons how to vote would produce similar drawings, meant that a mere similarity did not prove copying. However, it was accepted that an exact duplicate would infringe. Hence, the position would seem to be that only an exact duplicate of an icon could infringe copyright, provided, of course, that it was protected by copyright. Very few icons will be so protected as noted above.

USER INTERFACES

A user interface must be distinguished from a screen display even though the interface may be inevitably linked with or associated with the screen display. One point of view is that a user interface must be idea *per se*. On the other hand, certain elements of the interface could be considered to be expression, although such expression must be abstract because the screen display associated with it cannot be the interface itself. Two cases involved the user interface of the popular Lotus 1-2-3 spreadsheet software. The first decided that the menu system was protected by copyright.

Case

Lotus Development Corpn v Paperback Software International
740 F Supp 37 (D Mass 1990)

> The defendant developed a spreadsheet program known as VP-Planner. Because of the success of the plaintiff's Lotus 1-2-3

spreadsheet program, the defendant wanted to make VP-Planner compatible with Lotus 1-2-3 and, therefore, the defendant ensured that the arrangement of commands and menus in VP-Planner conformed to those in Lotus 1-2-3 so that it was possible to transfer spreadsheets from VP-Planner to Lotus 1-2-3 and vice versa, without prejudicing the functionality of any macros used in a spreadsheet. (A macro is a list of commands which are stored in a separate executable file, their purpose being to save keystrokes, the whole series of commands can be executed by a single keystroke rather than having to enter each command separately.) To achieve compatibility, the command language of VP-Planner was almost identical to that available with Lotus 1-2-3. Another advantage of using the same command language was that Lotus 1-2-3 users could transfer to VP-Planner without any need for further training.

The defendant claimed that he had not copied the program code of Lotus 1-2-3, so this was a case of 'non-literal copying'. Therefore, the central issue was whether the non-literal elements of the plaintiff's program were protected by copyright. The non-literal elements in question were the overall organisation and structure of the program, the content and structure of the command system, the screen displays and, especially, the user interface.

In a mammoth judgment in the District Court for Massachusetts, Judge Keeton held that the user interface of Lotus 1-2-3, in particular the two-line moving cursor menu, was protected by copyright and that the defendant had infringed that copyright. The defendant could not escape liability on the basis that this part of the interface was dictated by function because it was effected in different ways in different spreadsheet programs. For example, some use a list of letters (Visicalc uses 'BCDEFGIMPRSTVW-'), others use a three-line menu or pull-down menus. However, some of the other features such as the rotated 'L' used to contain the grid reference letters and numbers and the use of certain keys to call up commands and perform arithmetical functions, for example, the '/', '+', '-' and '*' keys were held not to be protected because they were common to spreadsheets, even though they were not essential (the Excel

spreadsheet does not use the rotated 'L'). Figure 3.5 shows
the basic screen display of Lotus 1-2-3 with the rotated 'L'
and moving cursor menu indicated.

Figure 3.5 Basic screen display for Lotus 1-2-3

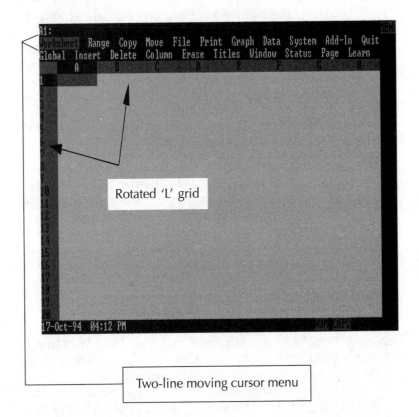

In his favour, Judge Keeton realised that it was essential to attempt to lay down a test which was helpful in practical terms. He said that, whilst ideas are not protected and expression is, it does not automatically follow that every expression of an idea is protected by copyright. Four things must be considered:

1. Originality: the expression must be original. That is, it originated from the author.
2. Functionality: if the expression does no more than embody elements of an idea which is functional in a utilitarian sense, the expression is not copyrightable.
3. Obviousness: if the expression is obvious it is inseparable from the idea and hence not protected by copyright.
4. Merger: if the particular expression is one of a quite limited number of forms of expression, then it is not copyrightable.

It was accepted that disentangling idea from expression was not an 'either-or' or 'black and white' matter but is a matter of degree and a distinction must be made between the generality and specificity of conceptualising an idea. A legal test for copyrightability was suggested, based on constructing a scale of abstraction from the most generalised conception at one end to the most particularised conception at the other end. The expression being considered was placed on this scale and a decision made based on choice and judgment. Indeed, the famous and respected Judge Learned Hand had suggested that this could only be done in an *ad hoc* way, for example, in *Shipman v RKO Radio Pictures* 100 F 2d 533 (2d Cir 1938). Such an approach does little to bring certainty to software copyright law.

It was not long before someone else made use of the Lotus 1-2-3 menu system and a similar scenario lay behind *Lotus Development Corp v Borland International Inc.*

Case

Lotus Development Corpn v Borland International Inc [1997] FSR 61, 1st Circuit Court of Appeal

This was an appeal against the judgment of Judge Keeton who had ruled that Borland had infringed copyright by using the Lotus Menu Command system in Borland's Quattro spreadsheet on a similar basis to the above case. Borland appealed.

The appeal succeeded because the court held that the menu command system was simply a method of operation. The court drew an analogy with the buttons on a video recorder, by which it could be operated. The United States Copyright Act expressly excludes methods of operation from copyright protection (section 102(b)). The fact that the Lotus designers could have designed the menu command system differently (suggesting that it was expression) did not take it out of the statutory exception.

Postcript: The United States Supreme Court affirmed the Court of Appeals decision in a split vote, *Computing*, 25 January 1996, p 8. However, because the vote was split equally (4:4), there was no substantive judgment from the Supreme Court. The issue is not yet beyond doubt.

Some earlier decisions now seem doubtful. For example, in *Autoskill Inc v National Educational Support Systems Inc* (1993) 994 F 2d 1476 (10th Cir) it was held that a keying procedure using the 1, 2 and 3 keys was potentially protectable and in *Brown Bag Software v Symantec Corpn* (1992) F 2d 1465 (9th Cir) it was suggested that menus and keystrokes were 'copyrightable' though, in the event, it was found that there was no infringement of these elements of the program.

Hence, a blow has been struck in favour of common interfaces and the earlier case of *Lotus v Paperback* overturned. However, that case is still of some interest because of Judge Keeton's *dicta* on the distinction between expression and idea and, ominously, the statutory 'method of operation' exception to copyright protection is not a feature of United Kingdom copyright law. It may, however, become an express feature of United Kingdom copyright law as a result of further harmonisation through European Directives and the TRIPS Agreement.

To summarise, it can be seen that the distinction between idea and expression is never going to be clear cut. In practice, the tests laid down in the first *Lotus* case and the *Computer Associates* case will do little to assist a judge in determining whether a particular element of a computer program is protected by copyright law, and this could contribute to the uncertainty of litigation in this area. The problem for software companies is that they cannot predict with any certainty what they can and cannot do with another company's computer program. Many will play safe and avoid similarities with other software and this will have a negative effect on the future development and cross-fertilisation of ideas, concepts and user interfaces. The movement towards universal standards and compatibility could be hampered. In the United States, some software companies have felt unable to appeal against what they considered to be restrictive court decisions because of the enormous expense associated with litigation in this area. They feared they would have been bankrupted by the costs if they lost the appeal.

SOLUTION TO EXAMPLE PROBLEM

The position under United States copyright law as described above will now be applied to the 'Jakesoft' problem described earlier in this chapter in the section on the idea/expression distinction.

Solution

It will be recalled that Jakesoft Inc intended to develop a word processing system and, to make its system more attractive to potential customers, it contemplated the following actions:

(a) to use a command system and basic screen display similar to the leading package, WORDWRAP;

(b) to inspect the program code of the spreadsheet system LILY A-B-C and examine LILY files in order to determine interface details so that the new word processor can import LILY charts.

The command system for WORDWRAP is probably not protected by copyright as a form of expression, being a method of operation (see the *Lotus v Borland* case). The screen display itself will be protected independently if not commonplace (see the *Digital Communications* case).

However, it is unlikely that the basic display is protected if it contains very little material. The determination of file interface details of the LILY program will infringe only if those details or their structure are copied in the new word processing program. Even if they are, if those details are constrained by the program's function so that no alternatives (or only slight differences are feasible) it may be a case of merger of idea and expression (see the *Whelan* case and the *NEC* case). In the United Kingdom, decompilation to obtain interface details may be permitted and in the United States, a defence of fair use may be available in appropriate cases; see Chapter 5.

IMPLICATIONS FOR THE UNITED KINGDOM

Three particular issues emanating from United States law are important in terms of their effect on United Kingdom law. United States cases have frequently been cited in argument in court trials in the United Kingdom, especially *Whelan v Jaslow*, *Lotus v Paperback*, and *Computer Associates*. In *Richardson v Flanders*, discussed in the following chapter, those cases were approved of and partially applied by the English judge. There are three issues from the United States:

1. The look and feel test and protection of program structure.
2. The idea/expression merger doctrine.
3. The extension of copyright protection to other non-literal elements, but not if deemed to be a method of operation.

Other issues, such as the protection of screen displays, are already well catered for in United Kingdom law and will be discussed in the following chapter.

On the subject of the look and feel doctrine, historically there is little English case law on the protection of the structure of copyright works. United Kingdom law has concentrated on the question of whether a substantial part of a work which has been recorded has been copied. Certainly, the idea/expression distinction is not so firmly rooted in United Kingdom law although there are ample judicial statements in favour of it such as in *Kenrick v Lawrence*, discussed in the previous chapter. The distinction is also implicit in copyright legislation. On the question of copyright and structure, there is one important House of Lords decision about a football coupon which lends weight to the argument that the structure of a computer program is a protectable element under copyright law.

Case

Ladbroke (Football) Ltd v William Hill (Football) Ltd [1964] 1 WLR 273

> The plaintiff designed a fixed odds football coupon. The defendant copied the overall layout by producing his own fixed odds football coupon although there were some differences, for example, in the fixtures and the odds. It was held that the coupon, which was laid out in the form of grids containing football matches and having various bets associated with them, was protected by copyright as an original literary compilation. The defendant had infringed that copyright by copying the general layout of the coupon. The football matches, the fixtures, changed from week to week and, indeed, the copyright subsisting in the fixture list itself belonged to the Football Association, so that, effectively, all that was left to protect was the layout of the football coupon; in other words, its structure.

It would seem that this case lays the foundations for the possible development of the scope of the restricted act of copying to include the structure of a computer program in addition to the actual program code itself. But, as noted, a structural similarity test may be easily defeated by a determined programmer. A test based on program function would be easier to apply but would give monopoly protection, which is counter to general copyright principles. In the end, the question of whether a computer program has been copied from another may be decided on the basis of the judge's subjective feelings which may have been influenced, to a greater or lesser extent, by expert witnesses. This is not at all satisfactory given that many judges have no more than a superficial understanding of computer technology.

The idea/expression merger is unlikely to find favour. It is very difficult to predict what the United Kingdom courts would make of a claim of infringement of a user interface. It is possible that judges would tend to look for some underlying work which would be infringed by copying the interface such as a screen display or preparatory material such as a flowchart. These issues will be discussed in more detail in Chapters 4 and 5 which concentrate on the United Kingdom position as it currently is, and as it is likely to develop in the future.

Finally, a brief note of the implications of Jakesoft's intended activities if they were subject to United Kingdom copyright law. As regards the command system, copying this might infringe copyright in preparatory materials such as specifications, drawings and flowcharts. Another option is that the command system can be considered to an abstraction, one step removed, from the expression of the software and it may be protected on the basis of non-literal copying.

Case

Corelli v Gray [1913] TLR 570

> The plaintiff had written a novel called *Temporal Power* and had alleged that the defendant had infringed the literary copyright in the novel by performing a dramatic sketch written by the defendant called '*The People's King*'. The plaintiff founded her case on coincidences and similarities between the novel and the sketch.
>
> Although there were relatively few coincidences in language, looking at the aggregate of similarities in the situation and dramatic incidents, the judge was of the opinion that it was impossible that this could be due to mere chance, and must have been the result of a process of copying or appropriation by the defendant. The defendant had incorporated dramatic incidents from the novel into his sketch. This case shows that copying can be non-literal and an absence of language similarity does not automatically mean that there has been no infringement of copyright.

Although there is potential protection for a screen display, if it is very simple it may be considered to be commonplace or the result of insufficient skill and judgment to attract protection. Otherwise, copying the screen display may infringe copyright in the screen display itself or in preparatory design materials such as a drawing showing a representation of the proposed screen display.

Chapter 4

The scope of copyright protection for computer programs and associated works

INTRODUCTION

In this chapter the scope of copyright protection for computer software in the United Kingdom is examined in detail. As noted in Chapter 1, computer software is not restricted to computer programs and includes other items such as computer data, programming languages, databases, flowcharts and user manuals. Computer programs have several other forms of works associated with them or with their development or use, and the copyright protection of these ancillary items may have the effect of extending the *de facto* protection of computer programs. In line with the approach taken in the United States, the protection of a computer program extends beyond the actual program code, whether source or object code, to 'non-literal' elements of the program, such as its structure, sequence of operations, user interface (possibly) and database structure.

The scope and boundaries of the restricted act of copying will be described first, in the context of a computer program, including developments in the United Kingdom on look and feel, followed by an examination of the protection of audio and visual works produced by the operation of a computer program. The copyright position of preparatory design material such as flowcharts and specifications will be discussed next. There follows a consideration of the acts permitted under copyright law with the exception of the act of decompilation which is of such import that it warrants separate treatment in Chapter 5 which addresses the thorny question of whether the reverse analysis of computer programs can be carried out without infringing copyright. Finally, other factors which may narrow the scope of copyright protection such as the controls over the abuse of the right and policy considerations are described. As before, case studies and examples are interspersed with the text with the aims of illustrating and clarifying the law in addition to providing a practical context. Statutory references are to the Copyright, Designs and Patents Act 1988 unless otherwise stated.

COPYING

There are several reasons why someone would want to make a copy of a computer program or other items of software such as databases, manuals and guides. At its simplest, and most common, copying consists of making duplicate copies, direct copies of programs copied from the original to new disks using, for example, the DOS command of DISKCOPY (to duplicate a disk) or COPY (to copy a single file or series of files) or the Windows file manager in addition to making photocopies of the accompanying documentation. The typical purposes are as follows:

- To enable the programs, files or databases to be used on a greater number of computers than permitted by the licence agreement. Typically, a company might obtain a single-user licence and then distribute many working copies throughout the organisation. The Federation Against Software Theft (FAST), the Software Publishers Association (SPA) and other organisations are active in stamping out such practices.
- To 'sell' as genuine, unauthorised copies. In one raid in Germany, pirated software with an estimated value of £37m was seized (*Computing*, 13 August 1998, p 4). Several computer dealers have been prosecuted successfully and given custodial sentences for this activity. The courts have shown a willingness to take this criminal offence more seriously and, in 1994, an Oxford computer dealer was jailed for six months for making unauthorised copies of WordPerfect (*Computing*, 11 August 1994, p 3). In 1997, the

owner of a computer supplier was jailed for three months for selling computers pre-loaded with pirated software (*Computing*, 1 May 1997, p 4).

• To make a back-up copy should the original copy become damaged or corrupted. This will be permissible in the majority of situations and, indeed, cannot be prevented in most cases as far as computer programs are concerned.

The first two of the above possibilities are not troublesome in terms of the law which is quite clear that such copying infringes copyright. In addition, there are a number of other legal remedies apart from those under copyright law. In the first case above, there will be a breach of the licence agreement and the copyright owner will be able to sue on that basis in addition to, or instead of, suing for copyright infringement. In the second case, there will be criminal offences associated with copyright law and with trade descriptions law and, possibly, even forgery and counterfeiting. In the third case, making back-up copies normally will be permitted under section 50A of the Copyright, Designs and Patents Act 1988 which specifically provides for the making of necessary back-up copies of computer programs by lawful users. A prudent licensee will guard against a proliferation of unauthorised copies by ensuring effective control and auditing of the use of computer software. Another form of copying is where it is done privately between friends. For example, a schoolboy makes a copy of a friend's computer game. There is little the computer industry can do about this apart from educating software users and attempts at copy-protecting software have, in the main, been unsuccessful. Whether such copying represents a serious loss in sales is a moot point.

Another form of copying is where computer software is used as a basis for developing a similar competing product. The programs and manuals are not copied literally. The program is used as a means to derive the new program. The know-how underlying the program is ascertained and used to write a new program. Often, to complicate matters, the new program is written using a different computer programming language. This form of non-literal copying is not without its difficulties for copyright law, and an important English case on look and feel, *Richardson v Flanders*, is discussed later and the implications of developments in the United States in this area have been discussed in the previous chapter and will be further discussed.

Copying – fundamental principles

The copyright in a computer program is infringed if a copy is made of the whole or a substantial part of it without the permission of the copyright owner. It has been noted that the question of substantiality has been interpreted by the judges on a qualitative basis and, theoretically, copying a relatively small part of a computer program can infringe copyright if that part is an important part of the whole. However, the fact that a computer program will not run without the part copied is not relevant to determining whether the part is substantial nor is the fact that the part copied is used frequently during the operation of the computer program, such as in the case of a small sub-routine which is executed many times; see *Cantor Fitzgerald International v Tradition (UK) Ltd* (1999) Times, 19 May, discussed in Chapter 2.

Admittedly it would be very convenient if an exact percentage could be quoted for the boundary between infringement and non-infringement, such as five per cent or ten per cent. However, each case must be examined in the light of its own circumstances, and in one case a High Court judge was prepared to contemplate that as little as 43 line similarities out of a total of 9,000 lines might amount to a substantial part although, in addition, there were structural similarities between the programs concerned as well as some common errors. As a consequence, it is risky to copy any part, however small, of another program, and it is far better to avoid any literal copying of the code of another program. If there has been, or appears to have been, some partial copying of another computer program, the following factors might well be taken into account by a judge in deciding whether the part taken is substantial and amounts to an infringement of copyright:

• Does the second program compete with the first?
• Is the part copied commonplace?

- Does the part copied contain a special or attractive feature of the first program?
- When looked at in isolation could it be said that the part copied was the result of skill or judgment?

It is essential to understand that, for a finding of infringement by copying a computer program, the court must be satisfied, on a balance of probabilities, that actual copying has taken place. The fact that two computer programs are similar does not inevitably mean that the copyright in the first program has been infringed. The act of copying must be proved. Theoretically, it is possible for two computer programs to be identical and to be the result of independent effort and skill. Of course, if two computer programs are very similar, this could raise a strong presumption that copying has taken place, and this is so especially where both programs have been written by the same person. A common example is an employee computer programmer who leaves his or her job and then writes another computer program which bears a striking resemblance to one written for the previous employer. However, even this is not conclusive and it can, at best, shift the burden of proof. Instead of the plaintiff having to show that his program has been copied by the defendant, the defendant will have the burden of proving that he or she did not copy the original program, a burden of proof which could be extremely difficult to discharge.

Example

Ada was employed by Whizzo Consumer Supplies Ltd where she wrote a computer program to select the speediest routes for Whizzo's delivery drivers. Ada is now employed by Whizzo's main competitor, Whamo plc and there she has written another computer program to calculate delivery routes. The two programs are not identical but there are several similarities, some of the smaller sub-routines are identical but these represent only a small part of the whole programs. The later program has several more features than the first one. Whizzo has just served a claim form on Whamo alleging infringement of the copyright in Whizzo's computer program. (Note that Whizzo and Whamo are the owners of the copyrights in the respective programs as Ada produced both as an employee in the course of her employment.)

Had Whamo employed someone other than Ada to write the program, they would have had little to fear. However, because Ada wrote the first program for Whizzo, this might mean that Whamo will have to prove that Ada did not copy from the first program. The fact that there are some similarities does not help Whizzo, and this might be aggravated if other non-literal similarities, such as the overall structure, menus or the sequence of operations performed by the two programs, are similar. Whamo should have made sure that Ada did not use any materials retained from her previous employment, only her knowledge of the general ideas underlying the Whizzo program. To go further, Whamo would have been well advised to instruct Ada to take steps to ensure that the two programs were as different as possible, even in respect of structure and flow. Deliberately using a different algorithm and computer language would help in this respect.

In addition to copyright, there may also be breach of confidence issues if the program written for Whizzo was in the nature of a trade secret (for example, nobody had ever thought of writing a program to perform such a function before). However, Ada's position in terms of future employability might be an important factor in determining whether the information was confidential. It might be considered that her knowledge of the program's function is part and parcel of her own skill and experience. Balancing an employee's duty of confidence to a previous employer and the employee's ability to make use of his or her knowledge and experience is not an easy matter.

Simply stated, there must be a causal relationship between the programs; the first must be the progenitor of the second for infringement by copying. An objective similarity between two programs does no more than raise an inference that there has been copying. If there is no obvious link between the programs such as in the case of an ex-employee, the plaintiff will have to prove that the defendant did, in fact, copy the original program. Figure 4.1 shows the situation where an employee writes a computer program for one employer and then leaves to write a similar program for a second employer.

Figure 4.1 Employees and copyright infringement

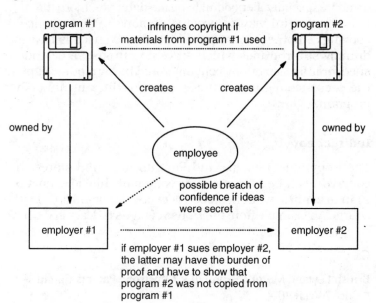

Certain factors can be identified as being important or useful in determining whether a defendant who denies copying has indeed copied. Bearing in mind that in civil trials the standard of proof is based on a balance of probabilities and, if one party's case is slightly better than that of the other, then the former will win the case. In the light of decided cases, the following factors appear to be useful:

- The presence of errors common to both programs. This can put the proof of copying beyond doubt; it then being a matter of determining whether the part copied represents a substantial part of the plaintiff's program.
- Whether the overall structure and sequence of operations performed by the programs are similar.
- The presence of literal similarities in the listings of both programs.
- Whether the first program contains information such as the name of the programmer embedded within the code. If the second program also contains this information it will be irrefutable proof of copying.

The insertion of the names of programmers or of the copyright owner, especially if encoded to make detection more difficult, is a very useful way to provide demonstrable evidence of copying. Another technique which may be used is to insert dummy sub-routines which serve no purpose; a defendant sued for infringement by copying would be hard put to explain the presence of such unnecessary routines in his or her program.

Indirect copying

The Copyright, Designs and Patents Act 1988 states that copyright can be infringed indirectly, but this does no more than to confirm what has been accepted for some time by the courts. An example from the House of Lords is described below.

Case

British Leyland Motor Corpn Ltd v Armstrong Patents Co Ltd
[1986] 2 WLR 400

The plaintiff manufactured the Morris Ital motor car (previously known as the Morris Marina) and also made spare parts for this model of cars. The plaintiff allowed other manufacturers to make spare parts for its cars in return for a modest royalty payment. The defendants decided to make exhaust pipes for the Morris Ital but refused to obtain a licence from the plaintiff. In order to make the exhaust pipes, the defendant obtained a exhaust pipe from a Morris Ital and, by measuring it to determine its shape and design (a process known as 'reverse engineering'), the defendant was able to make exhaust pipes for that make and model of car.

It was held that, by its actions, the defendant had indirectly infringed the copyright in the original drawings of the exhaust pipe, by copying the dimensions of a pipe made in accordance with the drawings. The drawing was an original artistic work of copyright and, in the case of artistic works, copyright is infringed by making a three-dimensional copy of a two-dimensional work (and vice versa). However, the House of Lords refused to enforce the copyright in the drawings in this instance on the basis that a

person who has bought a complex article which will need
replacement parts during its life has a right to obtain spare
parts in a free market.

This case clearly acknowledges the principle that copyright
can be infringed indirectly, and it would have made no
difference to the finding of infringement if the defendant had
not seen the drawings or even had not known of their
existence. In the past, most cases of indirect infringement
have concerned artistic works such as drawings. However,
computer programs are another type of work where the
concept of indirect infringement might be relevant. Of course,
there must be copying which in the British Leyland case was
done through the medium of a finished exhaust pipe. But,
what is the position where a person whom, having seen and
studied a computer program in operation, later decides to
write a new computer program to perform the same function
as the original program? Does he or she infringe the copyright
in the original program even though the person concerned
has not seen the actual code of the program, for example, by
inspecting a printed listing?

As noted above, by section 16(3), the Act recognises that
copyright can be infringed indirectly. Additionally, it
contemplates intervening acts which do not themselves
infringe copyright and the making of copies which are
transient or are incidental to some other use of the work.
However, where the copying is indirect, it is highly probable
that the code of the second program will be significantly
different to that in the first, even if both are written in the
same programming language. This fact might be sufficient
to defeat the possibility of a finding of infringement by indirect
copyright in these circumstances. In the United States, in
one case involving two programs for the design of signs,
banners and notices, it was suggested that copying the
format, structure and sequence of screen displays infringed
the copyright in the underlying programs. However, in a later
case this view was rejected on the basis that a screen display
cannot be a copy of part of the program because the same
screen display can be produced by various programs in
different ways. United Kingdom law could be stronger in this
respect.

Example

Ken Hacker is a stock control clerk who uses a computer program at work called STOCKER which keeps track of stock, orders for supplies, and produces daily reports highlighting which items need to be restocked in the course of the next week. Ken is a keen amateur computer programmer and has written several computer programs for his own entertainment. He realises that there is probably a good market for computer programs like STOCKER and he decides to write a program to do the same things with a view to setting up his own company to sell his new program.

Ken does not copy the program code for STOCKER (in fact it is in object code only and Ken can only write programs using the 'C' computer programming language). Therefore, Ken carefully observes the STOCKER program in use, including the input and output formats and their sequence. When it is finished, Ken's program looks similar to the STOCKER program in use, and the sequence of operations appears to be the same. The question is whether Ken has infringed the copyright in the STOCKER program bearing in mind that he has never seen the program code for STOCKER.

The chances are that the code for the STOCKER program and Ken's program will be quite different. STOCKER may even be written in a different high-level language. There will be little, if any, literal similarity between the two programs. It could be argued that Ken has infringed the copyright subsisting in the STOCKER program even though there is no similarity in the program code on the basis of indirect copying or that he has copied the structure (look and feel, discussed later) of STOCKER. Because of differences in the code, the latter is the more likely route but the former is not altogether a hopeless argument. In the British Leyland case, it was the shape of the exhaust pipe as indicated on the drawing that was important. The material with which the exhaust pipes were to be made and the thickness to be used were irrelevant. The defendant's exhaust pipes could have been very different in these respects. The two primary functions of the exhaust pipe had been copied, being to fit the particular model of car and to evacuate the engine's exhaust gases.

It would be different if Ken had used STOCKER only to gain inspiration and then decided to write a program to fulfil a similar purpose without considering the input and output formats and their sequence in the original program. In this case, there could still be structural similarities but these could be explained on the basis of coincidence, or as being a result of the application concerned dictating those parts of the program's structure. Ken would not have infringed copyright because he did not copy the structure or other non-literal elements, he merely made use of the basic idea, that is, a program to control stock, etc. However, Ken would have to be careful that he did not allow his recollection of the STOCKER program to influence him when he was designing the algorithm for his program and other features such as menus and file structure.

Back-up copies of computer programs

Persons and organisations using computer programs should take care to have back-up copies of their information which is stored on computer. This is an important feature of computer security even though computer equipment and storage media are very reliable. Without effective back-up systems, the failure of a large capacity hard disk can be catastrophic. This need to have back-up copies also applies to computer programs, whatever their nature and most software companies producing systems and applications software appreciate this and provide for the making of back-up copies in their licence agreements. Making necessary back-up copies now has statutory recognition as a result of the European Community Directive on the legal protection of computer programs by virtue of section 50A of the Copyright, Designs and Patents Act 1988.

Lawful users of computer programs (for example, licensees under a licence agreement) may make a back-up of a computer program if necessary for the purposes of his or her lawful use without infringing the copyright in the program. It is reasonable to assume that the word 'necessary' is used in a weak sense. Importantly, any term of condition, whether in a licence agreement or otherwise, which attempts to prohibit or restrict the making of such back-up copies is void and unenforceable. This defence to infringement came into force on 1 January 1993 but any terms or conditions in an agreement entered into before that date are unaffected.

Example

Robert obtained licensed copies of Fastwrite (a word processor program) and Vatman (an accounts package) during 1992. Samantha also obtained a copy of Vatman but not until April 1993. The Vatman software licence agreement contained a term prohibiting the making of any copies for whatever purpose but the Fastwrite agreement was silent on this point.

Samantha may make back-up copies of the Vatman programs because the term prohibiting the making of copies is void in so far as it purports to prevent the making of back-up copies necessary for Samantha's lawful use of the programs. Robert is bound by the term because his agreement was entered into before the new provisions on back-up copies came into force. However, as the Fastwrite licence was silent on the matter, Robert may safely assume that the courts would imply a term permitting him to make a back-up copy of the program if reasonably necessary to his use of the program.

It might be expected that section 50A would permit the making of one back-up copy only. Anything in excess might not be deemed necessary. However, the working of section 50A does not restrict the lawful user to a single back-up copy as it speaks of making 'any back-up copy of it which it is necessary for him to have for the purposes of his lawful use'. In practice it will depend on the circumstances. For example many computer systems are regularly backed-up on magnetic tape or a 'ZIP' device and a number of copies may be retained, having been made at different times such as daily, weekly, monthly, etc. Also, a separate tape back-up may be deposited with a company providing disaster-recovery services. Of course, such back-up copies are likely to have numerous works other than computer programs stored on them.

Even though making necessary back-up copies by lawful users may not be prohibited or restricted by a licence agreement, this does not extend to other materials provided with the program such as a database, thesaurus and documents such as user manuals. For example, photocopying a manual will infringe the literary copyright in the manual unless permitted by the licence. If the licence agreement is silent on the matter of back-up copies of these other materials, does this mean that the person who has obtained the software cannot, under any circumstances, make back-up copies of non-program items such as databases? In the absence of terms in the licence agreement to the contrary, the courts should be willing to imply a term allowing this were it would be reasonable to do so.

Ideally, the law's approach to making back-up copies should mirror good computing practice and reflect the needs of *bona fide* software users. There is nothing in the legal provisions to suggest that this is not so.

Section 56 of the Copyright, Designs and Patents Act 1988 deals with transfers of works in electronic form and the question of copies which are not transferred along with the original software, treating such copies as infringing copies. An example will serve to illustrate the workings of this provision.

Example

Boomerang Distributors Ltd obtain a word processing package, WORDWISE under a non-exclusive licence agreement. The agreement expressly permits the making of one back-up copy of the WORDWISE program (this would have been permitted in any case as discussed above). Boomerang use the word processing package and three copies of the programs are made, one for back-up purposes but the other two are put to use making a total of three working copies. Some years later, Boomerang obtain some new, more powerful, computers and new word processing software is obtained. Boomerang inspects the WORDWISE licence and note that it does not prevent the transfer of the licence to a third party. Boomerang therefore assign the licence to use WORDWISE to Krater Supplies Ltd and transfer the original copy of the program plus the single back-up copy.

Section 56 allows Boomerang to transfer the software because there were no express terms in the licence agreement prohibiting this, but they should have transferred all copies of WORDWISE and not retained any of them. The retained copies are treated as infringing copies leaving Boomerang liable to the owner of the copyright subsisting in the WORDWISE programs. Also, if the licence agreement only permitted the making of a single copy for back-up purposes, Boomerang is in breach of the licence agreement. This could, depending on the terms of the licence, bring the licence to an end, and this could make the purported transfer to Krater Supplies void. Krater should ask for an appropriate warranty from Boomerang when agreeing to the transfer of the licence.

The flowchart in Figure 4.2 shows the position concerning copies of computer programs when software is transferred to a third party. The flowchart takes account of the fact that copies may have been made in excess of those permitted under the licence agreement.

Figure 4.2   Transfer of licensed software

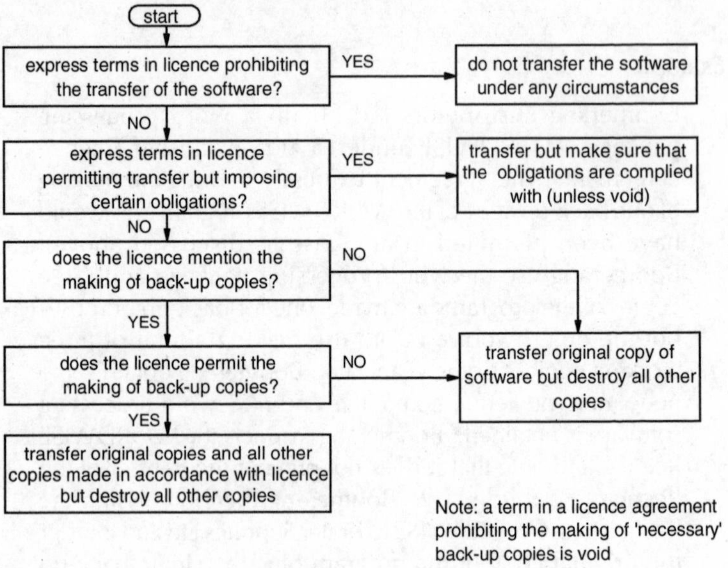

Note: a term in a licence agreement prohibiting the making of 'necessary' back-up copies is void

LIMITS OF OBJECTIVE SIMILARITY

If the original program is simply altered, perhaps in an attempt to disguise its origins or to improve it, the question of copying arises. In many cases, the two programs will be sufficiently similar to raise a presumption of copying which can shift the burden of proof in the case of ex-employee programmers. However, if the alterations are numerous, it may be less easy to infer that there has been copying. It is a relatively simple matter to change constituent parts of a program, for example, the screen displays, the names given to variables used in the program, the location of sub-routines and, where the language requires it, the line numbering. If these things are done, a line for line similarity between the two programs will be obscured. If the changes are merely cosmetic, it may still be possible to use a test of objective similarity based on the structure and sequence of the programs, for example, whether the flow of the program and the relative positioning of its constituent parts are similar. But even here, a determined programmer can rearrange the parts of the program to defeat this test. Re-writing the program in a different language will make it even harder to prove copying. For example, the highly structured nature of COBOL (using the 'four divisions' – identification division, environment division, data division and procedure division) will mean that a listing of a program written in COBOL will look quite different to the listing of a program written in BASIC by the same programmer to perform the same function. However, even though the structure of two programs may be different, any similarity in the sequence of operations carried out by the programs may suggest the possibility of non-literal copying.

Even more difficult is the situation where the new program is written using a totally different programming technique, using software tools and languages which are fundamentally different to those used to create the original program. In particular, the use of 'fourth-generation' languages is relevant to this discussion as they are dissimilar to traditional programming languages, such as BASIC and COBOL, in a way which goes beyond mere syntax. A program written in a traditional programming language is written line by line. A fourth-generation language is, in many respects, a tool which automates or simplifies the process of developing a computer system to a great extent. It is like a 'shell' into which the developer specifies attributes of the required system, such as the structure of database files and the operations to be carried out by the finished system. The file-handling and other operations such as report production are then performed by the fourth-generation system itself. The programmer designing the system will usually write some program code but much work is done by the fourth-generation language. The following example program written using dBase III+ (it will also run under the later versions, dBase VI and dBase V for Windows), which can be classed as a fourth-generation language, will give some idea of the difference, if the reader considers the amount of code required to perform the same operations (adding or altering records in a customer file containing several fields) if languages such as BASIC or COBOL were to be used. In particular, the words APPEND and EDIT would have to be replaced by many lines of code.

Example program written in a fourth-generation language environment

```
    *      Add/alter Customer details
    *      dBase 5.0 for Windows Version 30/12/96
    *      Copyright David Bainbridge 1991, 1996

    *      set up
USE CUSTFIL
    *      menu
STORE 0 TO CHOICE
DO WHILE CHOICE<9
CLEAR
?'CUSTFIL MAIN MENU'
?'_____'
?
?'1 - Enter more customer details'
```

```
?'2 - Edit customer details'
?'3 - List customer names'
?
?'9 - Close down'
?
INPUT'Enter your selection ' TO CHOICE
* perform operation
DO CASE
    CASE CHOICE = 1
    APPEND
CASE CHOICE = 2
    CLEAR
GO TOP
ACCEPT'Name/partname of customer to edit 'TO
    CUSTNAME
LOCATE FOR AT(UPPER(CNAME),UPPER(CUST
    NAME))<>0
DO WHILE .NOT. EOF()
    EDIT
    CONTINUE
ENDDO
CASE CHOICE = 3
    CLEAR
    LIST CUSTNAME
    WAIT
CASE CHOICE = 9
    CLOSE ALL
    RETURN
    ENDCASE CHOICE

    ENDDO
```

Case

Computer-Aided Systems (UK) Ltd v Bolwell (unreported) 23
August 1989, Chancery Division

Some of the plaintiff's ex-employees wrote a computer
program using a fourth-generation language called Progress

to carry out a similar function to the programs they had written in COBOL for the plaintiff. The software was for use in connection with vehicle leasing. The plaintiff cited the United States case of *Whelan v Jaslow* as authority for the notion that the structure of a computer program was a form of literary expression protected by copyright. The plaintiff applied for an interlocutory injunction to stop the defendants continuing to market their software. The case also involved issues of breach of confidence.

Mr Justice Hoffmann did not believe that a seriously triable issue was raised on the questions of copying or of the misuse of confidential information. The plaintiff had argued that the output formats and input layouts of the two computer programs would be very similar, especially as the defendants had designed the new system so that it was compatible with the plaintiff's system. The defendants had refused to allow the plaintiff to inspect their program, but it would be highly unlikely that there would be a sufficient similarity in the programs to infer that copying had taken place because of the conceptually different nature of the languages used. This was made forcefully by the defendants' expert witness who said that their system was constrained by the Progress language. The plaintiff's expert, a professor of computing, said that, because the output formats of the two systems were very similar, the way in which each stored and handled data would be likely to be very similar, *even if not directly copied*. Mr Justice Hoffmann said that this conclusion did not help the plaintiff because infringement of copyright required copying, lack of dissimilarity was not enough. Of the plaintiff's request for inspection of the defendants' program, Mr Justice Hoffmann expressed the opinion that this was little more than a fishing expedition.

Because of the different nature of the programming methods and languages used in the above case, the only plausible similarity could be in the structure of the databases used by the systems because of the efforts to achieve compatibility in this regard. Even though there would be some differences attributable to the different systems, features such as the number and description of fields and field lengths would be the same. This point was argued by the plaintiff but does not seem to have been taken seriously by the judge. However, if we accept that the structure and sequence of a computer program can be protected by copyright, it requires no novelty in thinking to extend this notion to the structural aspects to databases. Indeed, the European Directive on the legal protection of databases states in recital 15 that copyright protection for databases 'should cover the structure of the database'. Databases are discussed further in Chapter 6.

An important feature of the above case is that it illustrates the difficulty in reconciling the interests of a previous employer with the interests of the ex-employees who should be free to exercise their skill and knowledge for other employers (or for themselves) subject to copyright and limited confidentiality issues. Another interesting feature of this case is that it provides a good example of the frequent problem of diametrically opposed expert evidence. In a later case, the question of protection for the structure of a database was considered in more detail.

Case

Total Information Processing Systems Ltd v Daman Ltd [1992] FSR 171

It was argued that the field and record specifications for a database were protected by copyright. The particular details were expressed in the data division of a COBOL computer program which was intended to be one of a suite of programs.

Judge Paul Baker decided in the negative the preliminary issue that there was an arguable case that copying the field and record specifications was an infringement of copyright. He also rejected the submission that where a computer system comprised several programs, the whole compilation should be protected independently from the individual programs.

In his judgment, Paul Baker J said that if great steps where taken to keep the source code of a program secret, this inferred that the program was not protected by copyright. This view is unfounded in principle and there is absolutely no authority for it and has been strongly criticised by Mr Justice Jacob in *Ibcos v Barclays* as discussed in Chapter 2. He also disagreed with the view that a collection of programs could not be a compilation in which copyright subsists. The other parts of Paul Baker J's judgment must, accordingly, be treated with caution and have also been criticised. Certainly, in many cases, the field and record specifications of a database file will fail to attract copyright protection for want of originality. However, where the file's structure is complex and is the result of sufficient skill and judgment, there seems to be no reason why this element should not be protected, especially if it is expressed within the computer program. Figure 4.3 shows the field layout for a file which is the result of a reasonable amount of skill and effort and following this is a listing of the data division of a COBOL program for that file.

Figure 4.3   Field layout for a database file

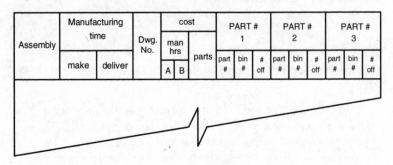

Example COBOL data division for file in Figure 4.3

```
DATA DIVISION.
FILE SECTION.
FD   assembly-file.
01   assembly-record.
     03   assembly-code          PIC X(8).
     03   manuf-time.
          05   make-time         PIC 999.
          05   delivery-time     PIC 999.
     03   drawing-no             PIC X(12).
     03   cost.
          05   manhours.
               07   manhoursA    PIC9(5).
               07   manhoursB    PIC9(5).
          05   parts-cost        PIC ££,££9.
     03   part1.
          05   part1-no          PIC X(10).
          05   part1-bi          PIC X(6).
          05   part1-off         PIC 999.
     03   part2.
          05   part2-no          PIC X(10).
          05   part2-bin         PIC X(6).
          05   part2-off         PIC 999.
     03   part3.
          05   part3-no          PIC X(10).
          05   part3-bin         PIC X(6).
          05   part3-off         PIC 999.
```

LOOK AND FEEL IN THE UNITED KINGDOM

The United States cases on the look and feel of computer programs (non-literal copying) have been cited in cases in the United Kingdom on a number of occasions. These cases have had some influence on the development of United Kingdom case law because of their persuasive (though not binding) authority. However, in 1993 one English judge decided to treat the American cases with special reverence and used them, in part, to decide a case in the High Court. The judge, Mr Justice Ferris, pointed out that there was a lack of English authority on non-literal copying in the context of computer programs. The case, *John Richardson Ltd v Flanders*, is of some importance, being the first English case to address fully the look and feel of computer programs and fills a large gap in copyright law in the United Kingdom.

Case

John Richardson Computers Ltd v Flanders [1993] FSR 497

The facts of this case are complex and provide an object lesson in how the development of computer programs should not be undertaken. There was a lack of evidence of the development of the two programs concerned and of what had or had not been agreed. Questions of ownership of copyright had not been properly resolved by the parties. The facts described below are a simplification of what the judge, with some difficulty, decided had actually happened.

Mr Richardson, the Chairman and Managing Director of the plaintiff company, was a pharmacist. He taught himself how to program a computer and wrote a program, using the BASIC programming language, to produce labels to attach to prescribed drugs (for example, containing the person's name, the name of the drug, the date and instructions on how to use the drug). Mr Richardson employed a programmer to improve the program and extend it to provide for stock control. Eventually, the defendant was employed by the plaintiff company and he re-wrote the program in assembly language for the BBC microcomputer. Later, the defendant left the employment of the plaintiff company but carried out further work to the program on a consultancy basis.

Eventually, the defendant wrote an equivalent program (to perform the same functions) for himself. This program was written in QuickBASIC for the IBM microcomputer. At around the same time, the plaintiff was also developing an IBM version of its program. There was some dispute as to what had been agreed between the parties (the defendant alleged that the plaintiff had known about his work on an IBM version for Eire) but the plaintiff sued when the defendant commenced marketing his program in the United Kingdom. It was alleged that the defendant had infringed the copyright in the plaintiff's BBC version (written in assembly language) and also was guilty of breach of confidence. As there was no literal similarity between the programs, one being in assembly language, the other in QuickBASIC, the judge had to consider non-literal elements such as structure, sequence, input and output formats and routines, facilities and options.

Mr Justice Ferris laid great store in the United States case of *Computer Associates Inc v Altai Inc*, the pinnacle of look and feel in America, and he said:

'There is thus nothing in any English decision which conflicts with the general approach adopted in the Computer Associates case . . . it would be right to adopt a similar approach in England. This means that consideration [of copying] is not restricted to the text of the code.'

In considering the non-literal elements of the program, Mr Justice Ferris identified seventeen objective similarities in the non-literal elements of the programs. Of these, three were deemed to be the result of copying a substantial part of the plaintiff's program and, hence, infringed the plaintiff's copyright. These elements were the line editor, amendment routines and dose codes.

The decision has been subject to much criticism. The three-stage test in *Computer Associates* was not applied in its entirety. Furthermore, it can be argued that the infringing elements, or some of them, were not substantial in a qualitative sense. In the *Ibcos v Barclays* case, Mr Justice Jacob was critical of the use of American precedents in the way done by Mr Justice Ferris. However, the two cases are instantly distinguishable as *Ibcos* was a case of literal copying whereas *Richardson* was about non-literal copying. Therefore, however much one may criticise Mr Justice Ferris's application of the look and feel test, he has brought it into United Kingdom law and this can only clarify the scope of copyright protection for non-literal elements of computer programs.

AUDIO-VISUAL DISPLAYS AND ASSOCIATED WORKS

A considerable amount of skill and judgment goes into the writing of a computer program, but that is not an end to the matter because the design of screen displays and sound effects also requires the expenditure of skill, effort and judgment. Although the Copyright, Designs and Patents Act 1988 grants direct protection to computer programs and preparatory design material for computer programs as literary works, this should not be considered to be the only way in which computer programs and preparatory materials are protected by copyright law. Screen displays will have been designed so that they are attractive, unambiguous and provide information in a clear and concise manner. In many instances, a great deal of work and thought will have gone into the design of the input and output interfaces of a computer program and in some cases, these elements will represent the largest portion of the computer program itself.

Computer output, such as printed reports, will generally be protected by copyright independently of the program, as literary or artistic works. However, questions arise about the scope of protection as regards the screen display generated by the running of a computer program, and whether this is protected in its own right. Four possibilities seem to exist (the first three also apply to sound effects and music generated by the operation of a computer program):

- copying a screen display indirectly infringes the copyright in the computer program containing the code used to generate the display;
- the screen display is protected by copyright as a work in its own right;
- the screen display will be protected as preparatory design material through the medium of any layouts and designs previously drawn on paper; or
- the screen display can be considered to be a photograph or a film.

Indirect infringement of program code

This is unlikely to provide adequate protection. In any event, if the display is an artistic work, such as in the case of a computer game, copying the display does not infringe the copyright in the underlying computer program, because it is not an infringement of the copyright in a literary work, to make an artistic work of it. Ignoring the screen display (or sounds), and studying the program code generating it is unlikely to help, because a display can be programmed in several different ways and it is unlikely that there will be much similarity between the code used to generate the original display and that used for the copy (in line with the approach in the United States). Even if the display is a literary work, such as in the case of a screen display giving guidance to the user as to how to proceed, then, if copying the display is to infringe the copyright in the program generating the display, it must be generated by a substantial part of the computer program. This will not usually be so unless a whole series of screen displays is copied which, collectively and qualitatively, represent a substantial part of the program or unless the screen display is particularly important and a feature of the program.

Screen displays and sounds as works of copyright

Screen displays and music generated by a computer program may be protected by copyright directly, in their own right, and this possibility has been accepted by Mr Justice Whitford. The 1988 Act expressly removes some potential overlaps in protection, for example by section 3(1) a dramatic work cannot be a literary work and, in the case of a conflict between copyright and the design right, by section 236 copyright takes precedence. However, there does not appear to be any fundamental bar to the notion that several different copyrights can subsist in a computer program. For example, the program itself will be a literary work for copyright purposes, textual information contained either within the program or in a separate computer file could be a literary work in its own right, any diagrams or pictures could be artistic works and any music or sound effects might be considered to be musical works and/or sound recordings.

Example

The Midwest Bank have developed a computer system which is used by the bank's pension advisers. The computer programs request information concerning an individual (for example, his or her age, employment status, present salary, etc) and use this to produce a report which is displayed on screen giving detailed advice as to the most appropriate pension scheme for that individual. Also available are various graphic displays such as bar charts and pie charts showing the financial implications of different payment schemes and the like. During the operation of the program various menus are displayed on the screen. The system also contains a hierarchical set of help screens which may be displayed during use.

The copyright position in terms of the various screen displays (and this will also apply to any print-out of a screen display) is as follows:

• *Menu screens* – these will probably be lacking originality, that is, the required skill and judgment to be protected, in other words, they are probably relatively commonplace unless they are special in some way. It could be said that they lack originality or are dictated by the function of the program. Copying a simple menu screen would not infringe the copyright in the underlying program. Of course, if the screen was complex or special or unusual in some way, it might be protected as a literary work (and/ or an artistic work if it includes graphics).

• *Input screen* – this may be like a template with prompts against which the user enters the appropriate details. Unless it is complex or special in some way it will be considered commonplace (with or without the addition of the client information).

• *Help screens* – unless trivial, these will almost certainly be protected as literary works collectively or individually, depending on which level corresponds to the notion of originality. The data for the screens is likely to be stored in a separate computer file (which may constitute a copyright database).

• *Report screen* – it is likely that this screen will be protected in its own right as a literary work because it appears to be the result of a reasonable amount of skill and judgment on the part of the programmer. (Some might consider it to be a computer-generated work.) Again, however, copying the screen display would not infringe the copyright in the program unless the code representing the screen display was a substantial part of the program.

• *Charts* – these are capable of protection individually as artistic works.

For copyright to subsist, by section 3(2), the work must be recorded in writing or otherwise (widely defined by section 178 of the Act). The content of the report screen and the charts will be influenced to some extent by the information entered by the user of the system. In the case of the report screen, if the program contains all the advice and a routine in the program matches the advice to the information entered by the user, we can say that the screen is recorded and any of the user's information which is included (such as the client's name, salary, etc) will be secondary in terms of creative effort.

However, in the case of the charts they will be more greatly influenced by the user's information (for example, the relative proportions of the pie segments will depend on the client's details). The program will contain the means of calculating and displaying the charts but the charts as displayed will not exist in the program as such. The charts should be protected, even if their only form of existence is as a screen display. It should be noted that artistic works are not required to be recorded in writing or otherwise.

In some circumstances, a computer program can comprise two or more works joined into one. Text screens generated by a computer program may be in the form of title screens, information giving guidance to the user of the program, input formats, such as a sequence of prompts alongside which the user enters information, or output formats such as reports (output might be directed to a file or the printer instead of, or in addition to, the screen). To be protected separately from the program, the textual information displayed must be original, it must 'originate from the author' and be the result of a minimum of skill or judgment. If this requirement is met, and it may not be in the case of simple title screens or input formats, then there is a possibility that the textual information is protected as a literary work in its own right. This accords with previous case law concerning conventional literary works. A title for a play or book or a phrase, for example 'Beauty is a social necessity, not a luxury', will not generally be protected by copyright as being too small.

The code for information and graphics to be displayed, and music or sounds to be generated, during the running of a computer program can be either contained within the program or stored in separate computer files which will be accessed by the program. By choosing to store information in separate files, the programmer may be increasing the likelihood of copyright protection for the screen display or sound effects. Each file can be considered to be a recording of a work in which copyright will subsist providing the other requirements are met (note that there is no requirement of originality for sound recordings). Modularisation of a computer system into separate programs and files is not uncommon and will, apart from easing maintenance and modification, produce the added bonus of strengthening copyright protection as well as creating a new separate copyright in the compilation of programs and files. Compilations and databases are mutually exclusive and it is more likely that such a modularised system is a compilation rather than a database as the latter is defined in terms of a collection of *independent* works; see Chapter 6. Separate computer programs forming part of an integrated software system cannot truly be said to be independent.

To a greater or lesser extent, many screen displays are the result of interaction between the user and the computer program. This is particularly so with computer games and the question of originality comes into play. However, even where the user exercises considerable control over the display and sequencing of different displays, there may be sufficient constants in the display which will not vary from user to user on which to find the basis of copyright, even though the relative positioning of elements of the display may vary. In respect of the individual frames generated, the user will not have any rights under copyright law because of a lack of originality (in terms of the user), and because they will not be recorded.

In all cases of screen displays, whether textual or graphical, the issue of separating idea from expression raises its head. In the United States, the courts have found infringement where the games in question have a similar 'total concept and feel' which is, in effect, an extension of the *Whelan v Jaslow* test to screen displays.

Case

Atari Inc v North American Phillips Consumer Electronics Corpn
672 F 2d 607 (7th Cir 1982)

This concerned an alleged infringement of the PAC-MAN computer game and, in particular, the screen displays generated during the game.

It was held that many aspects of the game such as the maze and connecting dots, were unprotected *scènes à faire*, being 'incidents, characters or settings which are as a practical matter indispensable, or at least standard, in the treatment of a given topic'. However, the portrayal of the graphics figures of the 'gobbler' and the 'ghost monsters' were held to be expression and protected by copyright.

Other cases in the United States suggest that screen displays may be protected in their own right by copyright, and that the sequence of screen displays is also a protected element. This could be useful if changes are made to the layout of individual screen displays but their overall sequence has been copied. Some commentators in the United States have argued that screen displays should be protected as literary or artistic works, but subject to a higher standard of originality than applies to conventional works. In principle, there is no justification for requiring a higher standard simply because the information concerned is displayed on a screen rather than being printed on paper.

Protection through preparatory materials

The direct copyright protection of screen displays has been the subject of a great deal of controversy, especially in the United States. However, the clearest and easiest route to protection is through the materials which have been used in the preparation of screen displays and sound. In most cases, computer professionals such as systems analysts and programmers will have produced a large quantity of materials on paper (some may have been produced directly using a computer) during the planning and development of a new item of computer software. These preparatory design materials will include layouts for text to be displayed, drawings for graphics screens and, in some cases, music, and many of them will be original for the purposes of copyright and are now specifically protected as a form of literary work, by section 3(1). There will be an indirect infringement of copyright in a single design for a screen display if the copyist reproduces a single screen of text or graphics. Assuming screen displays individually satisfy the minimum requirements for copyright protection, such as originality and a minimum of skill or judgment, the scope of copyright protection for computer screen displays is very strong. Copying a screen display will infringe the copyright subsisting in the preliminary drawings and designs associated with that particular screen display.

In principle, the scope of protection should be exactly the same as that possible when considering a screen display in its own right. That is, the display or the drawing should require the same standard of copyright originality and skill or judgment. However, because many judges feel more comfortable with paper materials, it may be that in practice, a higher standard might be required if the screen display is to be considered on its own. For this reason, even if a screen display can be produced on a computer without any written materials, it would be sensible to draft out the layout of the display on paper beforehand. The same principles apply if music is written by hand on paper before assimilation into the computer program. Copying the computer code generating the music will infringe the copyright in the hand written music. Similarly, copying the screen display will infringe the layout on paper which is preparatory design material for a computer program.

Screen displays as photographs or films

The Copyright, Designs and Patents Act 1988 contains some definitions which are, potentially, very wide. This is an attempt to produce legislation which will be sufficiently flexible to withstand future technological developments and change. As a result, the definitions in the Act for photographs and films could possibly apply to screen displays. A photograph (being a form of artistic work) is (by section 4(2)):

'a recording of light or other radiation on any medium on which an image is produced or from which an image may by any means be produced, and which is not part of a film.'

This could include a static screen display. Code representing the display stored on a magnetic disk could be deemed to be such a recording from which an image may be produced. The decisive factor is whether the code on computer storage media representing the screen display can be regarded as a recording of light or other radiation. In principle, this would appear to be a possibility. The definition of a film is even wider (section 5(1)):

'a recording on any medium from which a moving image may by any means be produced.'

(From 1 January 1996, the soundtrack accompanying a film is treated as part of the film for copyright purposes.)

This definition is so wide that it would certainly cover a moving screen display, such as occurs during the playing of a video game. The display is a moving image, and a magnetic disk or other computer storage must come within the meaning of 'any medium', and 'any means' must include computer technology. The copyright in the screen display, considered as a film, will be infringed, *inter alia*, if a copy is made of it. The link becomes a little tenuous if copying is carried out indirectly, for example, by someone who sees the screen display, makes some sketches on paper, and then writes some program code to reproduce the moving screen display, perhaps changing some of the figures and objects used in the display. The acid test will be whether the new screen display is substantially similar to, and derived from, the former, regardless of whether it is a direct or an indirect copy and whether any intervening acts infringe copyright. If the copier takes a photograph of the display, then copyright will be infringed even though the photograph is of a single frame of the moving display. Although photographs, being artistic works, have to be original, there is no such requirement for films.

Summary – audio-visual works

The issue of protection for screen displays is of immense importance to the computer software industry. An attractive screen display is important in the marketing of computer software. Protection of non-trivial screen displays (and music and sound effects) is fair and just, reflecting the considerable effort that goes into the creation and development of new, attractive and effective displays. The issue is not only important to the developers of computer games because carefully designed and attractive screen displays are also very important in more mundane applications. The screen display is the immediate interface between the user and the software and its value should not be underestimated. In line with copyright principles, anything which is the result of skill, work and judgment ought to be protected. Of course, very trivial displays should not, and will not, be afforded copyright protection.

On the other hand, it is desirable that computer software packages performing the same function as each other, for example spreadsheet systems, should exhibit a degree of standardisation so that it is easy for persons to change from one system to another with little or no retraining. One aspect which has hindered the acceptance of computer technology has been the great number of user interfaces around, which has added to the perceived difficulty of using computer software. Not only should varieties of a particular type of software have similar screen displays and user interfaces but there should be more synergy between different types of software. The advent of the Apple Mac and Microsoft Windows software for IBM computers has gone some way to bringing communality. However, there is a danger that strong protection for screen displays could greatly enhance the protection for computer programs, making it more difficult for rival companies to introduce competing software. Nevertheless, copyright protection does not generally give rise to monopolies, and it is important that competition is stimulated by allowing the development of rival computer programs, as long as they are a result of independent effort. But, by recognising concurrent copyrights in a computer program, the protection of computer programs is significantly strengthened, because the requirement of substantiality might not otherwise be met, for example, if a single screen display is copied. However, by modularising the program, a single screen display can be regarded as a work in its own right.

It is difficult to forecast whether judges will accept that a computer program can give rise to several copyrights, but to do so would require no novelty in thinking – a song has two copyrights, one in the music and one in the lyrics. However, there may be policy reasons for restricting a population explosion of copyrights in a single computer system, including a computer program and associated computer files. In the United States the emphasis has been on protecting the concept and feel of original screen displays independently from the computer program generating the display. Copyright law in the United Kingdom may admit several possible routes to copyright protection of screen displays and accompanying sound effects, the most promising of which is the copyright subsisting in the preliminary materials prepared for the purpose of writing a computer program, such as screen layouts, designs, sketches, and written music. In as much as these materials meet the basic requirements for copyright protection (originality and qualification), the protection of screen displays and sound effects is beyond doubt, without recourse to difficulties such as whether the code for a screen display is a substantial part of the computer program, whether the display is a film, or whether the program is partly a sound recording. Because a person copying a screen display will indirectly infringe any copyrights subsisting in the preliminary layouts and designs, software developers should make sure that they have retained all their preparatory design materials associated with their software. To do so could prove very important in any future legal actions taken to enforce their copyrights.

EXCEPTIONS TO COPYRIGHT INFRINGEMENT

What would otherwise be an infringement of copyright can be done with impunity if it is in the public interest. For example, the disclosure of a report outlining a company's plans to fix prices with another company contrary to the Restrictive Trade Practices Act 1976 (soon to be replaced by the Competition Act 1998) could fall within the meaning of public interest especially if the disclosure was made to an appropriate body such as the Monopolies and Mergers Commission (renamed the Competition Commission, as from 1 April 1999) rather than to a newspaper for payment. In addition to the public interest defence, the Copyright, Designs and Patents Act 1988 contains a number of exceptions to copyright infringement known as the permitted acts. These acts may be carried out without the permission of the copyright owner and do not infringe copyright, for example, if the act amounts to fair dealing for the purpose of research or private study, or for the purpose of criticism, review, or for reporting current events; sections 29 and 30. Other instances of the permitted acts relate to things done in relation to education, libraries and public administration, subject to careful limitations. The exceptions, known as the permitted acts, are tightly defined and limited in their application.

The Copyright (Computer Programs) Regulations 1992 made certain changes to the 1988 Act in pursuance with the European Directive on the legal protection of computer programs (the text of which is reproduced in Appendix 1). In particular, three new forms of permitted act were introduced and inserted into the Copyright, Designs and Patents Act 1988 as sections 50A to 50C. These permitted acts are as follows:

- Back-up copies, section 50A: the making of a back-up copy of a computer program by a lawful user if necessary for the purpose of his or her lawful use.
- Decompilation, section 50B: a lawful user may decompile a computer program to obtain the information necessary to create an 'interoperable' program, subject to specific conditions applying.
- Copying or adapting for lawful use, section 50C: a lawful user may copy or adapt a computer program if necessary

for his or her lawful use (this is really a non-derogation from grant provision).

By section 296A, the first two permitted acts may not be prohibited or restricted by any term or condition in any agreement such as the licence under which the program has been obtained, any such term being void to that extent.

A further 'permitted act' is buried in section 296A(1)(c) which states that 'the use of any device or means to observe, study or test the functioning of the program in order to understand the ideas and principles which underlie any element of the program'. This, too, may not be restricted or prohibited by any term in the agreement under which the relevant person has the use of the program. This is dealt with in the following chapter.

There is no specific control over terms purporting to prohibit or restrict copying or adapting for lawful use and, indeed, the Directive itself is not clear on this point. One of the recitals to the Directive suggests that the acts of loading and running a program necessary for its lawful use, including the correction of errors, cannot be prohibited by contract whereas Article 5(1) of the Directive suggests otherwise (see the text of the Directive in Appendix 1). This apparent contradiction can only be resolved by reference to the European Court of Justice. However, English common law may provide some control over restrictions on lawful use or error correction on the basis of non-derogation from grant as discussed further in the context of modification of computer programs in Chapter 10.

The decompilation permitted act and the act of observing, studying or testing a program to understand its underlying ideas and principles are discussed in the following chapter on reverse analysis.

Other permitted acts

In addition to the specific exceptions in sections 50A to 50C and section 296A(1)(c) of the Copyright, Designs and Patents Act 1988, a number of the other exceptions could be relevant. For example, fair dealing for the purposes of research or private study is such an act. Although the scope of this act has been curtailed in terms of computer programs (it no longer applies to decompilation, by section 29(4)) it may still be relevant in some cases. For example, it could apply where a student makes a copy of a printed sub-routine in a book to enable him or her to understand how it works or to study it further. It is unlikely to apply where a student copies an entire program although it is difficult to lay down hard and fast rules as the scope of the permitted act is difficult to predict. It must, of course, be fair but it is really a matter of looking at each case on its merits.

Another form of fair dealing is for criticism or review and this would allow, typically, the author of an article in a learned computer science journal to reproduce a short piece of computer program code for the purpose of commenting on that code, just as articles and books often contain quotations from other works. One proviso is that there should be a sufficient acknowledgement. Whether copying extracts of program listings for criticism or review amounts to fair dealing depends largely on the proportions of the extracts compared with the contribution of the author of the article. Short extracts and long passages should be acceptable but not the other way round. Needless to say, the permitted acts will not excuse a breach of confidence and extracts taken from programs that are secret may not be published without attracting legal liability unless such publication is with the permission of the owner of the programs.

There used to be a provision in section 66 of the Copyright, Designs and Patents Act 1988 for the Secretary of State to order that copies of computer programs (and films and sound recordings) rented to the public are to be treated as licensed by the copyright owner, regardless of the owner's wishes in this respect. No such order was made and the section was replaced on 1 December 1996 with a new section which covers only *lending* to the public of literary, dramatic, musical or artistic works, sound recordings or films. The copyright owner will be recompensed for such lending by a reasonable royalty or other payment as agreed or in default of such agreement, as determined by the Copyright Tribunal. No order will be made if, or to the extent that, there is a licensing scheme certified for the purposes of the new section 66.

As computer programs, databases subject to copyright and preparatory design material are all literary works the other permitted acts for literary works also apply. These include copying and other use for educational purposes, by libraries and archives, public administration, etc. By and large, these exceptions to infringement are tightly drawn and fairly narrow. In practice, they will be relevant in a handful of cases only. For further details of these permitted acts, reference should be made to one of the specialist texts on copyright or intellectual property listed in the bibliography to this book.

CONTROLS OVER ABUSE OF COPYRIGHT

The United Kingdom's membership of the European Community means that Community law prevails over inconsistent United Kingdom domestic law. One of the objectives of the European Economic Community, enshrined in the Treaty of Rome 1957 (now known as the EC Treaty), is to ensure competition is not distorted within the common market and particularly, Article 82 of the Treaty prohibits abuses of dominant positions within the common market (or a substantial part of it) as incompatible with the common market if trade between Member States is affected. Some examples are imposing unfair purchase or selling prices, or limiting production. Would Article 82 be available to counterbalance the effect of a very strong copyright law? It should be noted that patents and copyrights do not, *per se*, fall foul of Article 82; the European Court of Justice is quite prepared to recognise such rights and will not usually order compulsory licences unless some other significant abuse is present, such as charging unfair prices for a product. However, although the Court will recognise the *existence* of such rights, it might be prepared to interfere with the *exercise* of the rights if that is in conflict with the Treaty of Rome, although it will take a realistic view of activities which might be considered to fall within the scope of the normal exploitation of copyright even permitting, in some circumstance, different royalty rates in different Member States.

Case

RTE & ITP v Commission [1995] FSR 530

RTE in Eire and ITP and BBC in the United Kingdom, being broadcasting organisations or associated companies, controlled listings of television programmes. Each published a weekly guide (such as the TV Times or Radio Times) but refused to make available in advance their schedules of programmes to other publishing companies. Magill TV Guide Ltd attempted to publish such listings in a weekly guide but was prevented by injunctions granted on the grounds of copyright infringement.

The Commission found that there had been a breach of Article 86 (now Article 82) and the European Court of Justice confirmed this. The court pointed out that the broadcasting organisations had a *de facto* monopoly in the information used to compile the listings and, as such, they occupied a dominant position.

Each of the organisations published weekly guides to their own programmes. No one published a comprehensive guide to all television programmes and it was clear that there was a demand for such a product. By refusing to grant licences, the broadcasters were abusing their dominant position. They had excluded competition by this refusal because the information was not available from any other source.

The European Court of Justice, by confirming the decision of the European Commission, has shown that it is prepared to use Article 82 in the context of copyright law. This is so, even though it was thought that, pending full harmonisation of copyright law throughout Europe, determination of the application of the law in this area was a matter for national legislation. The decisive feature of this case is that the information was not available elsewhere. Applied to computer software, it is possible that a refusal to license (perhaps selectively) an industry standard operating system could contravene Article 82 where the owner of the copyright is in a dominant position, as a number of software companies clearly are.

Restrictive trading agreements and concerted practices are also controlled, under Article 81(1). An example is where a powerful software company imposes onerous obligations on its licensees such as by requiring them to obtain other products in addition to the licensed software. Another example is where several organisations get together and pool their intellectual property rights so that, collectively, they can control the market and volume of supplies, prices and conditions.

Great care is needed when drawing up agreements between companies, whether for licensing the exploitation of intellectual property or imposing different pricing structures in different Member States. Problems in terms of computer software include the identification of an unfair selling price, or licence fee, in respect of an item of computer software which is unique, possibly because would-be imitators have been frightened off by the prospects of infringement actions. It is possible that, in respect of computer programs, the abuse in question would have to be fairly blatant before an action would be likely to succeed. Mergers, take-overs and reciprocal licensing agreements seem much more vulnerable. However, simply being in a dominant position does not, *per se*, fall foul of the provisions in the EC Treaty.

Another factor is that Article 81(1) only applies to large organisations as there is a *de minimis* 'rule of thumb' used by the Commission being at least a five per cent market share and an aggregate turnover of at least 300 million ECU.

Microsoft gave undertakings to the United States Justice Department and to the European Commission to the effect that certain types of restrictive provisions in licence agreements would no longer be used. The full detail of the undertakings with the Commission have not been fully publicised (Q Archer, 'Transatlantic Cooperation and the Microsoft Case' [1996] 12 *Computer Law and Security Report* p 101).

(Note: Articles 85 and 86 of the EC Treaty were renumbered Articles 81 and 82 during 1999 as a result of the Amsterdam Treaty).

Provisions similar to Articles 81 and 82 are soon to be implemented on a national scale under the Competition Act 1998. Subject to some exemptions, section 2 of that Act will control agreements between undertakings, decisions by associations of undertakings or concerted practices which may affect trade within the United Kingdom and have as their object or effect the prevention, restriction or distortion of competition within the United Kingdom. Section 178 prohibits, except in specific excluded cases, any conduct on the part of one or more undertakings which amounts to an abuse of a dominant position in a market if it affects trade within the United Kingdom. The dominance of a position is judged in relation to the United Kingdom or any part of it.

Whereas EC competition law applies where trade between Member States is affected, the new Competition Act will apply where trade within the United Kingdom is affected. This also extends to effects in any part of the United Kingdom. Examples of the type of behaviour that could be subject to investigation by the Competition Commission include a software licence that requires the licensee to bundle the software with any hardware he or she sells or where an on-line database which contains information which cannot be derived from any other source is being licensed in a restrictive manner.

Chapter 5

Reverse analysis

INTRODUCTION

In the case of a work of literature, it is possible to discover the ideas encapsulated in the work simply by reading it. The ideas are available to anyone who takes the trouble to read the work, and without having to do anything which infringes copyright. It is possible to produce another work of literature which is based upon the same fundamental ideas without infringing copyright, although care must be taken not to copy the plot (rather than the basic idea), if one considers the plot to be a more detailed plan involving characters, scenarios and the sequence of events. Closely following someone else's detailed plot could amount to an infringement of copyright, even if the literal similarity between the two works was slight. Even so, the ideas, plot and expression are all transparent to the reader of a novel.

This is not so with computer programs. It may be possible to determine some aspects of a computer program by using the program, but to gain the level of insight available in the case of works of literature, usually it will be necessary to convert the computer program into a different form of code to give access to the ideas and methodology underpinning the program. Alternatively, other techniques may be used such as recording the output of the program or the effect on the performance of the program of various input values. The ideas, techniques and principles used in the creation of a computer program are often hidden from the user. A computer program is opaque in these respects. If the computer program in question is in object code, disassembly may be required so that the ideas and techniques can be ascertained, and this act falls within the meaning of making an adaptation, an act restricted by copyright. If the program is in source code form, say it is a BASIC program running in interpreted mode, the program must be loaded into the computer's random access memory (RAM) to be inspected, accessed via a text editor or printed out. All of these acts fall within the restricted acts of making a copy which includes making transient copies and would apply to a copy loaded into RAM, or making an adaptation of the program.

Major aspects of a computer program which are of interest to other developers of software (or hardware) are the interfaces of the computer program. The interface of a computer program includes the form and structure of the files it creates and uses, its allocation and management of computer memory, its interaction with peripheral devices, and its input and output formats. The manner in which the program interacts with the user is another form of interface.

Bearing in mind that ideas and techniques are usually less accessible in computer programs than in other forms of copyright, it seems only proper that this imbalance should be redressed, and it should be possible to discover these ideas and techniques without infringing the copyright subsisting in the program if done for certain purposes. Obviously purpose is important here, and it seems reasonable to make a distinction between the purpose of creating a program which is compatible with the original and will operate with it and the purpose of making a program which will directly compete with the original one. This problem has been squarely addressed by the European Community in its Directive on the legal protection of computer programs which was implemented in the United Kingdom in 1992. The permitted act of decompiling a computer program is also highly relevant in this respect but, before looking at the protection of ideas and principles and decompilation, it will be helpful to consider the scope of the act of making an adaptation, decompilation being one form only of this.

MAKING AN ADAPTATION

In circumstances where a computer program is re-written in another computer language, the restricted act of making an adaptation will be relevant. Section 21 of the Copyright, Designs and Patents Act 1988 defines the restricted act of making an adaptation, and for computer programs an adaptation is an arrangement or altered version of the program or a translation of it which *includes*:

'. . . a version of the program in which it is converted into or out of a computer language or code or into a different computer language or code, [otherwise than incidentally in the course of running the program.]' (The words in square brackets were repealed by the Copyright (Computer Programs) Regulations 1992.)

Because the definition of translation for computer programs is not exhaustive, it is possible that other activities not described above come within its umbrella. Translation obviously includes the acts of compiling, disassembling or decompiling a computer program. It seems entirely possible that it goes even further, and also applies to the manual conversion of a computer program from one language to another, just as translating a novel from French to English would be an infringement of the copyright in the original French novel. Therefore, re-writing a computer program in a different high-level language, for example re-writing in BASIC a program originally written in COBOL, is making an adaptation, an act restricted by copyright. The definition of translation refers to 'conversion' so the original program must have been used as a model for the new program, it must at least have been referred to by the person writing the new program. Even if the express definition of translation does not cover manual translation (which is unlikely), the ordinary meaning of translation would include this, and the judges would be likely to use the ordinary meaning in addition to the express definition.

Compiling a computer program means converting a high-level language source code program into object code, being the machine code which can be directly understood by the computer. A permanent version of the program in object code form is created which can then be used and operated without the source code version. This must be contrasted with interpreting, a process by which a high-level source code computer program is temporarily converted, line by line, into object code during the operation of the program. This is not as efficient as running a compiled version of the program. Assembling a computer program means converting a low-level assembly language program into object code. The reverse process of disassembly produces assembly language from an object code version of a computer program. Disassembly unlocks the ideas and techniques contained in the object code version of the program. Decompiling a program to retrieve the original high-level language source code is possible only if the exact version of the high-level language is known. However, this is not usually undertaken and has many difficulties associated with it. Non-executable labels and remark lines are not converted to object code during compilation and, thus, will not be retrievable. There is a problem with terminology because people quite often talk about decompiling a computer program when what they really mean is the process of disassembly; that is, converting the object code into the assembly language version of the program. However, in legal terms, this confusion does not really matter, because both decompilation and disassembly are caught by the meaning of making an adaptation.

Figure 5.1 shows the relevant acts which can be done in relation to a computer program, and which may fall within the meaning of translating a computer program. Some of the acts clearly come within the meaning but, in respect of others, this is less certain. Say that a computer program has been written, either in a high-level programming language such as BASIC or a low-level language such as Z80 assembly language. (BASIC is a good example because it can be run in interpreted or compiled form; not all computer languages can be.) The legal meaning of making an adaptation would certainly seem to cover the act of compiling or assembling the computer program. It will now also apply to the direct use of the BASIC source code program which is interpreted during use, as this is conversion done incidentally in the course of running the program and is no longer excluded by the definition of making an adaptation even though no permanent object code version of the program is produced. If the object code version of a program, produced by compiling or assembling the original source code program, is later disassembled to derive an assembly language version, that process too falls within the meaning of making an adaptation.

Figure 5.1 Translation in relation to a computer program

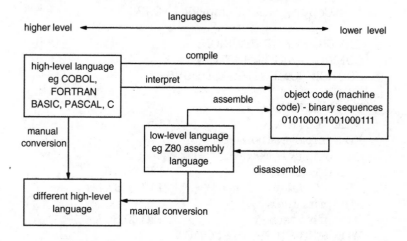

Some might argue that the wide meaning of translation in respect of computer programs bridges the idea/expression dichotomy because re-writing a computer program in a different high-level language involves going back to the basic ideas and principles rather than making a line for line translation, and the programmer will not be particularly concerned with converting the actual code of the original program. The two example programs below do the same, very simple, thing. They both print out information from a file which simply consists of employee names and their salaries. One is written in COBOL, the other in BASIC.

Example COBOL program

```
IDENTIFICATION DIVISION.
PROGRAM-ID print-employee-file.

*       This is a simple program to
*       print out details from a
*       file containing two fields
*       per record
*
*       Copyright D.I.Bainbridge 1992


ENVIRONMENT DIVISION.
CONFIGURATION SECTION.
SOURCE-COMPUTER. ICL 2955.

DATA DIVISION.
FILE SECTION.
FD      employee-file.
01      employee-record.
        03  name                    PIC X(26).
        03  salary                  PIC 9(6).
FD      print-file.
01      print-record                PIC X(80).
WORKING STORAGE SECTION.
77      endfile-flag                PIC XXX VALUE SPACES.
01      print-line.
        03    name-out PIC X(26).
        03                          PIC X(6).
        03    salary-out            PIC ££££,££9.
        03                          PIC X(40).


PROCEDURE DIVISION.
print-employee-file.
        OPEN    INPUT employee-file
                OUTPUT print-file
PERFORM UNTIL endfile-flag = "EOF"
        READ employee-file
        AT END
                MOVE "EOF" TO endfile-flag
```

```
      NOT AT END
        MOVE name TO name-out
        MOVE salary TO salary-out
        WRITE print-record
          FROM print-line
      END-READ
    END-PERFORM
    CLOSE employee-file
        print-file
    STOP RUN.
```

Example BASIC program

```
1000 REM  PROGRAM TO PRINT EMPLOYEE FILE
          'EMPFILE'
1010 REM  FILE CONTAINS TWO FIELDS PER
          RECORD
1020 REM  COPYRIGHT D.I.BAINBRIDGE 1992
1030 REM  ******************************
1100 REM  OPEN FILE
1110 OPEN "I",#1,"EMPFILE"
1120 REM  ******************************
1200 REM  GET INFO FROM FILE AND PRINT OUT
1210 WHILE NOT EOF(1)
1220      INPUT#1,EMPNAME$,SALARY
1230      PRINT EMPNAME$;
1240      PRINT TAB(32) USING'######,';SALARY
1250 WEND
1260 CLOSE#1
1270 END
```

Comparing the two example programs, it can be seen that to write a program in BASIC from an original COBOL program, the programmer will have little concern for the detail of the COBOL code itself because of substantial differences in the syntax, file-handling, and structural aspects of the two languages. All the programmer requires is the ideas or the purpose behind the COBOL program; he or she will reduce the COBOL program to its basic algorithm and from this algorithm (not from the COBOL source code) the programmer will be able to produce a BASIC program. (In this simple example, one might wonder why the programmer was not able to discover the basic idea and purpose simply by running the program.) The new program will not 'look and feel' like the original program, so the objective similarity test leading to an inference of copying will not be satisfied. Of course, the more alike the two languages are, the more likely it is that the programs will exhibit similarities, for example, if the languages are PASCAL and some forms of BASIC. But, if an objective similarity is missing (semantic, syntactical or structural), as it often will be in such circumstances, should the conversion fall within the meaning of adaptation? Bearing in mind that copyright is not intended to give rise to monopolies, does the law give disproportionate protection to computer programs through the concept of making an adaptation?

Translating a computer program is not like translating a literary work from one language to another, such as from French to English. Making a translation of a novel is an adaptation, but here we are talking about a conversion from one language to another word by word, phrase by phrase and sentence by sentence. Consider a novel written in French. If a person reads the novel and decides to write a novel *loosely* based on the same plot in English, but without referring back to the original French text, it is submitted that the novelist does not infringe the copyright in the French work. The French work has not been translated, either directly or indirectly. Of course, care must be taken not to follow the plot of the French novel too closely, using the same scenes and characters. Why should computer programs be treated differently?

One way around this problem is for the courts to construe the word 'convert' to mean a line for line conversion from one language to another. However, this would defeat the control of programs which are compiled or disassembled because a line for line nexus may be lacking. A compiled version (object code) may have several lines of code corresponding to a single line of the source code. What is clear is that the fairness or otherwise of the meaning of 'translation' depends on the nature of both the original program and the program which is subsequently produced. A wide meaning will make it very difficult to produce a program to fulfil a purpose similar to another program if the programmer has some knowledge of the original program. This could be an undesirable constraint on the activities of ex-employees who should be free to use their skill and experience elsewhere providing the function of the original program is not in the nature of a trade secret. A narrower interpretation will fail to cover a simple compilation of a source code program into object code. Although, in this case, if the owner of the copyright in the source code program has himself compiled it into object code, it would seem that the object code program is protected by copyright independently of the source code version. If there are difficulties in showing the presence of sufficient skill and effort, particularly if the compilation is carried out automatically using a compiler program, the object code version could be considered to be an adaptation of the source code program or even a computer-generated work.

REVERSE ANALYSIS

Reverse analysis is the process by which ideas and principles contained and expressed in a computer program (in whatever form), are made transparent and available by means of an operation such as disassembly of an object code program. This is translating the object code into another form of code or computer language and will thus infringe the copyright in the object code program, unless the copyright owner has expressly or impliedly authorised this, or it is covered by the permitted act of decompilation, discussed later in this chapter.

Reverse analysis may also be carried out by studying or testing the operation of a computer program in order to gain access to its underlying ideas, principles and algorithm.

Reverse analysis is important in the computer industry, particularly with respect to the development of computer programs which have to interface with other programs, data files created by other programs or with computer hardware. The key word describing this feature of working with other programs is 'interoperability'. Many computer software developers argue that it is vital that they are allowed to disassemble and decompile other programs so that they can develop other software and hardware which will be interoperable, that is, work with or alongside existing programs or transfer data to and from other programs.

The equivalent acts in the world of hardware, computer or otherwise, are to take something apart to determine how it works, or to measure and examine an article to find its precise shape and configuration. For example, a motor car manufacturer might develop a braking system involving a new technique and others will be tempted to take it apart to obtain an insight into how it works (if the system is the subject matter of a patent, then this information will be contained in the patent specification, a document which is available to be public). Spare parts manufacturers sometimes carry out reverse analysis to find the shape and dimensions of spare parts such as exhaust pipes and car body panels so that they can make replacement parts. Design law will allow them to do this in many cases.

Ideas and principles

In terms of computer software, reverse analysis may be used to find out about the entire workings of a computer program including the precise code making up the program. This will involve disassembly of the computer program and, even if no further use is made of the information thus gained, it will infringe copyright as it is making an adaptation, unless the decompilation exception applies. Alternatively, reverse analysis might be carried out in a less direct way, simply by using and observing the operation of a computer program. This can give a lesser degree of insight into the basic ideas and flow of the program and will not infringe copyright *per se* if the person so doing has a licence to use the program. Indeed, the European Community Directive on the legal protection of computer programs, the text of which is reproduced in Appendix 1, states that a lawful user of a program can observe, study or test the functioning of the program in order to determine the ideas and principles which underlie any element of the program, in the course of loading, displaying, running, transmitting or storing the program as he or she is entitled to do, for example, by virtue of a licence agreement; Article 5(3).

Section 296A(1)(c) of the Copyright, Designs and Patents Act 1988 contains the equivalent provision which cannot be prohibited or restricted by any term in an agreement under which the person so observing, studying or testing the program has use of that program.

Ideas and principles are not protected by copyright and this provision is needed so that the user of a program cannot be prevented from gleaning the ideas and principles underlying the program. It may be a matter simply of observing the program in use so that its underlying ideas and principles can be determined. In other cases, it may be a matter of monitoring the computer output, for example, where the program controls an industrial process, by recording the signals transmitted from the computer. Other means might be employed such as applying test data to the program or recording the flow of the program under differing parameters. This particular provision does not extend to the act of decompilation which is restricted to a 'permitted objective' as discussed later in this chapter. A further point is that the subsequent use made of the information thus obtained may itself infringe copyright.

Example

Lynne acquires a copy of a program to forecast winning lottery numbers. She observes and tests the program thoroughly and thereby deduces the algorithm used by the program as a basis of selecting the sequences of numbers. She then writes her own program based on the same algorithm. However, in doing so, she structures her program in the same way as she was impressed with the 'elegance' of the program's flow.

It is likely that Lynne may have infringed the copyright in some of the non-literal elements of the original program. Indeed, the basic algorithm itself may be deemed to be a non-literal element. The fact that her act of observing, studying and testing the program does not infringe copyright if it goes beyond a basic idea or principle does not mean to say that she may copy ideas and principles in her own program *if they are considered to be non-literal elements protected by copyright.* Section 16(3) of the Copyright, Designs and Patents Act 1988 makes it clear that it matters not whether any intervening acts themselves infringe copyright. That being so, although ideas and principles are made accessible and transparent, they may not be used if to do so would infringe copyright.

Copyright infringement, if any, will be dependent upon the nature of the subsequent use of the information obtained in this way, and even then the subsequent use may fall within the exceptions to copyright infringement. However, if this method is followed, great care must be taken not to copy screen displays, menu systems and non-literal elements. Figure 5.2 shows different forms of analysing a computer program, and whether they constitute an infringement of copyright.

Figure 5.2   Reverse analysis and purpose

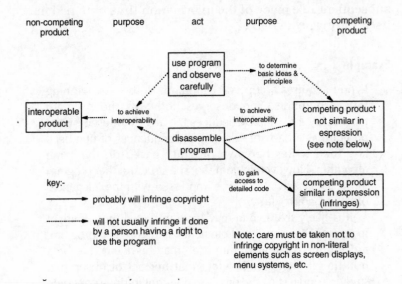

Simply using a computer program to determine its basic ideas and principles and then writing another computer program in accordance with those ideas and principles, *per se*, will not infringe copyright, providing nothing further is taken from the original program. Studying a program in use will make its functionality readily available together with some knowledge of the manner in which it interfaces with the user and the general nature of input and output data.

Before the changes made as a result of the Directive on computer programs, reverse analysis would usually have been judged on the basis of the permitted act of fair dealing, especially for research purposes. There was very little case law to assist in determining the scope of fair dealing in terms of any work let alone computer programs. Obviously, it must have been based on notions of fairness. In the first edition of this book, the author reckoned it would permit reverse analysis for the purpose of making a compatible program that could interoperate with the original program but that it would not extend to reverse analysis where the purpose was to make a competing program where the expression of the second program was similar to that of the first program. Subsequently, a case in the United States gave a further indication of the scope of the permitted act, although this was 'fair use', the American equivalent of fair dealing.

Case

Sega Enterprises Ltd v Accolade Inc (1992) US App LEXIS 26645

The plaintiff made a computer games system comprising a console and a large number of games cartridges. Each cartridge contained an access code that was checked for by the console before the game could be played. The defendant produced games cartridges which were compatible with the plaintiff's consoles. It did this by disassembling the plaintiff's games cartridges and comparing the resulting code. A common piece of code occurred in all the games cartridges and the defendant correctly believed this was the access code. The defendant copied this piece of code and inserted it into its games (the code itself was a very small part of the total code of the plaintiff's programs).

It was held that the defendant's reverse analysis was fair use under United States copyright law. Otherwise, the plaintiff would achieve a monopoly over functional elements of his program, accepting that the access code, part of the interface between the console and the cartridge, was a functional element unprotected by copyright. Thus, the defendant was entitled to rely on the defence even though it had disassembled all the plaintiff's programs. The fact that the plaintiff's trade mark was displayed when using the defendant's cartridge did not assist the plaintiff as it was said that trade mark rights could not be used as a way to overcome the fair use defence.

It is likely that a similar approach would have been taken in the United Kingdom before the changes to copyright law precipitated by the European Community Directive. Compliance with the Directive has not significantly changed the position as regards decompilation and occasions when it is permitted. However, the new provisions have brought more precision and predictability though some of the potential for flexibility provided by the fair dealing defence necessarily has been sacrificed.

Decompilation and interoperability

Computer programs have to interact with other things apart from computer memory, as shown in Figure 5.3. A great many computer systems involve the use of computer files and databases, records of information stored on a computer or on storage media; for example, a list of employees' names, addresses, salaries, tax code, etc. Programs also have to interact with other programs, hardware and peripheral devices and, last but not least, the person using the system. To interact with any of these, the computer program must use an interface, being a method of transferring data to and from the computer program or computer memory being used by the computer. For example, the interface with the user may involve a keyboard or mouse and a pull-down menu system. An interface with a data file must contain details of the structure of the file and nature of the data stored therein. Access to details of these interfaces will usually involve reverse analysis in the form of disassembly. The interface itself will be expressed in computer program code, usually having been written in assembly language and converted into machine code (object code).

Figure 5.3   Elements available after disassembly

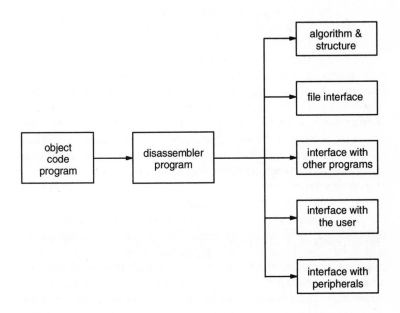

There is now a specific permitted act of decompilation, provided for by section 50B inserted by the Copyright (Computer Programs) Regulations 1992. A lawful user of a copy of a computer program expressed in a low-level language may, subject to certain conditions:

- convert the program into a version expressed in a higher-level language, or
- incidentally, in the course of so converting the program, copy it.

Thus, in certain circumstances, an object code program can be converted into its source code without infringing copyright. For example, the following conversions are possible:

machine language program   —>   assembly language program
machine language program   —>   high-level language program
assembly language program   —>   high-level language program

In all of these cases, a program in a low-level language has been changed into the equivalent program expressed in a higher language.

Although the permitted act is referred to as decompilation, its expression in terms of low-level and higher-level languages makes it clear that it applies also to disassembly. In any case, it is clear that the word 'decompilation' is now being taken by many to mean or include disassembly although, strictly speaking, the two acts are different though having a similar effect; that is, moving further away from the machine language of the computer's processor.

The conditions under which decompilation is permitted are pivotal to the scope of the exception to copyright infringement. It must be necessary to decompile the program to obtain the information necessary to create an independent program which can be operated with the program decompiled or with another program (this is known as 'the permitted objective') and the information so obtained is not used for any purpose other than that permitted objective. It is important to note that it is not necessary that the program decompiled is the one with which it is intended to interoperate.

The conditions above are declared not to be met if:

- the information necessary to achieve the permitted objective is readily available, or
- the act of decompiling is not confined to the permitted objective, or
- the information is supplied to any person to whom it is not necessary to supply it in order to achieve that objective, or
- the information is used to create a program which is substantially similar in its expression or to do any act restricted by copyright.

In some instances, the owner of the copyright subsisting in a computer program might be willing to divulge the necessary information to the person wishing to develop an interoperable program. The information may even be published. The copyright owner might be pleased to see the development of other programs that will operate with his or her program as this might enhance its sales.

It is important to note that the scope of fair dealing has, for computer programs, been restricted to exclude decompilation which can only be performed in accordance with the above act. The permitted act of decompilation cannot be prohibited or restricted by any term or condition in an agreement, such terms or conditions being void, by section 296A, unless the agreement was entered into before 1 January 1993, the date on which the new provisions came into force. Now that the decompilation provisions have been described, it will be useful to consider how they will work in practice by way of some examples.

Example 1

Jingle Inc distributes an operating system for the Weller personal computer. Tupper Equipment makes a laser printer and Snodgrass Ltd market the 'industry standard' fourth-generation database package.

Buzfuz Software plc buy a Weller PC complete with operating system, a Tupper laser printer and a copy of the Snodgrass 4GL package. Buzfuz decompiles the Jingle operating system programs to discover how they use the computer's memory so that Buzfuz can develop applications software for the Weller PC. The information is also used to determine the interface with the Tupper printer. Buzfuz then prints out the computer code of a sample database file created with the Snodgrass 4GL with the intention of creating a compatible 4GL.

Buzfuz can rely on the exception to infringement in the case of the Jingle operating system's program, providing the conditions are met, particularly that the information is not readily available. It often is for operating systems or, if not, the copyright owner might be prepared to divulge the necessary interface details free of charge or a little cost. Although Buzfuz is seeking hardware compatibility it is, in reality, the ability to interoperate with the operating systems programs and the programs in the laser printer that is required. Buzfuz can then use this information in developing its interoperable programs.

The 'decompilation' of the database file is, however, not covered by the exception as a database file is not a computer program and the exception is not applicable. However, in this case, Buzfuz may be able to rely on the normal defence of fair dealing. This defence may be successful if the purpose is to use the information to make a compatible, non-competing product such as a word processor or spreadsheet that has file transfer capabilities with the Snodgrass 4GL. It is less likely to succeed if Buzfuz's intention is to make a direct replacement for the Snodgrass 4GL. The matter is, however, not beyond doubt.

Example 2

Bardell Software produces a leading word processing software package. Pickwick Computer Systems obtain a copy and decompile it to discover how it interfaces with document files so that:

• Pickwick can produce a spreadsheet program that can transfer data to and from Bardell's word processor,
• Pickwick can produce a spreadsheet program that has file compatibility with Dodson Corporation's spreadsheet (this is known to be compatible with Bardell's program), and
• Pickwick can develop a word processing package with file transfer facilities to and from Bardell's word processor.

Bardell had previously refused to furnish Pickwick with the necessary information and Pickwick do not intend to divulge it to anyone else nor to use it for purposes other than achieving compatibility. All of Pickwick's proposed actions should be permissible and within the scope of the exception to infringement. Figure 5.4 shows this diagramatically.

Figure 5.4 Interoperability examples

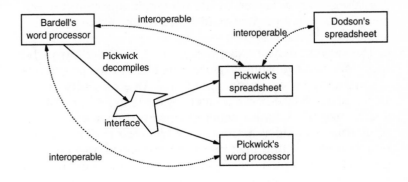

One proviso must be added to the second example. The wording of section 50B defines the permitted objective in terms of the creation of an independent program which 'can be operated with the program decompiled or with another program'. This suggests that the purpose must be to operate the new program simultaneously with the 'target program'. This is precisely what is intended in the first example above in relation to the computer's operating system and the printer's software.

To clarify this issue, the text of the Directive on the legal protection of computer programs must be examined (see Appendix 1). Article 6 simply states the purpose as being to '. . . achieve the interoperability of an independently created computer program with other programs' (subject to a number of conditions). The appropriate recitals to the Directive reinforces the author's view that simultaneous interoperability is not essential. One recital defines interoperability as the 'ability to exchange information and mutually to use the information which has been exchanged'. This confirms that the decompilation permitted act should apply to facilitating the transfer of data files and the like from one program format to another, just as in the second example. It should also permit the creation of appropriate filters providing the expression of the decompiled program is not copied should it represent a substantial part of that program, subject to what is said below.

The decompilation exception cannot be relied on if the expression, or a substantial part thereof, of the first program is taken and used in the new program. One difficulty facing 'decompilers' is whether they can copy the relevant information (for example, the interface code) and insert it into their own new program. Consider a piece of code, several lines long, representing an interface between a program and another program. The person decompiling must not perform any acts restricted by copyright unless covered by the permitted act itself. Can the interface code be incorporated into the new program?

1. If the interface code is insufficiently original or too trivial for copyright protection in its own right or if it does not represent a substantial part of the decompilation program it may be copied.
2. If the interface code is protected by copyright (either in its own right or as a substantial part of the program decompiled) it is submitted that two possibilities exist:
   a) if some new code, having the same function, can be written from the ideas and principles underlying the interface then that must be done and the actual expression of the interface must not be copied;
   b) if it is not possible to write code to perform the same function in any different way then, on the basis of an implied licence, the code can be copied, otherwise the permitted act is illusory in such cases.

The second scenario above is not entirely implausible and does accord with the approach taken in the United States in the *Sega v Accolade* case. However, one point that can be made is that the move toward facilitating interoperability of computer programs does call into question the validity of the approach in cases such as *Lotus v Paperback Software* (since overruled on the basis that the menu system was a method of operation) in terms of United Kingdom law. Other 'non-literal' copying cases should also be viewed with some suspicion, even

Richardson v Flanders discussed in the previous chapter, although this case was decided on the basis of the law prior to the changes made to copyright law. However, two points should be borne in mind. First, determining interfaces (such as a user interface) by observing a program or studying a listing of the program in its original form does not involve decompilation and is not covered by this exception, though other exceptions may apply such as that allowing observing, studying or testing to gain access to the underlying ideas and principles. Second, compatibility is in the wider interests of acquirers and users of computer software.

The question of the lawfulness of reverse analysis of computer programs is of immense importance to software developers. The changes brought about to copyright law in respect of decompilation, although representing something of a compromise, must be welcomed for the increased certainty that they bring. Some doubts as to how the provisions will work in practice remain.

The following case touches on reverse engineering of computer programs and other software.

Case

Mars UK Ltd v Teknowledge Ltd (1999) Times, 23 June, Chancery Division

> Mars made coin-operated and coin-changing machines which contained sophisticated encrypted software used to check whether coins were legal tender. The software included programs and data and was installed on PROM chips (programmable read only memory) and EEPROM chips (electronically erasable programmable read only memory). The latter could be re-programmed. Mars claimed it owned copyright and a database right in respect of the software. Teknowledge reverse engineered the chips to discover the algorithms, data and program code with a view to re-programming EEPROM chips to take account of newly introduced coinage. Teknowledge did not argue about subsistence of copyright or that it had carried out the reverse engineering or other acts but argued that it could rely on the common law 'right to repair' defence in *British Leyland*

Motor Corpn v Armstrong Patents Co Ltd [1986] 2 WLR 400.
Mars also claimed that Teknowledge was in breach of
confidence in respect of the encrypted software.

On the copyright issue, Mr Justice Jacob said that sections
50A–50C of the 1988 Act provided a complete statutory code
as far as a defence based on reverse engineering of computer
programs was concerned. In the circumstances,
Teknowledge was unable to avail itself of those provisions
as what it had done was outside the specific provisions (it
had not decompiled for the purpose of interoperability).
Furthermore, the *British Leyland* defence had been narrowed
in scope by *Canon KK v Green Cartridge Co (Hong Kong)
Ltd* [1997] AC 728 (a case involving rights in respect of toner
cartridges for laser printers and photocopying machines).
Although the European Directive on the legal protection of
databases authorised Member States to adopt defences
'traditionally authorised under national law' in respect of
databases, the judge thought it far from certain that a
common law defence had been so authorised. Parliament
had not made specific provision for an appropriate defence
in the regulations implementing the Directive.

Mr Justice Jacob, in a previous case, *Hyde Park Residence
Ltd v Yelland* (1999) Times, 24 March, said that a general
public policy defence would apply only if the court was
reasonably certain that 'no right-thinking member of society
would quarrel with the result'. The 'right to repair' defence
was part of this general public policy defence but, in the
present case, he did not consider the test satisfied and said
that there was no overwhelming public policy principle to
allow persons obtaining the machines to reverse engineer
them with a view to re-programming them for new coins.

On the issue of confidence, Mr Justice Jacob decided that
Mars failed to demonstrate that the encrypted information
had the necessary quality of confidence about it. Although
that was sufficient to defeat the claim, he then considered
whether, as the information was encrypted, this was
equivalent to giving a person who had acquired a machine
notice that the information was confidential and that it must
not be decrypted. The judge was unimpressed and he said
that the fact of encryption merely sent a message that the

owner of the information did not want anyone to gain access to it. This was not sufficient to impose an obligation of confidence on a person acquiring a machine. Ownership of a machine brought with it an entitlement to reverse engineer it to see how it worked.

The general defence of public policy (or public interest) is quite narrow in its application and there are relatively few cases where it has succeeded. Strictly speaking, as the Copyright, Designs and Patents Act 1988 is such a comprehensive piece of legislation, it could be argued that it provides a complete and exhaustive code on copyright. However, section 171(3) of the Act states that the copyright provisions do not affect 'any rule of law preventing or restricting the enforcement of copyright, on grounds of public interest or otherwise'. Subsequent case law has demonstrated that the *British Leyland* defence survived the passing of the 1988 Act though its scope was restricted in the *Canon* case.

Mere encryption of information, such as computer data or program code, does not automatically impose an obligation of confidence. Where machinery incorporating confidential information is sold, it may be possible to impose an obligation of confidence by contractual means with an express prohibition on reverse engineering.

Chapter 6

Databases

INTRODUCTION

A computer database is a collection of information stored on computer media. The information may be a list of clients and their addresses or the full text of various documents or a set of co-ordinates relating to a three-dimensional building structure or a collection of representations of pre-Raphaelite paintings. The range of things which may be included in a computer database is enormous. The information contained in the database may be confidential and protected by the law of breach of confidence but what is the copyright position? The simplest way of looking at a computer database is to consider the work it represents, for example, a printed listing of names and addresses, a printed set of documents or drawings of buildings or a collection of paintings. Those works may be protected individually by copyright as literary or artistic works as appropriate but the collection of works may also be protected additionally and separately by copyright and/or the database right, notwithstanding the separate copyrights subsisting in the individual works. This is an important point. In terms of databases, copyright can exist at two levels, at the level of the individual works contained in the database and at the level of the database itself as a form of work in its own right. The database may have protection by the database right which came into existence on 1 January 1998.

Prior to 1 January 1998, databases were protected by copyright as literary works, being compilations. However, the

Copyright, Designs and Patents Act 1988 now excludes databases from compilations and, if protected by copyright, databases are a separate and distinct form of literary work. The Copyright and Rights in Databases Regulations 1997 made the necessary changes, bringing also a new requirement for originality for databases and other provisions specific to copyright databases. The Regulations, which implemented the European Directive on the legal protection of databases (OJ L77, 27.3.96, p 20), also introduced a new database right, intended primarily to protect databases which are the result of a substantial investment but which may not necessarily be protected by copyright as databases. Before looking at the present position regarding the protection of databases, the position prior to 1 January 1998 is described.

DATABASES BEFORE 1 JANUARY 1998

The Copyright, Designs and Patents Act 1988, before amendment on 1 January 1998, made no specific mention of databases but it was clear that they were protected as compilations and subject to the usual rules that applied to literary works generally. Thus, they had to be original, that is, the result of the author's own work without copying another database and involving a minimum of skill and judgment in their creation. The other implications of literary works such as the qualification, authorship, ownership, acts restricted by the copyright and the permitted acts would all have applied to copyright databases without exception. However, there was some doubt as to whether a database of artistic works would qualify as the definition of a literary work was as follows:

> '"literary work" means any work, other than a dramatic or musical work, which is written, spoken or sung, and accordingly includes . . .'

This part of the definition remains the same now and the problem is that it is difficult to envisage writing, speaking or singing an artistic work. However, the Directive on the legal protection of databases specifically mentions artistic works as being included in the meaning of what is to be understood by the term 'database'. That being so and notwithstanding this ambiguity in the definition of literary work, there should now be no doubt that a database of artistic works will be subject to a database copyright and the database right if all the other requirements are present for those rights.

The following example indicates the working of copyright in relation to databases before 1 January 1998.

Example

In 1997, XYZ Supplies Ltd had a computer database containing names, addresses, telephone and fax numbers of customers. This database had been developed over a couple of years and it was usual for a new customer's details to be entered directly into the computer by XYZ's 'tele-sales' staff without a written record being made.

The customer database was protected by copyright as an original literary work (assuming a modicum of skill and judgment was involved in compiling the database, for example, if the design of the database structure required skill and judgment or if the tele-sales staff had to exercise judgment in deciding whether to accept a new customer or what his or her initial credit-rating should be). Being a compilation, it was a literary work by section 3(1). By storing the information in a database, it was recorded in 'writing or otherwise' as required by the Act ('writing' was defined widely by section 178 and includes any form of notation or code regardless of the method or medium of storage – this definition has not been changed). Even if the database was never printed out on paper, it was protected by copyright.

We will return to this example at the end of the chapter to see what the position is now in respect of such a database if in existence prior to 1 January 1998 or if made after that date.

Some databases do not take a great deal of skill or judgment in their design and creation. An example is a simple database of names and addresses or a database containing a schedule of goods and their retail prices. The design of the structure of the database will take little time using, for example, database development software such as dBase V for Windows or Microsoft Access. What will take more skill and judgment, and usually considerably more time even with a simple database, is the design of forms and reports. Of course, if very detailed, these designs may be considered to be works of copyright in their own right but the question remained, before 1 January 1998, whether the database was a copyright database. The following discussion on 'sweat of the brow' looks at developments in the United States, which were very influential in the lead up to the European Directive, and compares this with the position in the United Kingdom before 1 January 1998.

Sweat of the brow

Some databases were compilations of works which were themselves subject to copyright, an example being a database containing a selection of contemporary romantic poems. Copyright would have subsisted in each poem as well as in the whole as a compilation providing it was the result of a design or selection process requiring skill and judgment. Even if the poems themselves were out of copyright (for example, a collection of eighteenth-century love sonnets) the database itself may have been the subject of copyright. It had been recognised by the courts that a compilation of commonplace materials taken from the public domain may have had sufficient originality to qualify for copyright protection. However, the database as a compilation must have been the result of some skill and judgment. But the difficulty was determining the position if the making of the database did not require skill or judgment but merely the expenditure of effort or expense. Once it had been decided to compile the database in question, there was little or no room for skill or judgment. The Supreme Court of the United States had to consider such a problem.

Case

Feist Publications Inc v Rural Telephone Service Co Inc (1991)
111 S Ct 1282

> The United States Supreme Court held that the 'White Pages' of a telephone directory were not protected by copyright

because, comprising simply of names arranged in alphabetical order together with addresses and telephone numbers, its creation required no skill and judgment. It was the result of effort alone. However, the 'Yellow Pages' in a telephone directory could be the subject matter of copyright because there was some skill and judgment in devising the classification system and individual works of copyright, such as pictorial advertisements, were contained within that section (although in a subsequent case it was held that taking substantial extracts from the yellow pages did not necessarily infringe copyright). Thus, something more than the mere 'sweat of the brow' is required in the United States to bestow copyright upon a work.

A great many databases could be classified as being the result of no more than the sweat of the brow. In some cases, where the database is, for example, a list of customers, their addresses, buying preferences and accounts this will not be a serious issue. Such a database is likely to be afforded some protection by the law of breach of confidence. The database may not be made available to any other organisation and may have little or no intrinsic commercial value as a database. However, a collection of data is a valuable commodity in its own right and a growing number of organisations are involved in 'list trading', that is, selling copies of their customer databases to other organisations. In other cases, the database will have been specifically made for commercial exploitation. The significance of denying copyright protection to some databases is very worrying and is one of the reasons for the European Directive on the legal protection of databases. This, and the implementing Regulations, are discussed later in this chapter.

Of course, *Feist* is an American case and is not necessarily applicable in the United Kingdom and, prior to the changes to the protection of databases, there were a number of cases in the United Kingdom involving allegations of copyright infringement of databases such as given below. The author is not aware of any case in the United Kingdom in which it was held that a computer database was not protected by copyright.

Case

Waterlow Directories Ltd v Reed Information Services Ltd [1992] FSR 409

Both parties published directories of solicitors' firms and barristers' names and addresses. The defendant obtained a copy of the plaintiff's directory and noted those names not included in the defendant's directory. Using a word processor, the defendant sent letters to those firms of solicitors and barristers, inviting them to appear in the new edition of his directory. The plaintiff's directory contained some 12,620 names and the defendant had used about 1,600 of them in the manner described above. The defendant also made use of the plaintiff's directory to compile a list of solicitors and barristers in public authorities and industry (a feature which the defendant's directory did not have). Over ten per cent of the list compiled by the defendant did not appear anywhere else other than in the plaintiff's directory.

The plaintiff was granted an interlocutory injunction. Whilst it might be possible for a person to use information in a directory to compile another, that person could not simply reproduce the entries from the directory to compile his own. Here there had been clear copying by reproducing the names and addresses using a computer with word processing software. The defendant had not contested the subsistence of copyright in the plaintiff's directory. The issue was whether the part taken was a substantial one. It was held that there was a strong case that that was so.

Directories of lawyers were in issue in another, earlier, case which was decided under the Copyright Act 1956. The case was actually decided in 1989 but not reported until 1995.

Case

Waterlow Publishers Ltd v Rose [1995] FSR 207

The plaintiff published a lawyers' directory. The directory containing details of solicitors had been compiled from a list of practising solicitors obtained from the Law Society. Each solicitor was then sent a form asking for further details.

The information returned was used to compile a database of solicitors. The database was then sorted into order and used for typesetting and publication. The defendant used names and addresses from the plaintiff's directory to send out forms with proposed entries for solicitors to approve or correct. The defendant used the returned forms to compile a database but the plaintiff obtained an interlocutory injunction, although it did not seek any relief when the case came to full trial. The defendant claimed damages to compensate him and this was refused by the trial judge because he held that the defendant had infringed the plaintiff's copyright. The defendant appealed to the Court of Appeal.

The appeal was dismissed. The Court of Appeal confirmed that the defendant had infringed the plaintiff's copyright by reproducing a substantial part of the plaintiff's directory in his forms. The Court of Appeal approved the following statement of the trial judge, his Honour Andrew Blackett-Ord:

'I will read a sentence from *Morris v Ashbee* (1868) LR 7 Eq 34, the judgment of Vice-Chancellor Giffard. He says at 41: "The simple upshot of the whole case is, that the plaintiff's directory was the source from which they compiled very material parts of theirs, and they had no right to resort to that source. They had no right to make the results arrived at by the plaintiff the foundation of their work or any material part of it, and this is what they have done."

Mr Rose argued that he only used the existing directory to get in touch with the solicitors and that his work was then based upon the forms returned to him by the solicitors to whom they were sent. There were something like 50,000 forms and the names and addresses to which they were sent were all obtained from the [plaintiff's directory] . . . In my judgment that goes beyond the lawful use of an existing publication and amounted to an infringement of the plaintiff's copyright.'

The fact that the plaintiff did not claim relief at the full trial did not entitle the defendant to damages on the basis that he had been prevented from publishing his directory because of the injunction.

In *Waterlow v Rose*, Mr Rose had argued that his directory was to be based only on information supplied to him by solicitors in response to the forms and that he would design his directory along different lines with a different layout and that, by exercising his own skill and judgment, he would not be infringing copyright. That submission was rejected. In many cases, the forms would be returned unaltered and the court considered it unlikely that those 20 per cent of solicitors that failed to return the forms would be omitted from the directory as claimed.

The case is instructive, building as it does on authorities from Victorian times, in showing that making use of someone else's database in the design of a new database was likely to infringe copyright unless done with permission. Also, a finding of infringement did not require that the structure of the database be copied. Such case law demonstrated that the legal protection of copyright in databases was potentially very strong in the United Kingdom. We will now turn to the position after 1 January 1998. There have been some significant changes.

CURRENT PROTECTION OF DATABASES

As the use and power of information technology continues to increase at an impressive rate, it is vitally important that strong and effective protection is available for computer databases as well as for computer programs and other works. For many organisations, their most valuable information technology resource will be their computer data, perhaps more so than the computer programs. Databases may be used by organisations internally in their day-to-day operations or they may be developed for the purpose of commercial exploitation by selling copies of databases or by providing others with on-line access to the databases. They may range from directories, customer lists and schedules to multimedia products and massive databases containing a multitude of works of copyright which can be accessed via the Internet. It is clear that the work involved in creating, maintaining, extending and improving such databases should result in some form of property right to control subsequent use and access, particularly as the investment required may be quite substantial. Granting proprietary rights to the owners of databases can be justified on simple economic grounds. For some databases, the creative flair of the author also ought to be recognised on moral grounds.

Directive 96/9/EC of the European Parliament and of the Council of 11 March 1996 on the legal protection of databases (OJ L77, 27.3.96, p 20), which is reproduced in Appendix 2, required implementation before 1 January 1998. It is described briefly below, following which the United Kingdom's implementing Regulations will be looked at in detail.

Directive on the legal protection of databases

The Directive recognises the importance of databases in the field of information technology, describing databases as a 'vital tool in the development of an information market within the Community'. The need for a stable and uniform legal protection for databases is seen as critical to the investment in modern information technology by the Parliament and Council to the European Union. Hence the need for a Directive to provide an effective level of protection for databases and to harmonise the law throughout the Community.

The Directive has a number of features of some interest. First, it provides for two forms of rights, a copyright not far removed from the previous 'compilation' copyright under prior United Kingdom law, and a new *sui generis* right, intended to provide a shorter-term protection for databases which fail to reach the standard required for copyright protection but which are the result of a substantial investment. By recognising that some databases may fail to be protected by copyright, the Directive appears to have adopted the sweat of the brow principle under United States copyright law. The sole criteria for subsistence of copyright in a database is that it constitutes the 'author's own intellectual creation'; Article 3(1). This phrase would seem to exclude databases that are a result of effort or expense only. However, the recitals to the Directive make it clear that copyright protection will extend to the structure of the database.

Second, the Directive applies to paper databases as well as computer databases. This is in line with the policy behind the data protection Directive, controlling the processing of personal data relating to individuals. Article 1 of the database Directive states that it concerns the legal protection of databases in any form. Previous United Kingdom copyright law did not differentiate between paper and electronic databases. Article 1(2) of the Directive describes a database as meaning:

'a collection of independent works, data or other materials arranged in a systematic or methodical way and individually accessible by electronic or other means'.

Computer programs used in the manufacture or operation of databases which are accessed by electronic means are excluded, being separately protected in any case. The recitals to the Directive make it clear that a thesaurus or index used with a database is part of the database. With modern programming techniques and software development tools it is, however, not always an easy task to distinguish between database and program. Some databases contain executable instructions. A database file may include forms and reports with associated macros and queries, all contained within the same computer file.

The Directive sets out the rights of the owner of the copyright and database right and contains a number of exceptions to both rights. Some degree of flexibility is granted to Member States in relation to the exceptions. As the Directive has been implemented by the Copyright and Rights in Databases Regulations 1997, there is little to be gained by describing its contents in great detail. Where there are actual or potential discrepancies between the Directive and the Regulations or where the Regulations are imprecise, reference is made to the Directive in the following sections. Of course, where a provision in a Directive is mandatory, clear and unambiguous, it will override any contradictory national implementing legislation. In other cases, where a provision in the implementing legislation is ambiguous or needs further explanation, the Directive may be useful in clarifying that provision or in defining its scope.

At this stage it may be worth looking at Figures 6.1 and 6.2 which set out the basic mechanisms for copyright and database right as provided for by the Directive.

Figure 6.1 Database copyright as set out in the Directive

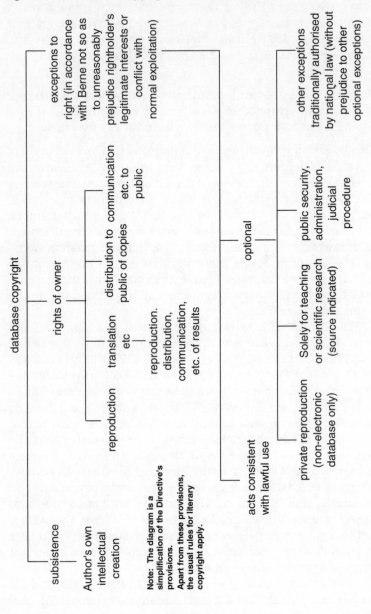

Figure 6.2 Database right as set out in the Directive

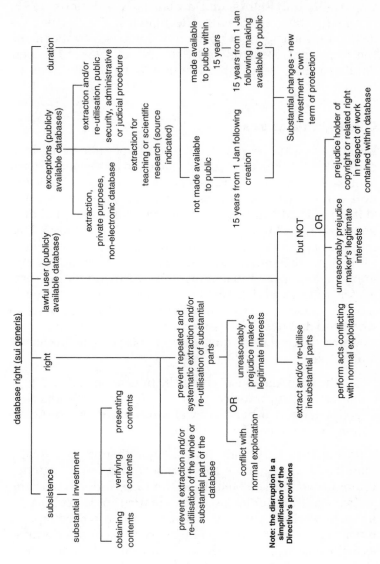

The Directive was implemented in the United Kingdom by the Copyright and Rights in Databases Regulations 1997, hereinafter referred to as the Regulations. The Regulations dealt with the copyright position of databases by modifying the Copyright, Designs and Patents Act 1988. The new database right is provided for directly by the Regulations themselves.

Copyright databases

Databases, whether electronic or on paper (for example, a card index system) are expressly included as a separate form of literary work and, to the list of items in section 3(1), clearly non-exhaustive, of things which are literary works, 'database' is added. It is also made clear that compilations, another form of literary work, do not include databases. This removal of potential dual protection is important particularly as there are differences between some of the exemptions that apply to databases and compilations. As mentioned earlier, a literary work is described as being something which is written, spoken or sung and there was some doubt as to whether a database of artistic works could be a literary work. However, the Directive is quite clear on this point and recital 17 states that:

> '. . . the term "database" should be understood to include literary, artistic, musical or other collections of works or collections of other material such as texts, sound, images, numbers, facts, and data . . .'

This appears very wide and, although not specifically mentioned, presumably the phrase 'other works' catches dramatic works. The recital goes on to exclude 'a recording or [*sic*, "of"] an audiovisual, cinematographic, literary or musical work as such . . .'. Thus, a video recording of a musical performance or of a film recording actors performing a Shakespeare play will not, on their own, form a database. However, a collection of such works could be a database such as a systematically arranged collection of film clips. Furthermore, as a general rule by recital 19, a compilation of several recordings of musical performances on a CD is outside the scope of the Directive (as far as both database copyright and the database right are concerned) and will remain to be protected as a compilation. The reason for this is that making the collection fails to meet the requirement of being an intellectual creation for copyright or a substantial investment for the database right. The recital states this is so 'as a rule' so this does not appear to be conclusive and there may be such collections which, because of their complexity or imaginative input of the person making the collection, may qualify for either copyright or the database right or both. It is submitted that this is likely to be quite rare.

A new section 3A is inserted into the Copyright, Designs and Patents Act 1988. This defines a database and sets out the requirement from the Directive for subsistence. First a database is defined in section 3A(1) as meaning:

> 'a collection of independent works, data or other materials which –
> (a) are arranged in a systematic or methodical way, and
> (b) are individually accessible by electronic or other means.'

This follows the definition in Article 1(2) of the Directive very closely. It should be noted that the definition extends to collections of things other than 'works'; otherwise only databases containing independent works of copyright could be protected as databases. The inclusion of 'data or other materials' means that there is no need for the constituent parts of the database to be works of copyright or to be substantial or significant in any way. For example, a database of film titles together with the names of leading actors, directors and producers together with year of making and of release could be protected (providing the database is deemed to be an intellectual creation) even though all the independent items of information are too small or trivial to qualify for copyright protection in their own right. There is no express exclusion of computer programs from the definition of database nor any express inclusion of any thesaurus or index system. Of course computer programs are protected as another form of literary work (as is preparatory design material for a computer program). The Directive states that protection may also apply to thesauruses and index systems and there seems to be no reason why this should not be so under the Copyright, Designs and Patents Act 1988 as amended. These elements of a database may be considered to be non-literal elements.

The test for originality for a database is, closely following the Directive, given by section 3A(2) which states that a literary work consisting of a database is original:

> '. . . if, and only if, by reason of the selection and arrangement of the contents of the database the database constitutes the author's own intellectual creation.'

The skill in selecting and arranging the contents is rewarded by granting a copyright but, in many respects, it is not an easy matter to say just what this means and where the boundaries lie.

Selection *and* arrangement are required. Selection means choosing the contents of the database whilst arrangement may be more to do with the design of the database. It could mean ordering the contents within the database (something which may be automatic or specified by the creator of the database, depending on the development software used) or it could mean the work in designing the fields (what set of information is stored about a particular entry) or both. The example in Figure 6.3 indicates a portion of a database created by the author (it is one of the databases which are available from the author – see the back of the book for details). In designing the database, first it must be decided what information is to be included. In the example, some of the fields are shown (Name, Ref, Court, Keywords, etc). This part of the design is the arrangement of information within each record (that is, relating to one entry in the database). There is then an ordering of entries. Here, the cases are arranged in alphabetic order (there are three shown and, in the example, not all the information in each entry is visible).

Figure 6.3 Arrangement of database

NAME	REF	COURT	KEYWORDS	LEGIS	FACTS	HELD
ANDERSEN CONSULTING v CHP CONSULTING LTD	(unrep) 26 July 1991	Chancery Division	computer program - breach of confidence - inducing breach of contract - licence - employee -		The defendant was a firm providing software maintenance and which was made up of ex-employees of the plaintiff, a software company producing a software package called LEASEPAC. This was licensed to finance houses and banks and dealt	The injunctions were refused. The balance of convenience lay with the defendant. The harm alleged to be done to the plaintiff was minimal. An injunction would be unlikely to be granted at the full trial and the defendant would be
ANTON PILLER KG v MANUFACTURING PROCESSES LTD	[1976] 1 Ch 55	Court of Appeal	Anton Piller order - breach of confidence - copyright - enter premises and inspect and remove documents		The defendant was UK agent for the plaintiff which claimed that the defendant was disclosing confidential information about a new converter to other German Companies and also infringing the plaintiff's copyright. The plaintiff applied ex parte for	The appeal was allowed. The court had an inherent jurisdiction to grant an order requiring the defendant to "permit" the plaintiff's representatives to enter the defendant's premises and inspect and remove material which was
APPLE COMPUTER INC v COMPUTER EDGE PTY LTD	[1984] FSR 481	Federal Court of Australia	copyright - subsistence - computer program - object & source code - literary work - adaptation - hard-wired	s.10(1) Australian Copyright Act 1968	The defendant imported computers called WOMBATS into Australia. They were copies of the famous APPLE II personal computer, and silicon chips in the WOMBAT computers contained all the APPLE operating systems programs. The defendant could	At first instance (see [1984] FSR 246) it was held that copyright did not subsist in the programs as literary works. The judge placed great reliance on English copyright cases including EXXON CORPORATION v EXXON
ASHLEY v	(1994) 159	Divisional	goods -	s.14 Trade	Ashley supplied books on mail	Counsel for Ashley

Record 1 of 60

In many cases, the person who decides what type of information is to be included by designing the fields or internal structure of the database will not be the person who selects just what information is to be included in the contents. One person, the database designer, will create a 'blank database' and the user of the database may be the person who enters information, data or works into it. There may be some collaboration between the two, such as where the designer consults the user to determine the user's requirements. Where this is so, the normal rules for joint authorship apply as they do generally for literary works and the database will be a work of joint authorship only if the contribution of each is not distinct.

Example

Jenny is an estate agent and she wants a database which can contain details of freehold houses for sale including a photograph, plans, descriptions of rooms and their dimensions, council tax details, information about services, etc. Jenny asks a self-employed computer programmer, Rod, to create a suitable database system. Rod does this using database development software and tests it out using some test data, photographs and plans given to him by Jenny. Once the system has been thoroughly tested, Rod installs it on Jenny's computer and removes all the test data. Jenny then starts using the system and, in a few weeks, she has a database of over 100 properties.

It could be argued that the database is a collaborative work in which the contribution of each author is not distinct (after all, Jenny had some input into the design process) and the database as a database is a work of joint authorship and, unless there has been an assignment of one of the joint owner's copyright to the other, a work with joint owners, Jenny and Rod. Of course, any works contained within it such as photographs and plans will have their own copyright. However, as Rod took no part in deciding which properties the details of which were to be entered into the database, it would seem strange if he could be deemed to be the joint author in respect of the database as it now stands.

If Jenny employs an assistant, Ella, who is to be responsible for entering details of leasehold properties and rented accommodation into the database then, as far as the content is concerned Jenny and Ella are not joint authors as their contributions are distinct. Jenny enters details of freehold houses, Ella enters details of leasehold and rented properties and accommodation. They will each be the author of their respective parts of the database. The problem is, has Ella been responsible for any arrangement (apart from simply entering the details in a particular order)? And, in the case of Rod, has he been responsible for any selection of the contents? As both are required for originality, this could throw doubts on subsistence of copyright where two or more people are involved in the creation of a database.

To be protected by copyright, databases are required to be intellectual creations in respect of the selection and arrangement of their contents. This derives from the Berne Copyright Convention, Article 2(5) of which states that:

'Collections of literary or artistic works such as encyclopaedias and anthologies which, by reason of the selection and arrangement of their contents, constitute intellectual creations shall be protected as such, without prejudice to the copyright in each of the works forming part of such collection'.

No such limitation (that is, 'intellectual creation') is placed on literary and artistic works generally, presumably as all such works could be considered to be intellectual creations *per se*. It should be noted that the definition of 'literary and artistic works' in the Convention is very wide and includes, for example, dramatic works and musical works as well as a great many other forms of works.

The use of the above test in copyright legislation is new to the United Kingdom. (A similar requirement for originality of computer programs in the Directive on the legal protection of computer programs was not inserted into the Copyright, Designs and Patents Act 1988 by the implementing regulations.) It is therefore necessary to give the meaning of the phrase 'author's own intellectual creation' some thought. Of course, the first two words simply indicate that the database is the result of the author's own work – it has originated from the author in the normal copyright sense as used traditionally in the United Kingdom. The phrase as a whole could be said to require a conscious act of creation, that the author has used his or her mind to make the decisions relating to selecting and arranging the contents of the database. Put that way, the result does not have to be unique or particularly innovative in any way, it is simply the application of the human mind to a particular problem (designing a database) which results in the creation of the database. If that view is taken, then the standard does not appear to be much different to the test for originality for other literary works being that the work originated from the author and was the result of at least some skill and judgment.

An alternative view is that the test sets a higher standard and requires the exercise of intellect going beyond a mere exercise of mental faculty and the result must go beyond the mundane or commonplace. One factor in favour of this view is that, if a low standard were used in accordance with that traditionally applied in the United Kingdom, there would be little point in introducing the new database right as very few databases would fail to attract copyright protection. The author of this book takes the *via media* and suggests that the answer lies between these extremes. In other words, to be protected by copyright, a database must be the result of some basic ingenuity. Although a test of novelty has no place in copyright law, it may be that this is determined objectively along similar lines to the design right, that is, that in addition to originality in the traditional sense that the work originated from the author, the resulting database must not be commonplace in terms of the selection and arrangement of its contents. Thus, a simple database containing names, addresses and telephone numbers of customers would fail to attract copyright protection. On the other hand, a database such as that described in the example earlier (a database of properties used by estate agents) would be a work of copyright. The essential question could become whether, because of the types and nature of databases already in use and widely known, the selection and arrangement of the contents of the database under consideration is obvious and required no feat of intellect going beyond the mundane.

Requiring an intellectual creation seems to rule out the possibility of a computer-generated database, that is, one made in circumstances such that there is no human author unless the intellect of the person who devised the programs to create the database is taken into account. Computer-generated works are discussed in more detail in Chapter 9.

The normal rules on qualification for copyright in section 153 and following sections apply, that is qualification by virtue of the author or country of first publication. The extension to other countries of this form of copyright will apply subject to any orders made under section 160 denying such copyright to authors of other countries if those countries do not provide equivalent protection to British copyright databases.

Rights, infringement and exceptions

Many of the provisions in the Act which apply to literary works generally also apply in respect of database copyright. Thus the first owner of the copyright is the author unless made in circumstances where the author is an employee creating the database in the course of employment. The special rules that apply in respect of Crown copyright, parliamentary copyright and copyright belonging to certain international organisations such as the United Nations also apply. What has been said about ownership in Chapter 1 applies equally here.

The rights of the owner are those as for literary works generally and this is consistent with the Directive (although the Directive uses slightly different terminology). However, the meaning of adaptation in section 21 is modified and specific mention of databases is made. For a database, adaptation means an arrangement or altered version of the database or a translation of it. A database may undergo an arrangement where the ordering of its contents is changed or where another database is created by taking a sub-set of the database (for example, by omitting one or more of the fields). A translation could be where a database of English poems is translated into Spanish or, possibly, where a database created using one form of database development software is converted so as to be used with another form of database software. All of these will result in an altered version as will the addition or deletion of particular entries or sets of information.

As far as the permitted acts are concerned, these apply as they do in relation to literary works generally with two exceptions. First, section 29 is modified and fair dealing with a database for research or private study is limited to non-commercial research and an indication of the source of the database must be given. Second, a new section 50D is inserted into the Copyright, Designs and Patents Act 1988 which is basically a non-derogation from grant provision. It allows a person having the right to use a database or any part of it to do, in exercising that right, anything necessary for the purposes of access to and use of the contents of the database or that part of the database. This is backed by section 296B which prevents the exclusion or limitation of this right by means of terms or conditions in any agreement under which the person has the right to use the database.

Database structure and copyright

The issue of software compatibility is not restricted to the computer program and its user interface. It should also apply to the format and structure of files generated by, or used by the program, for example, a database or a file containing the formulae, calculations, text, numbers and format for a spreadsheet. It would seem reasonable to suggest that the same arguments for protecting the structure of databases and data files should apply as they apply to the structure of a computer program, as discussed in Chapter 3. In other words, structure should be deemed to be a form of expression independent of the information contained in a database. Indeed, recital 15 to the Directive on the legal protection of databases expressly states that copyright protection of databases should extend to the structure of the database.

A considerable amount of skill and effort may be expended on the design of the structure of a database. For example, the designer will have to determine what type of information will be stored in the database, in what form it should be stored, and how the database will interact with the computer program. The first part of the database may be reserved for information dealing with the interaction between the file, the program and the hardware, as well as containing details of the structure, such as field sizes, field names, etc. More than one database may be involved, for example, in the case of a relational database. Figure 6.4 shows how two example databases for keeping records of customers and transactions concerning them might be structured.

Figure 6.4 Structure of a relational database

Basic Information	Field information			
	Format			
	Printer set-up			
	Ref. to related files			
FILE No.1	ID	Name	Address	Status
	03207	J Smith	3 New Street	A3
	03815	F Bloggs	21 Old Road	B1

FILE No. 2	ID	Date	Transaction
	03815	08/02/95	+ 135.75
	03815	09/02/95	- 85.41
	03207	09/02/95	+ 14.00

Compatibility of database structure is obviously an important point to be considered by a person developing a new item of software. If the database structure of a competitor is selected, it means that previous customers of that competitor might be prepared to change to the new software because of the compatibility of databases generated by the two software packages.

Example

Satinsoft Inc intends to write a system for dealing with customer accounts. The leading package is Cashflow by Brittle Software. Satinsoft wants to capture a large part of Brittle Software's market share and it becomes clear to Satinsoft that its new system must be compatible to the extent that the existing databases built up by users with the Cashflow software must be able to be directly used with the new software. To achieve this, Satinsoft obtains a copy of Cashflow, uses it and examines the structure of the databases it creates and uses. When Satinsoft's software is available it attracts a lot of Brittle's customers because it has more features and can produce a greater variety of reports. Brittle is upset when it finds out that the Cashflow database can be used directly with the new software. Brittle sues for infringement of the copyright (a) subsisting in the Cashflow program, and (b) subsisting in the structure and arrangement of the database.

If Satinsoft has not copied the Cashflow program or its command system or its screen displays (including the structure and sequence of those elements) or other 'non-literal' elements, then the copyright in the program will not have been infringed. However, it is possible that the structure of the database is protected by copyright as a form of expression and there may be an infringement of this. In the United Kingdom judicial acceptance of copyright in database and file structures has been mixed. In *Total Information Processing Systems v Daman* [1992] FSR 171, Judge Paul Baker said that the data division in a COBOL program (this defines the file structure and nature of variables in the file and used by the program) was not a substantial part of a program. However, in *Ibcos Computers Ltd v Barclays Mercantile Highland Finance Ltd* [1994] FSR 275, Mr Justice Jacob said (at 303):

> '. . . there may well be a considerable degree of skill involved in setting up the data division of a program . . . and its construction may well involve enough skill, labour and, I add, judgment, for it to be considered a substantial part of the program as a whole.'

Certainly, to accept that the structure of a database or data file can be protected by copyright is a logical extension of the *Computer Associates* case, discussed in Chapter 3. Often, the design of the database structure is a central and fundamental step in the development of a software package. The view of Mr Justice Jacob is the better one and is the view most likely to be followed in subsequent cases, especially as the Directive confirms that protection of a database extends to its structure. The content of the database, being created by the individual users, could be protected by copyright independently of the program and the database including its structure. To give some idea of the skill involved in the design of a database structure, an example of a data division in a COBOL program is shown in Figure 6.5. It should be noted that considerable thought will have been given to the determination of the structure before the data division can be written.

Figure 6.5 Data division of COBOL program

```
010   FD    PRINTER LABELS ARE OMITTED.
020                 DATA RECORDS ARE PRINTLINE DXCRP.
030   01    PRINTLINE.
040         02    FILLER      PICTURE    IS    X(4).
050         "     PL1         "          "     X(12).
060         "     PL2         "          "     X(8).
070         "     PL3         "          "     X(18).
080               03    PL4   "          "     X(4).
090   01    DXCRP
100         02    FILLER      PICTURE    IS    X(8).
110         "     R1          "          "     9(4).
120         "     FILLER      "          "     X(5).
130         "     R2          "          "     9(4).
140         "     FILLER      "          "     X(5).
150         "     R3          "          "     9(4).
160         "     FILLER      "          "     X(5).
170
180   FD    TEMPRINT LABELS ARE OMITTED.
190                 DATA RECORDS ARE INP.
200   01    INPUT.
210         02    HOURSIN     PICTURE    IS    9(4).
220               RATEIN      "          "     9(6).
230               STATIN      "          "     9(2).
240               OTIMIN      "          "     9(8).
250
260   FD    TEMPRINT LABELS ARE OMITTED.
270                 DATA RECORDS ARE OUP.
280   01    OUP.
290         02    HOURSOUT    PICTURE    IS    9(4).
300               STATOUT     "          "     9(2).
310               OTIMOUT     "          "     9(8).
320
330   WORKING STORAGE SECTION.
340   01    COUNTER     PICTURE    IS    99.
350   01    DATIN       "          "     9(8).
360   01    NEWBAL      "          "     9(8).
370   01    OLBAL       "          "     9(8).
```

Moral rights in databases

Moral rights include the right to be identified as author (identification), the right to object to a derogatory treatment (integrity) and the right not to have a work falsely attributed and apply, *inter alia,* to literary works with some exceptions. For example, the moral rights of identification and integrity do not apply in the case of computer programs. The Directive confirms that moral rights belong to the creator of a database and should be exercised in accordance with national law and the Berne Copyright Convention. Thus, the author of a copyright database will enjoy moral rights in accordance with sections 77 to 89 of the Copyright, Designs and Patents Act 1988. As applies in the case of other works, the identification right must be asserted and the rights may be waived. Furthermore, the identification right and the integrity right are subject to a number of exceptions, for example, the right to be identified as author does not apply to anything done by or with the authority of the copyright owner where the work was created in circumstances such that the author's employer was the first owner of the copyright.

Moral rights do not subsist in relation to non-copyright databases which are subject only to the database right. Of course, moral rights may subsist in relation to individual works contained within a database, whether that database is protected by copyright, the database right, both or neither.

Database right

The database right is a new right which is intended to afford protection to databases which, although not original in the sense required for copyright purposes, are deserving of protection because they represent a substantial investment and involve a financial or commercial risk in their making. Although not a true copyright, this right conforms to the traditional English economic approach to copyright in that granting protection rewards the investment and risk in creating new forms of expression, thereby encouraging and accelerating the dissemination of ideas and information. Though lacking some of the attributes of a true copyright, it can reasonably be described as a quasi-copyright.

The database right, described in the Directive as a right *sui generis* (unique), is intended, primarily, to give protection to databases (as databases) which fail to measure up to the test of the author's own intellectual creation for copyright subsistence. Nevertheless, the right will apply to many copyright databases and the dual form of protection (multiple protection if the individual works within the database are works of copyright in their own right), may prove to be very useful as there are some differences in the scope of the rights, infringement and the exceptions to infringement. The owner of the rights in a database may find that he succeeds in litigation on the basis of one right if not the other.

Nature of the database right

The first thing to consider is the existence and nature of the database right. Fundamentally, it is a property right which subsists in a database if there has been a substantial investment in obtaining, verifying or presenting the contents of the database; regulation 13(1). In this context, 'substantial' means substantial in terms of quantity or quality or a combination of both and 'investment' means any investment whether of financial, human or technical resources.

Thus, a database which is the result of a significant financial investment should fall within these requirements even though it is not particularly innovative or difficult to compile. For example, a database of customer preferences derived from an extensive mailing of questionnaires could be protected by the database right. This will involve a substantial investment of financial, and possibly human, resources in obtaining the contents of the database. Another example is where someone has combined several databases from different sources (so as to create a data warehouse) and has spent considerable time in verifying the accuracy of the contents of the database. In this case, the investment is in verifying the contents. In another example, a person may use sophisticated computer software to generate attractive forms and reports displaying the contents of the database. Here, there has been a substantial investment in technical and human resources in presenting the contents.

It matters not if the contents of the database are themselves works of copyright or whether the database also qualifies for copyright protection. The database right does not prejudice such other copyrights which may still be enforced by their respective owners. Where dual protection is available for a database, it is possible that the owner of the copyright and the owner of the database right are different persons, for example, if their rights have been assigned separately. Similarly, if the database contains works of copyright. The person commercially exploiting or using the database will need to ensure that he or she has all the requisite assignments of rights or licences.

What the database right gives to its owner is a right in action in respect of anyone who, without the owner's consent, extracts or re-utilises all or a substantial part of the database. The meaning of 'extraction' and 're-utilisation' are obviously important and they are fairly technical. They are defined in regulation 12 as follows.

> '"Extraction", in relation to any contents of a database, means the permanent or temporary transfer of those contents to another medium by any means or in any form; and
> "re-utilisation", in relation to any contents of a database, means making those contents available to the public by any means.'

It may seem strange that the rights afforded by the database right do not mirror those for copyright but this reflects that the primary purpose of this right is to protect investment. The definition of 'extraction' is strange. It talks of the *transfer* of the contents which suggests that the contents are physically moved to another medium rather than simply copied to another medium. However, the act of extraction, in view of the purpose of the database right and taking into account the recitals to the Directive, must cover transfer by way of making a copy in another medium. Recital 38 points out the risk to the database maker of someone copying and rearranging the contents electronically without consent to produce a database having identical content but which does not infringe copyright. Hence, the need for the database right but clearly this envisages that a copy has been made. Recital 39 talks of the danger of misappropriation of the results of financial and professional investment in making the database and recital 42 indicates that the conduct to be targeted is the making of parasitic competing products and also the carrying out of acts which cause significant detriment to the investment. Taking these points into consideration, it is clear that extraction covers copying in all its forms, whether permanent or temporary. A transient copy made in a computer memory should also be within the meaning of extraction.

Re-utilisation will occur where, for example, a person without the consent of the owner of the database makes copies on CD-ROM for sale to the public or makes a copy of it available on the Internet.

The database right is infringed by any person who, without the consent of the owner, extracts or re-utilises all or a substantial part of the contents of the database; regulation 16. However, in some circumstances, a series of insubstantial extractions or re-utilisations may infringe if repeated and systematic. The Directive indicates that this will be so where it 'conflicts with a normal exploitation of the database' or where it 'unreasonably prejudices the legitimate interests of the maker [that is, owner] of the database'; Article 7(5). The regulations give no further clue simply than to say that the repeated and systematic extraction or re-utilisation of insubstantial parts may amount to the extraction or re-utilisation of a substantial part of the contents of the database. Not a very convincing test especially, as the word 'substantial' is defined as meaning substantial in terms of quantity or quality or both.

Example

Fiscal Software Ltd owns a database of all the world's currency exchange rates which it updates continually. Gerald subscribes under terms that he is to access it for his own private purposes. Gerald has a number of clients in South Africa and Australia. Gerald builds a gateway from the database via his access link to his own Web site where he displays the current exchange rate against the British Pound for the South African Rand and the Australian Dollar for his clients to inspect. Everytime there is a change in those rates, the gateway software detects the change and copies the new rate onto the Web site. However, compared to the whole database, the amount of information extracted is tiny.

Even though the contents of the database extracted and re-utilised in this way is insubstantial in a qualitative and quantitative sense, they may be deemed to be substantial for the purposes of the database right. Gerald is extracting and re-utilising those contents in a repeated and systematic manner. Such use may harm the legitimate interests of Fiscal Software Ltd by possibly depriving Fiscal Software Ltd of the chance to grant direct access to Gerald's clients.

Maker and owner of the database right

A database must qualify for protection by the database right in a way similar to, though by no means identical to, qualification for copyright. Qualification is by virtue of the maker of the database and it is to the meaning of 'maker' that we will first turn.

Under regulation 13, the maker of a database is the first owner of it. Regulation 14 sets out rules for determining who the maker of the database is for the purposes of the database right. The maker is the person who takes or took the initiative in obtaining, verifying or presenting the contents of the database and assumes the risk of that investment. Again, investment relates to investment of financial, human or technical resources. If a database is made by an employee in the course of his or her employment, the employer is regarded as the maker of the database subject to any agreement to the contrary. The provision for employee makers is almost unnecessary as it would be rare for the employee to take the initiative in the making of the database or, indeed, assume any risk of investment. Even in terms of the investment of human resources, it is the employer who makes that investment and who takes the risk. A salaried employee takes no risk, unless his or her job or prospects depend on success.

A database may be made jointly by two or more persons. Unlike the case with copyright where the contributions of each author must not be distinct, there is no requirement for this for the database right. The makers will be joint makers if they collaborate in taking the initiative and assuming the risk of investment, whether or not their contributions, in the database as made, can or cannot be separated out. For example, it may be that three persons work together to create a database in circumstances such as one of them obtains and verifies the data, another works on presentation whilst a third person's main contribution is financing the making of the database.

Similar to the position with copyright, there are no provisions for ownership of commissioned works. In terms of copyright, a person commissioning the creation of a work of copyright by a self-employed person or by anyone else other than an employee would be wise to obtain an assignment of that copyright from the person creating it (or a licence if that would be satisfactory). For the database right, the definition of 'maker' almost suggests that a person commissioning another to create the database would still be the maker. If the other is paid on a hourly or weekly rate, it is the commissioner who could be said to take the risk. However, if the consultant is paid a lump sum for the work, he also bears some of the risk. In any case, because investment may also be of human and technical resources, it is more likely that both persons will be deemed to be joint makers of the database. Therefore, for the avoidance of doubt, it would be sensible to expressly provide for ownership.

Example

> Andrew decided to create and regularly update a database of second-hand car prices to be made available on-line to the public so that individuals can consult the database for a modest payment. He thought this would be very attractive and commercially viable. The prices would be obtained from a variety of sources and reflect 'forecourt' prices. Setting up the database and putting it on-line required a significant investment of capital and Andrew approached Betty with

an outline plan and cost-appraisal with a view to Betty financing the scheme. Betty studied the plan carefully and made some suggestions as to what should be included in the database, for example, photographs of cars to be obtained from manufacturers under licence. Andrew and Betty intend to set up a limited company, ElectroCars Ltd, to exploit the database with Andrew and Betty as co-directors. With Betty's approval, Andrew has agreed to pay Charlie to help him obtain the information to be included in the database and to pay Deborah to design the database and input the information after checking it. Both Charlie and Deborah are paid a fixed sum for this work. Deborah has bought the database development software herself. Andrew and Deborah jointly designed the Web site.

At first sight it would seem that Andrew, Betty, Charlie and Deborah are all joint makers of the database. However, as the maker is the person who takes the initiative *and* assumes the risk, it could be argued that Andrew and Betty are the only joint makers as it is only they that have done both. Charlie and Deborah may have assumed some risk but have they really taken the initiative? Deborah may have done so as the initiative applies to verifying and presenting the contents. If Betty did not make suggestions as to the information to be included, could she be said to have taken any initiative in obtaining, verifying or presenting the contents? In the end, it is difficult to say with any certainty just who the joint makers are. This demonstrates the unsatisfactory nature of the definition of 'maker'. Fortunately, the Directive gives some guidance and recital 41 states that the maker of the database is the person who takes the initiative and risk of investing but this excludes sub-contractors, in particular, from the definition of maker. Thus, if we consider Charlie and Deborah to be sub-contractors (a reasonable assumption), they will not be joint makers along with Andrew and Betty. It will be the latter two who are the joint makers, subject to any doubt about Betty's role if her contribution does not go beyond simply financing the scheme.

In any case, should any doubt, however slight, remain, Andrew and Betty should ask Charlie and Deborah for an assignment of any database rights and other rights in the database and its planned exploitation (Deborah will probably have a copyright in the pages of the Web site, possibly as joint author with Andrew). When ElectroCars commences trading, the database right and other rights (and benefits of licences) should be assigned to the company.

Apart from provisions relating to databases made by employees there are also provisions for 'Crown database right', where a database is made by her Majesty or by an officer or servant of the Crown in the course of his or her duties, and for 'parliamentary database right', where a database is made by or under the direction or control of either House of both Houses. In the latter case, the House of Commons and House of Lords shall be considered to be joint makers of the database.

The database right is not available to everyone, basically it is limited to persons and bodies in the European Economic Area (EEA). Regulation 18 sets out requirements for qualification for the right. To qualify, the maker, or if jointly made, at least one of the makers, was at the material time:

- an individual who was a national of an EEA state or habitually resident in the EEA,
- a body incorporated under the law of an EEA state and which, at that time, had its central administration or principal place of business within the EEA or had its registered office within the EEA and the body's operations are linked on an ongoing basis with the economy of an EEA state, or
- a partnership or other unincorporated body formed under the law of an EEA state, having its central administration or principal place of business within the EEA.

The 'material time' is the time when the database was made or, if it was made over a period of time, a substantial part of that period.

There is no provision in the Regulations for extending the database right to makers outside the EEA. However, Article 11(3) of the Directive includes a mechanism for extending the database right to databases made in third countries (outside the EEA) by the Council acting on a proposal by the Commission. This will occur where agreements are made with third countries which will offer reciprocal and equivalent protection to EEA databases.

Dealing with the database right is exactly the same as for copyright and sections 90 to 93 of the Copyright, Designs and Patents Act 1988 (assignment and licences, prospective ownership and exclusive licences) apply to the database right as they apply to copyright. Thus, an assignment of the database right must be in writing, signed by or on behalf of the person making the assignment. Similarly, exclusive licences must be in writing, signed by the owner of the database right. Presumably, the concept of beneficial ownership will also apply in appropriate circumstances to the database right in a similar fashion to how it applies to copyright.

Duration of database right

Given that the database right is perceived as a purely economic right which has been designed to protect databases of commercial value which fail to meet the more exacting requirements for copyright (notwithstanding that a database may be protected by both rights), it is not surprising that the duration for this right is somewhat less than for copyright. The basic term of protection is fifteen years from the end of the calendar year during which the making of the database was completed but, if during that period the database has been made available to the public, the right does not expire until fifteen years from the end of the calendar year during which it was made available to the public.

Of course, many databases are subject to change, whether a periodic updating and reissue or a continual process of change. This begs the question of whether a new database right can come into being in a pre-existing database and, if so, when that new right expires. The approach taken by the Directive and implemented by the Regulations is to qualify a modified database for a new period of protection when it has undergone a substantial change; regulation 16(3). This requires a substantial change resulting from an accumulation of successive additions, deletions or alterations which would result in the database being considered to be a substantial new investment. 'Investment' is interpreted, as before, in terms of financial, human or technical resources and relates to obtaining, verifying or presenting the contents of a database. The Directive makes it clear, in recital 55, that a substantial investment bringing a new term of protection may be the result of a substantial verification of the contents of the database.

The rules as to the database right apply to databases made before or after 1 January 1998 and because of the changes made by the regulations to the protection of databases, there are some transitional provisions in the Regulations. They are as follows:

- any agreement (for example, a licence agreement) made before 1 January 1998 is unaffected by the Regulations;
- anything done before 1 January 1998 or after that date in pursuance of an agreement made previously does not infringe the database right;
- where a database was created before 27 March 1996 (the date the Directive was published) and was a copyright work immediately before 1 January 1998, it shall continue to be protected by copyright for its full term; and
- where the making of a database was completed on or before 1 January 1983 and on 1 January 1998, the database right subsisted in the database, that right continues for 15 years beginning with 1 January 1998.

The workings of the rules on duration can be illustrated by the following examples.

Examples

Sampson Ltd, Hercules plc and Goliath Ltd are builders' merchants selling building materials. Sampson Ltd completed making a database of building material and their prices on 1 May 1992 for its own internal use. Hercules plc completed making its own database of building materials on 1 October 1998 with the intention of making it available to the public via its Web site. It was made so available as from 10 January 1999. Goliath Ltd completed making its equivalent database on 25 June 1999 and made it available to builders on CD-ROM from 10 October 1999. Updates are sent to subscribing builders every six months. Some time later, during 2003, Goliath Ltd released a new version on CD-ROM which contained many more entries than previously, reflecting the company's expansion into the supply of road building and other materials. Figure 6.6 indicates the duration of the database right in each of these examples. It is assumed that simple updating of the prices of materials, *per se*, is not such as to cause the databases to be considered to be substantial new investments.

Sampson Ltd's database was made after 1 January 1983 and would be protected by the database right on commencement of the right (1 January 1998) and will continue to enjoy the right until fifteen years from 1 January 1998; that is, until midnight 31 December 2012. As Sampson Ltd's database was created before 27 March 1996, if it enjoyed copyright protection then, it will continue to have copyright protection for the normal term; that is, until the expiry of 70 years from the end of the calendar year during which the author (or last surviving author if it was a work of joint authorship) died. Although impossible to say with any certainty, it seems likely that such a database would have attracted copyright protection when it was made even though it is unlikely to be viewed as a work of copyright if made on or after 1 January 1998 under the new regime.

Hercules plc's database was made available to the public on 10 January 1999 and the fifteen-year period expires on midnight 31 December 2014; that is, fifteen years from the end of 1999.

Goliath Ltd's database right in respect of the original database expires on midnight 31 December 2014 but because of new additions can be considered to be a substantial new investment and, as this database was first made available during 2003, the right in respect of this version of the database continues until midnight 31 December 2018. The database in its original form will still be protected by the database right until the end of 2014.

Figure 6.6 Duration of database right in examples

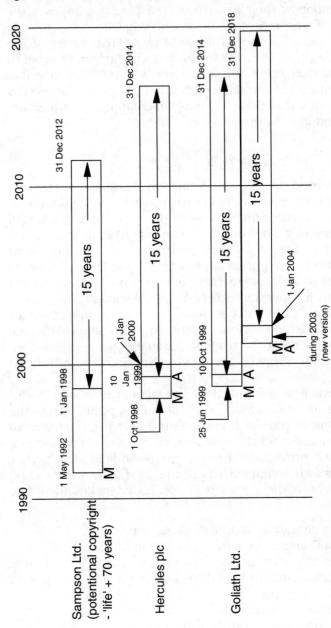

Makers of databases should keep records of the creation and modification of their databases. The Directive imposes the burden of proof regarding the date of completion of a database on the maker of the database, that is, the owner of the database right. The maker also has the burden of proof in showing that there is a new right where a database has undergone a substantial modification. There are, however, a number of useful presumptions which apply and which are described later in this chapter.

Exceptions to database right

The database right is fairly limited by defining it in terms of extraction or re-utilisation of the contents of the database. There are further limitations to the right by a number of exceptions to it. For example, the meaning of extraction or re-utilisation does not cover lending by an establishment accessible by the public (for example a public library) for no payment or for a payment which does not exceed what is necessary to cover the costs of the establishment. There must be no direct or indirect economic or commercial advantage to the establishment. However, this does not extend to making a copy of the database available for on the spot reference use, for which the normal rules on extraction and or re-utilisation apply.

There is also a fair dealing provision available for lawful users of databases made available to the public where the extraction of part of the contents is for the purposes of illustration for teaching or research for non-commercial purposes providing the source is indicated. Further exceptions are contained in Schedule 1 to the Regulations and mirror some of those available under copyright law and relate to:

- parliamentary and judicial proceedings,
- Royal Commissions and statutory inquiries,
- material open to public inspection or on public registers,
- material communicated to the Crown in the course of public business,
- material in certain public records, and
- acts done under statutory authority.

There is a further exception which is, in effect, a non-derogation from grant provision. Lawful users of databases made available to the public may extract or re-utilise insubstantial parts of the database (or part of a database if their lawful use is restricted to part of a database) for any purpose. Unlike equivalent provisions for copyright, this is not limited to acts consistent to the lawful use but is limited to insubstantial parts. This 'right' may not be taken away by any term or condition in an agreement governing the lawful use in question and any such term or condition shall be void to that extent.

There is also an equivalent to a permitted act under copyright law where it is reasonable to assume that the right no longer subsists in the database in question. The extraction or re-utilisation of a substantial part of a database does not infringe the database right if done at a time, or in pursuance of an arrangement made at a time, when it was not possible by reasonable inquiry to ascertain the identity of the maker (or any of the joint makers) of the database and it was reasonable in the circumstances to assume that the right had expired.

The doctrine of exhaustion of rights applies to products placed on the market anywhere in the Community by or with the consent of the owner of any rights subsisting in the product such as a copyright, patent or trade mark. The Directive makes it clear in recital 43 that this doctrine does not apply to the right to prohibit re-utilisation in respect of a database made available on-line. The owner's rights are not exhausted by doing this. Nor is the right exhausted as regards a material copy of the database or any part of it made by a person accessing it by on-line transmission. However, if copies have been sold within the European Economic Area (EEA), for example on CD-ROM, by or with the consent of the owner of the database right, any right of the owner to control resale within the EEA is exhausted to the extent that such resale shall not be taken to constitute extraction or re-utilisation of the contents of the database.

Presumptions

There are some useful presumptions for the database right similar to some of those that apply to copyright works. These presumptions show the importance of placing the name of the maker of a database and the year it was first published on the database or copies of it.

A name purporting to be that of the maker of the database placed on the database or copies thereof shall be presumed correct until the contrary is proved. It is also presumed that the database was not made in circumstances that an employer would have been considered to be the maker nor in circumstances where Crown or parliamentary database right would have applied. Furthermore, where copies of the database are published with a label of mark stating that a named person was the maker of the database and that it was first published in a specified year, that label or mark is admissible in evidence and presumed correct until the contrary is proved. In other words, a defendant sued for infringing the database right has the burden of proof and must adduce evidence of the falsity of that statement. We saw in Chapter 2 the benefit of the equivalent presumptions under copyright law in the case of *Microsoft Corpn v Electro-Wide Ltd* [1997] FSR 580.

Licensing schemes and licensing bodies

The Regulations include provisions for licensing schemes and licensing bodies in respect of the database right, similar to some of those that apply to copyright works. This could apply, for example, where a collecting society licences the use of particular databases where the owners have joined the scheme and distributes the income derived amongst those owners. The jurisdiction of the Copyright Tribunal is extended accordingly to cover references of proposed schemes, references of disputes and applications for the grant of a licence to the Tribunal.

Database right – summary

The database right can be seen as a response to concerns over the protection of commercially valuable databases which might fail to attract copyright protection. Whilst of much narrower scope, the right can be viewed as a quasi-copyright and a number of the provisions in the Copyright, Designs and Patents Act 1988 which apply to copyright works also apply to the database right, examples being the provisions on assignment and licensing. Other copyright provisions which are applied to the database right are those relating to rights and remedies of the owner and of the exclusive licensee. Thus, injunctions, damages or accounts and additional damages are available. Exclusive licensees may bring an action for infringement, normally by joining the owner of the right unless leave of the court is obtained to proceed alone. The provisions relating to orders for delivery up and seizure of infringing copies of copyright works do not, however, apply.

It is clear that the database right may be a useful adjunct to copyright and it may also be useful in its own right. There remain a number of problems however. The subsistence of the right and, especially, the question of whether changes to a database will result in a new right are as yet uncertain. This is partly because of the vagueness of the language used in the Directive and the Regulations and because new concepts of subsistence are used, such as investment and assumption of risk. The prudent database maker will be careful to keep detailed records of the creation and modification of databases so that he or she can demonstrate that it conforms to the requirements for subsistence. Placing the name of the maker and year of first publication on copies of the database are also sensible precautions which could prove very useful in an infringement action.

Although the right is limited to the particular acts of extraction and re-utilisation, the full panoply of remedies are available with the exception of delivery up and destruction, making this right potentially very important. It has already been claimed in one case, *Mars UK Ltd v Teknowledge Ltd* (1999) Times, 23 June, described in Chapter 5, though not challenged by the defendant. Nevertheless, the author suspects that most owners of databases will seek to rely on copyright and use the database right as a back-up form of attack only.

OTHER ASPECTS OF DATABASES

In many cases of computer databases, there will exist a hard copy (that is, a print-out) of the information contained therein.

If the hard copy was the first to come into existence (that is, the database was created using the hard copy) then anyone copying the computer database will infringe the copyright in the hard copy. On the other hand, if the database existed first, making a copy of the hard copy will infringe the copyright in the database. Copyright will subsist in the first to be created whether it be the computer database or the written or printed copy. Furthermore, under the new provisions, paper databases are protected also.

A great deal of data stored on computer is available remotely, through telecommunications systems or the Internet. There are a growing number of systems which contain information relating to companies, abstracts and indices, current events, sport and news or the full text of documents. These types of databases will normally be stored on a central computer or file server and many will be protected as works of copyright in their own right unless the information previously existed in another form, in which case copying the database, or a substantial part of it, will infringe the copyright in the pre-existing work or works. Even then, the copyright in the database and/or the database right will be infringed. The agreement under which the database was made available should provide for copyright and database right issues, such as whether a print-out may be made of part of it, and what use may be made of the database and its contents. That agreement probably also may provide for rights and obligations in excess of those resulting from copyright law.

In many cases, subscription computer databases will come within the meaning of a cable programme, which is any item included in a cable programme service, being, by section 7, a service consisting wholly or partly of sending visual images, sounds or other information by means of a telecommunications system (but not by wireless telegraphy). It does not matter whether the information is received simultaneously by two or more users, or at different times in response to requests by different users. Making a copy, for example by making a photograph of any image forming part of the cable programme, infringes copyright. The Copyright, Designs and Patents Act 1988 is not clear as to the extent of copying in relation to cable programmes but it would, presumably, extend to capturing a screen image generated by a cable programme as computer data to be stored in a computer in addition to making a photograph. (Incidentally, 'photograph' itself is widely defined by section 4(2) and is not by any means restricted to the normal meaning of a negative or a print taken from a negative.) The utility of protection as a cable programme for subscription databases is twofold. First, infringement of the copyright in a cable programme will occur even if the copyright in the material transmitted has expired. Second, infringement by copying depends on whether the part taken is substantial and this is measured against the whole of an original work of copyright but only against a single image in a visual cable programme service.

Example

> Nanette, without permission, used a full text retrieval system containing the full text of legal cases in her local University library. She retrieved the full text of two cases, one dating from 1873, the other from 1958. She stored the entire text of the 1873 case on her floppy disk and also stored one screen of information from the 1958 case which comprised a total of 75 screens.
>
> Nanette has infringed the copyright in the cable programme twice (for each retrieved document). As regards literary copyright, the copyright in the text of the 1873 case has expired and she has only taken 1.33 per cent of the second case which may not amount to a substantial part. However, Nanette has infringed the cable programme copyright in the second case because she took the whole or a substantial part of one image, even though there were 75 such images.

The above example shows the type of circumstances when cable programme copyright might prove useful. By accessing the system without permission, Nanette may also be guilty of the unauthorised access offence (computer hacking) under section 1 of the Computer Misuse Act 1990.

POSTSCRIPT

Earlier in this chapter an example was given of a computer database containing details of customers and the copyright position as regards the database prior to 1 January 1998. We now return to the example and what the situation is now if the database was created before 1 January 1998 or on or after that date.

Example

To remind ourselves, XYZ Supplies Ltd have a computer database containing names, addresses, telephone and fax numbers of customers. This database had been developed over a couple of years and it was usual for a new customer's details to be entered directly into the computer by XYZ's 'tele-sales' staff without a written record being made. It appeared that, before 1 January 1998, the database was protected by copyright as a compilation.

(a) Database created on or after 1 January 1998

There is some doubt as to whether such a database would be protected by copyright if it was created on or after 1 January 1998 as it is questionable that it is the 'author's own intellectual creation'. If it is, it will have protection until 70 years from the end of the calendar year during which the last surviving author dies (it may be a work of joint authorship). XYZ Supplies will be the first owner of the copyright if, as seems likely, it was created by its employees. Whatever the copyright position of the database as a database it is highly unlikely that the contents, taken individually, will be works of copyright.

If the database is not protected by copyright, which seems the better view, it should be protected by the database right, being the result of a substantial investment in accordance with the Regulations. It does not appear that the database will be made available to the public. If, for example, the making of the database was completed on 1 July 1999, the database right in that version will continue until the end of 2014. Of course, it is somewhat artificial to talk in terms of a date when the making of such a database is complete. From its original design and setting up, containing no records, it will grow over time, with new records being added from time to time. At one date, it may contain 50 records, at another date 1,000 records and later still, some 10,000 records. At what time can the making of the database be said to be completed? One approach might be to say when it is first used for its intended purposes, for example, for marketing or accounting purposes. If a date can be fixed (and it will be for the maker to claim and justify that date), eventually, as the database undergoes successive additions, deletions or alterations, a new database right will spring to life in the database in its new form. Again, it will be difficult to fix this date in relation to databases such as that owned by XYZ Supplies and, again, it will be for the owner to claim a date and be prepared to justify it in the event of litigation. It is important, therefore, that the owner keeps good records of the creation and development of the database, including keeping older copies for comparison if a new right is claimed.

(b) Database created on 1 January 1995

In this and the following examples, if copyright subsisted in the database as a compilation, it will continue to be protected by copyright for its full period. If the database would qualify for copyright protection on the basis of the new rules, from 1 January 1998, the database will be protected by copyright under the new provisions relating to databases. However, it appears that, if the database would fail to be protected by copyright under the new regime, it will continue to be protected by copyright from 1 January 1998 as a compilation. The regulations are not altogether clear on this point but the Directive states that if, at the date of publication of the Directive (27 March 1996) the database did not fulfil the new criteria for eligibility for copyright protection, the remaining term of protection under the previous national law shall not be curtailed.

As the database was created on or after 1 January 1983 and the database right appears to subsist on 1 January 1998, the database right will continue to subsist until the end of 2012, that is fifteen years from 1 January 1998; regulation 30.

(c) Database created on 1 January 1997

Assuming the database would fail to meet the criteria for protection under copyright under the new rules, as this database was created after the date of publication of the Directive (27 March 1996), there can be no copyright protection for it; regulation 29. However, the database right will subsist on the database for fifteen years from 1 January 1998. Of course, if the database is made available to the public before the end of that period, the fifteen years will run from the end of the calendar year during which it was first so made available. Furthermore, a new database right will arise if there are successive additions, deletions or alterations such that it is considered to a substantial new investment.

(d) Database created on 1 January 1982

This example is highly unlikely to happen in reality as the vast majority of databases undergo continual or periodic modification and it would be quite remarkable if a database created in 1982 was still in use in a similar form without having undergone considerable changes, giving birth to new rights. Nevertheless, this is another example of one of the transitional provisions.

If the database was protected by copyright, that will continue to run for its normal term, that is, 'life' plus 70 years. If it was not protected by copyright, having been made before 1 January 1983, by virtue of regulation 30, the database right does not subsist in the database. However, had it been made on or after 1 January 1983, it would have enjoyed the database right for fifteen years beginning with 1 January 1998.

As a final note, it must be remembered that database copyright and the database right apply to paper databases as well as electronic databases. Many of the imponderables concerning copyright in databases and the database right may not fall to be fully decided by the courts until 2013, the time the database right will expire in relation to databases in existence prior to 1 January 1998.

It could be argued that the new rules as to the protection of databases do nothing but confuse issues of protection and infringement. Perhaps a better approach would be simply to say that anyone who takes or uses a substantial part of a database, including an accumulation of insubstantial takings, without consent ought to be exposed to the danger of an infringement action. After all, trespass to land is trespass, however slight.

Chapter 7

Electronic publishing

INTRODUCTION

The phrase 'electronic publishing' is one lacking precise
definition. However, section 178 of the Copyright, Designs
and Patents Act 1988 defines 'electronic' as meaning
'actuated by electric, magnetic, electro-magnetic, electro-
chemical or electro-mechanical energy and "in electronic
form" means in a form usable only by electronic means'.
This wide definition certainly covers all forms of works
stored digitally on magnetic tape or disk or on an
integrated circuit. It also covers works made available via
a telecommunications system, whether a broadcast or by
cable. Further, it should apply to CD-ROM because lasers
operate in a particular bandwidth in the electro-magnetic
spectrum and the information stored on such devices,
whilst 'read' by a laser, is only made accessible by virtue
of electronic means.

The implications of using magnetic media such as
magnetic disks and tape have been discussed in previous
chapters. What is of particular concern in this chapter
is the position where software is published or made
available on CD-ROM, for example, as part of a
multimedia product, or on the Internet. Electronic mail
may also pose problems. Apart from looking at the legal
position in terms of copyright and related rights, the
practical difficulties are considered. First, CD-ROM is
discussed.

CD-ROM AND DVD

At the present time, compact disks based on laser technology are generally available in read only memory form. Given the massive storage capacity of this form of medium it is not surprising that there is substantial research into the development of a re-recordable form of optical disk. The fact that the information is stored by using laser beams to etch a pattern into the surface of the media makes the dream of having the read/write flexibility of magnetically stored data some way off. Magnetic mini-disk technology is developing in ever impressive ways but, eventually, a form of storing data in massive quantities whereby it can be modified and re-written an infinite number of times will be developed. DVDs (digital versatile disks) are a newer form of CD-ROM with greater storage capacities.

In spite of the apparent difficulty of the 'WORM' (write once/read many) attribute of CD-ROM, it has become a very versatile and popular medium by which copies of all manner of works are sold. Databases, dictionaries and encyclopaedic works are commonly made available on CD-ROM. Computer programs and applications software packages are frequently distributed on this media. Where the information changes over time, to overcome the difficulty of WORM technology, it is common to make the works available on a subscription basis with new CD-ROMs being delivered every few months or so.

Normal principles apply to works made available on CD-ROM. Thus, computer programs and databases are protected as literary works. A suite of computer programs will give rise to two levels of copyright. Each program will be subject to copyright and there will also be a compilation copyright reflecting the skill and judgment in selecting and arranging the individual programs. In the same way, a database compiled from individual works of copyright may also have a copyright as a database and/or be protected by the database right. Issues of subsistence of copyright and infringement are as for programs and other items of software stored in other ways, such as on magnetic disks.

The single most important aspect of CD-ROMs is that, in many cases, a large number of individual works are stored on them. In practice, this can make it very difficult for the publisher to ensure that he or she has all the permissions and licences required. In some cases, hundreds of licences must be obtained and administered. The issues and difficulties flowing from the use of CD-ROMs as a publishing medium include:

- some CD-ROM products (such as a multimedia encyclopaedia) contain works of varying ages owned by different copyright owners;
- varying forms of copyright works may be included, such as literary, dramatic, musical and artistic works (such as drawings and photographs), films and sound recordings;
- some of the older works included may be subject to revived or extended copyright; it may be difficult to trace the copyright owner in some cases in respect of such works;
- some of the works may be out of copyright but may not previously have been published, in which a publication right might arise;
- there may be moral rights in relation to many of the works included on the CD-ROM;
- the publisher may have existing licences or assignments of copyright for some of the works but these agreements were based on older forms of publishing and may not cover publication on CD-ROM;
- some of the works may be subject to rights other than copyright, for example, registered trade marks, passing off or rights in designs; and
- the dissemination of some of the works may give rise to liability for defamation or criminal offences such as under the Official Secrets Act 1989 or the law of blasphemy.

These issues are best addressed by means of an example.

Example

Early in 1997, Electro-Publishing plc decided to publish a multimedia product on the life and times of famous artists from the period 1850 to 1950. Apart from representations of paintings, the product would contain photographs of various scenes and persons (for example, photographs of the artists and their models and photographs of the places where the artists lived and worked), contemporary and newly written descriptions and critiques of the artists' work, biographies of the artists and, where available, film of the artists at work and relaxing. The CD-ROM would also contain excerpts from appropriate musical compositions. Figure 7.1 shows some of the works to be included in the product.

Before proceeding, Electro-Publishing plc's head of product development, Catherine, made a complete list of all the various works to be included in the product (existing and to be commissioned) and, for those in existence, noted whether copyright still subsisted and, if so, she recorded the name of the copyright owner. She made a note of any of the authors of the various works (or directors of films) who were still alive at 1 August 1989 and found that Florence (a biographer) died in 1990 and Kenneth, who directed one of the films, an extract of which is to be included, was still alive. The film was made in 1938 and first shown to the public in 1939.

Catherine discovered that some works, particularly some of the extracts of films, were subject to revived copyright. She then tried to fill any gaps such as the identity of those copyright owners not yet ascertained. She did this by contacting organisations such as the Society of Authors and the Design and Artists Copyright Society. For one work, a description of the formative years of the pre-Raphaelites, the then present copyright owner could not be found but the work was purported to be by a certain Harold Snipe who was known to have died in Fiji in 1930. He did not have any children and it was not known who inherited his estate.

In researching the project, Catherine was fortunate to discover some previously unpublished letters written by Edward, one of the artists featured, The letters were in the possession of Nancy, Edward's great-granddaughter. Edward died in 1876.

Vellum Publishing Ltd is an old established publishing company which, some 28 years earlier, published a small book covering some subject-matter that Electro-Publishing plc wished to include in its CD-ROM (for example, some sketches made by, and biographies of, artists).

Electro-Publishing plc wanted to include in its new work a contemporary description of the controversial religious views of a small group of artists who were active at the turn of the century. It was decided to commission Sir James Harvey-Heedless to write this.

Figure 7.1 Works included in multimedia product

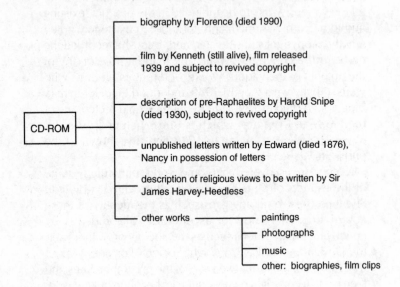

CD-ROM
- biography by Florence (died 1990)
- film by Kenneth (still alive), film released 1939 and subject to revived copyright
- description of pre-Raphaelites by Harold Snipe (died 1930), subject to revived copyright
- unpublished letters written by Edward (died 1876), Nancy in possession of letters
- description of religious views to be written by Sir James Harvey-Heedless
- other works
  - paintings
  - photographs
  - music
  - other: biographies, film clips

Discussion

It will be apparent that the work in classifying the copyright position of all the works to be included could have been quite immense. It was important to determine which works were still in copyright, which were subject to extended or revived copyright, the identity of the then current owner of the copyright, whether there were moral rights subsisting in the work and so on. In some cases, it may not have been possible to ascertain all of these things.

In the example, the following points can be made as regards copyright subsistence and moral rights.

- Where copyright subsisted (not being revived copyright) Catherine would simply have to approach the copyright owner for a licence.
- The work on the pre-Raphaelites, apparently by Harold Snipe, was subject to revived copyright as he died between 50 and 70 years ago. Section 104 of the Copyright, Designs and Patents Act 1988 contains a presumption to the effect that, unless the contrary be proved, Harold would have been presumed to be the author and to have written the work in circumstances such that he would be considered to be the first owner of the copyright. By regulation 23(4) of the Duration of Copyright and Rights in Performances Regulations 1995, if Catherine was unable, by reasonable inquiry, to ascertain the name and address of the person entitled to grant permission to authorise the acts envisaged, Electro-Publishing plc would not infringe copyright. In other cases of revived copyright (such as Kenneth's film), Electro-Publishing plc may have made use of the relevant work subject to paying a reasonable royalty after giving reasonable notice to the copyright owner (regulation 24). Of course, it was unlikely that Kenneth had the copyright in the film as, until 1 December 1996, the director of a film was not considered to be one of the authors of it and it was the person making the arrangements necessary for the creation of the film who was considered the author and, unless an employee, the first owner. In reality, it was likely that the film company which appointed Kenneth would have owned the copyright.
- As Florence was alive at the time of commencement of the 1988 Act, she would have had moral rights (to be identified and not to have her work subjected to a derogatory treatment). As she had died recently, the rights were exercisable by her estate. Catherine would have to check whether Florence asserted her right to be identified (if so, she must have been identified as author of her work). Although film directors now have moral rights in respect of their films, Kenneth does not have the right to be identified as the director nor the right to object to a derogatory treatment of the film because the film was made before commencement of the 1988 Act; paragraph 23 of

Schedule 1 to the Act. This limitation does not apply to literary, dramatic, musical or artistic works providing the author did not die before commencement. Therefore, it does not matter when Florence wrote the biography: assuming that she did not write the biography in the course of employment, she would have had moral rights in it providing she did not waive those rights. If acknowledging her as author was a problem, Electro-Publishing plc could have considered asking who had her moral rights (whoever Florence willed the right to or, failing specific mention in her will, the person who owned the copyright) to waive the moral rights (probably for a payment). However, the moral rights would not have been onerous except for the fact that it is not necessarily as easy to 'roll the credits' on a multimedia product as it is a traditional work such as a film. Any person using the CD-ROM would soon get bored at having to view a list of all the contributors to the product before using it.

Edward's letters were as yet unpublished and the copyright in them long since expired. However, as from 1 December 1996, a publication right could exist in works which are first published after the copyright has expired by virtue of regulation 16 of the Copyright and Related Rights Regulations 1996. This has the following implications in the context of the multimedia product:

- publication is defined as including making the work available to the public by means of an electronic retrieval system;
- the right arises in previously unpublished literary, dramatic, musical or artistic works or films;
- the right endures for 25 years from the end of the calendar year in which the work was first published;
- the person who 'owns' the right is the owner of the physical medium in which the work is embodied or on which it is recorded.

In the example, Edward's great granddaughter would have owned the right, assuming that she was the owner of the original letters. Electro-Publishing plc would have needed to draw up a licence agreement with her to allow the company to have included the letters in its new product. Of course, even if the publication right did not exist, Electro-Publishing plc would probably have to have paid Nancy simply to get access to the letters.

It may have been worthwhile for Catherine to contact Vellum Publishing Ltd to see if it had any current licences covering publication of some of the works and, if so, whether Vellum was interested in assigning the benefit of those licences to Electro-Publishing plc. However, great care must be taken to make sure that the rights granted covered the acts that Electro-Publishing plc proposed to do. The licences may have been couched in terms of publishing in paper form only. Hopefully, they were expressed in terms of publication 'in any form now known or hitherto discovered'. Even so, the licences must be such as they could have been assigned. It may have been that assignment was only possible subject to the consent of the licensor. The licences must also have been checked for their duration and any other limitations. Overall, it may have been better to approach the copyright owner direct for new licences, unless those granted to Vellum Publishing Ltd were exclusive licences (or copyright was assigned to Vellum).

There may have been a number of new works included in the CD-ROM product which were commissioned by Electro-Publishing plc. It would have been important that the formal agreements with the persons involved included terms dealing with assignment of copyright (or the grant of exclusive licences) in favour of Electro-Publishing plc. Moral rights must also have been addressed. It may have been that Electro-Publishing plc intended to obtain waivers of moral rights by the authors involved.

Other terms in the agreement might include warranties from the authors that they were entitled to grant the rights covered and suitable indemnities in case they did not and, especially in the case of Sir James Harvey-Heedless, an indemnity in case the work included defamatory or blasphemous material.

All the assignments and licences obtained by Electro-Publishing plc must have taken account of the intended use of the multimedia product. For example, it may have been made available over a network or the CD-ROMs may have been rented out or lent. The licences would have to mirror the permission granted by Electro-Publishing plc to the persons acquiring the product and all users of the product. For example, if it was intended that extracts should be printed out or downloaded, an appropriate term must have been included in the licence. The licences might have contained a term requiring Electro-Publishing plc to incorporate a suitable copyright notice into the software to be displayed when it was accessed.

Finally, in the case of assignments and non-terminable exclusive licences, where the consideration is £60,000 or over, stamp duty of one per cent will be payable.

ELECTRONIC MAIL

Electronic mail (e-mail) is used to transmit electronically information from one person to another or others. E-mail differs from subscription databases in that it is a medium for sending information as well as receiving it, and because it is not primarily intended to be a means of access to large databases. It is, as its name suggests, a method of sending and receiving messages, documents and other information. Quite often, especially if the message is brief, there may not be any written or printed record of it. In other cases, very large documents may be transmitted along with an e-mail message as attachments.

Example

Jenny from London sent to John in Manchester an e-mail message about her views for a forthcoming meeting, with a list of items which she thought should be included on the agenda. Jenny composed the message at her computer terminal and then transmitted it to John on Tuesday. John was out of the office until Friday when he read the message and printed it out.

The message was recorded for copyright purposes, at the latest, when John printed it out. It was probably recorded earlier in a permanent or semi-permanent form on the computer to which either Jenny's or John's terminal is attached. For copyright to subsist in the message, it must be original. That is, it must be Jenny's own independent work and she must have expended a minimum amount of skill or judgment in its creation. This will be so unless the message is extremely brief and commonplace in nature.

If someone, such as a computer hacker, intercepts the message before it is sent or during its transmission, it may not yet be in a sufficiently permanent form for copyright to subsist in it and the computer hacker, although he or she may commit offences such as the unauthorised access to a computer or the interception of a communication, there may be no copyright infringement at that stage. It depends on whether the information has been 'recorded' and it is likely that some form of permanence will be required. If the information is 'volatile' when captured by a third party, there can be no infringement at that stage. Note, however, that taking a copy which is itself volatile or transient can infringe the copyright in a permanent work by section 17(6) and even displaying a work on a television screen or visual display unit is reproducing the work in a material form.

If a person sends an e-mail message to another person and attaches a document in which copyright subsists to the message without the permission of the copyright owner, there could be two infringements of copyright. The sender will infringe copyright by making a copy of the document on his or her computer and the person receiving the document may make a copy on his or her computer disk and/or by printing the document. The sender could also be liable for authorising the receiving person's infringement of copyright and, if the sender has access to the document under a licence agreement, contractually liable for a breach of that agreement. If the person receiving the copy of the document did not know or had no reason to believe that copyright subsisted in the document (fairly unlikely as having reason to believe is tested objectively), damages may not be available against that person although other remedies such as an injunction or an account of profits may be granted to the copyright owner.

If a work transmitted by e-mail is sent to more than one person, whether simultaneously or not, it seems likely that this also falls within the meaning of a cable programme service. Because it is possible using e-mail to send messages and documents to large numbers of persons, copyright can be infringed many times, at a stroke, either by making copies of the work or by including it in a cable programme service. However, the Internet itself provides the greatest opportunity for copyright infringement on an impressive scale.

THE INTERNET

The global telecommunications network that forms the platform for the Internet brings the ability to disseminate information on an hitherto unprecedented scale. Whilst this feature can be seen as creating wonderful opportunities in many ways, it poses enormous problems in terms of intellectual property rights (and the laws of defamation and breach of confidence and the criminal law relating to pornography) which result from a number of factors including the possibility of making all types of works available to millions (or even billions) of people world-wide, the lack of harmonisation of relevant laws, the impossibility of effectively policing the use of the Internet together with jurisdictional issues.

Web pages as a cable programme service

Many persons and organisations now have 'Web pages' allowing them to make large quantities of material available on the Internet and commercial uses are growing very quickly. For example, it is possible to contact a florist in Miami, view selections of flower arrangements and place an order for delivery in New York, paying by credit card. This can be considerably cheaper than going through a local florist in the United Kingdom. Alternatively, a bunch of 'virtual flowers' can be transmitted to the recipient's computer.

If information placed on the Internet, say on a Web site, is deemed to be 'sent' to the persons 'calling' at the site and accessing the information, it would appear that operating the Web site is providing a cable programme service within section 7 of the Copyright, Designs and Patents Act 1988. Having been placed on a Web page, the information is passively waiting until callers gain access to it or retrieve it. The following Scots case indicates that there is at least a case for saying that a person running a Web site is operating a cable programme service. If this is so, it has a number of important implications.

Case

Shetland Times Ltd v Dr Jonathan Wills [1997] FSR 604, Court of Session, Outer House

> The pursuer (plaintiff or claimant) operated a Web site on the Internet on which it made available news items which appeared in printed editions of its newspapers. Once its Web site was well established, the pursuer hoped that it would attract advertisers wanting to place advertisements on the front page of the Web site. The defender (defendant) also had a Web site and included on its pages headlines taken verbatim from the pursuer's Web site. Persons accessing these headlines on the defender's Web site could, by clicking on them, access the pursuer's news items in such a way any advertising material on the pursuer's front page would not be seen. The pursuer's front page could, accordingly, be by-passed. The pursuer sued for infringement of copyright in the headlines.
>
> Lord Hamilton, in granting an interim interdict (Scots equivalent of an interlocutory or interim injunction), accepted that it was at least arguable that the pursuer was operating a cable programme service within section 7 of the Copyright, Designs and Patents Act 1988 and, by copying the headlines, the defender had infringed the copyright in them by including them in his cable programme service.
>
> Section 7(1) defines a cable programme service in terms of '. . . *sending* visual images, sounds or other information by means of a telecommunications system, otherwise than by wireless telegraphy . . .' (emphasis added). The definition goes on to give the purpose as being, *inter alia*, for reception

'. . . at two or more places (whether for simultaneous reception or at different times in response to requests by different users) . . .'. This is not inconsistent with the provision of information on the Internet.

The defender argued that, in any case, the exception in section 7(2)(a) applied, that is, where an essential feature of the service is that it is interactive. Lord Hamilton did not accept this contention as, although persons accessing the Web site could send messages and communicate with the pursuer via the Internet, that was not an essential feature of the service.

There are two important implications to this case. First, the inclusion of a work of copyright (other than a typographical arrangement but, importantly, including a cable programme), in a cable programme service is a restricted act under section 20. This is in addition to and without prejudice to the performance of any of the other restricted acts such as copying. A 'cable programme' is any item included in a cable programme service and the author of a cable programme is deemed to be the person providing the cable programme service in which the programme is included. Taken together, these provisions suggest that, with respect to infringing works made available on the Internet, the owner of the Web site and, possibly the Internet access provider, infringe copyright and the infringement takes place in the country from which the information is sent to the person calling at the site.

The second point is that infringing a cable programme by copying extends to making a photograph of the whole or any substantial part of any image forming part of the cable programme; section 17(4). This is very wide, given the wide definition of photograph and the fact that a cable programme is *any item* included in a cable programme service.

Another interesting aspect of this case is that the judge accepted that it was at least arguable that the headlines, some of them comprising at least eight words, could be literary works in which copyright subsisted as they were put together for the purpose of conveying information. This seems to run counter to the general view that small or trivial items of information such as names, slogans or titles of books and films are not protected by copyright under the *de minimis* rule discussed in Chapter 2. Of course, there is no reason why a headline could never attract copyright. Essentially it is a question of whether it is the result of the expenditure of sufficient skill and judgment so as to be a 'work'. Most headlines and other small works will fail that test but they may still be considered to be 'other information' and, hence, cable programmes and infringed as such by an unauthorised taking.

Position of service providers

Access to the Internet is generally obtained through a service provider. A number of these organisations provide access relatively inexpensively or even free and the service normally comes with electronic mail and bulletin board facilities. The position of the service provider is not altogether clear in the context of copyright infringement. For example, say a subscriber makes copyright material available through the Internet without the permission of the copyright owner. Is that person liable for any infringing copies made by persons downloading the material? Is the service provider responsible as a facilitator by authorising infringement?

A person placing copyright material on the Internet without the permission of the copyright owner infringes copyright by making a copy of the work. He or she may also be liable for authorising others to take copies as a person infringes copyright by authorising another to perform a restricted act. There is no need for there to be a message encouraging others to make copies and the concept of tacit authorisation should suffice. Persons accessing material through the Internet need to be careful and to check the copyright position. Even if the copyright owner has placed the material on the Internet himself or herself, this does not necessarily mean to say that a copy may be taken. Responsible copyright owners placing material on the Internet will include a copyright notice specifying the extent of the use that can be made of the work. Removing such notices could soon become a criminal offence as discussed at the end of this chapter.

Service providers are potentially at risk as it may be claimed that they are authorising infringement of copyright. Certainly, in the United States this is a possibility as demonstrated by the case of *Playboy Enterprises Inc v Frena* 839 F Supp 1522 (M D Fla 1993) in which infringing copies of photographs from Playboy magazine were placed on a bulletin board by customers of the on-line service provider. More recently, the Church of Scientology attempted to obtain injunctive relief against a service provider, one of whose subscribers had posted copyright materials belonging the Church on the Internet.

Case

Religious Technology Center v Netcom On-Line Communications Services Inc (unreported) 21 November 1995, District Court for the Northern District of California

> An ex-minister of the Church of Scientology who was disillusioned with the Church placed some of its documents on the Internet via a bulletin board operator which subscribed to Netcom. The Church claimed that the documents were works of copyright and also trade secrets. In an application for summary judgment, the judge refused to grant the injunction asked for. He said that the plaintiff had not proved direct or vicarious copyright infringement. However, he went on to say that allegations of contributory infringement were triable because Netcom had been informed by the Church that the infringement was occurring.

In the United Kingdom, under circumstances where the service provider knows that infringing material is being made available through its service, it could be liable for authorising infringement. The service provider is in a position to control the use of its service and can remove material it knows to infringe copyright. This is different to the position where the person alleged to have authorised infringement has no control at all.

Case

Amstrad Consumer Electronics plc v The British Phonograph Industry Ltd [1986] FSR 159

> Amstrad made dual cassette tape players which could be used to make copies of music cassettes. Obviously, there was a significant danger that many persons who bought these

machines would use them to make infringing copies of sound recordings. The advertising copy, with phrases such as 'You can even make a copy of your favourite cassettes', did not ease the music industry's concerns.

By section 16(2) of the Copyright, Designs and Patents Act 1988, copyright is infringed by a person who, without the licence of the copyright owner does, *or authorises another to do*, any of the acts restricted by the copyright. However, it was held that simply making and supplying machines which could be used to make infringing copies of music cassettes was not sufficient to make Amstrad or a retailer of the machines liable for infringement of copyright. Amstrad could not be said to be authorising infringement of copyright because it had no control over the way its machines were used once they had been sold.

The problem for Internet access providers is that they do have some control over how works are accessed or used. The same applies to libraries and other organisations which allow their customers, clients or employees access to the Internet and to CD-ROMs. Service providers' contracts with subscribers usually contain terms whereby the person using the service warrants that he or she will not infringe copyright. Other organisations which could be in a position to be sued for authorising infringement would do well to make sure that their contracts contain appropriate terms. Where there is no contract, the use of prominent notices would seem sensible.

Copyright is a territorial right. Although United Kingdom copyright is extended to nationals of other Berne Convention countries, the general rule is that, to infringe United Kingdom copyright, the infringing act must be done in the United Kingdom. One exception is in terms of authorising infringement of copyright.

Case

ABKCO Music & Records Inc v Music Collection International Ltd
[1995] RPC 657, CA

A Danish company granted a licence to an English company to make and issue to the public recordings of the plaintiff's sound recordings in the United Kingdom and Eire. It was held that, providing the act which infringes is done in the United Kingdom, it does not matter if the authorisation comes from elsewhere. Thus, a person from outside the United Kingdom can infringe copyright by authorising a person within jurisdiction to carry out an act which infringes. Both persons will infringe copyright.

An Internet service provider could be caught by a form of secondary infringement, though this depends on whether such a service is deemed to be a cable programme service or not. By virtue of section 24(2) of the Copyright, Designs and Patents Act 1988 it is an infringement of copyright to transmit a work, without the licence of the copyright owner, by a telecommunications system knowing or having reason to believe that infringing copies will be made by means of the reception of the transmission in the United Kingdom or elsewhere.

It does not matter where the reception takes place but the definition of 'infringing copy' provides some territorial limitation as, in relation to infringing copies made outside the United Kingdom, the copy must have been imported into the United Kingdom or it is proposed to so import the copy. Furthermore, had the copy been made in the United Kingdom that act would have to have been an infringement of copyright or a breach of an exclusive licence agreement relating to the work.

A limitation on this form of secondary infringement is that the transmission must be otherwise than by broadcasting or inclusion in a cable programme service. As indicated in the *Shetland Times* case, discussed earlier, it appears that operating a Web site falls within the definition of operating a cable programme service. That being so, this form of infringement does not apply to those parts of the service deemed to be cable programme services. However, and as indicated by the judge in the *Shetland Times* case, parts of the Web site may be severable. Some parts may fall to be considered as a cable programme service whilst others, for example, by being predominantly interactive such as an e-mail service or bulletin board or discussion group, may not be considered to be a cable programme service. For these latter parts, the secondary infringement in section 24(2) may still apply.

The latter part of the test of knowledge for the secondary infringement, 'having reason to believe', is an objective test based on whether a reasonable person, having knowledge of the facts known to the defendant, would have reason to believe that infringing copies will be made.

An Internet service provider may also be liable for joint infringement but this would have to be quite deliberate as joint infringement requires two or more persons to act in concert pursuant to a common design. Joint infringement is more likely to occur where a person allows and encourages another to use his computer equipment to perform infringing acts.

Example

> Dodgy Dealers Ltd is a company which imports and sells 'grey imports' (famous brand goods which are bought outside the European Community and which appear to have been sold there by or with the consent of the trade mark owners). As part of its marketing campaign, Dodgy Dealers decided to set up a Web site. Kevin, the managing director, told Mary, an employee of the company, to include substantial extracts from advertising literature and price lists published by the English and French manufacturers of goods such as perfumes, fashion clothing and sunglasses which Dodgy Dealers had just imported from the Ukraine. Kevin gave the material to Mary and asked her to scan this in and place it on Dodgy Dealer's Web site. Mary did this.
>
> Dodgy Dealers, Kevin and Mary are all joint infringers of copyright. It does not matter whether Kevin or Mary did not know whether what they did infringed copyright. Knowledge is not required for copyright infringement although it can affect the availability of damages, though not other remedies. Dodgy Dealers Ltd is a joint infringer as the acts were done in the course of its business.

Copyright offences on the Internet

United States copyright is not identical to that in the United Kingdom and one of the weaknesses of the criminal offences under United States copyright law was that the prosecution had to show that the infringement was done deliberately with a view to commercial gain.

Case

United States v LaMacchia 871 F Supp 535 (D Mass 1994)

A student from Massachusetts Institute of Technology operated a bulletin board and encouraged others to use it to exchange commercial software. It was reckoned that over $1 million of software was copied, including software packages such as WordPerfect. However, because the student had no motive to gain from his activities in a commercial sense, a prosecution under the United States Copyright Act was bound to fail. Therefore, he was prosecuted under the Computer Fraud and Abuse Act 1986 but the indictment was dismissed as the court would not allow a 'back-door' prosecution for something that was not a criminal act under copyright law.

Of course, the student in the case above could have been sued in the civil courts and, certainly, in the United Kingdom he would be liable for authorising infringement, a case where additional damages might be awarded, particularly if he had derived a large profit from the exercise.

Whether such an act in the United Kingdom would expose him to criminal prosecution depends on the interpretation of section 107 of the Copyright, Designs and Patents Act 1988. Most of the offences therein are concerned with commercial activity. However, one of the offences covers the act of distributing an article otherwise than in the course of business to such an extent as to affect prejudicially the owner of the copyright. It is questionable whether by placing the software on the Internet a person 'distributes' it. A further difficulty is the meaning of 'article'. Is a copy of software which has been placed on the Internet an article? There is some support for the view that it is. The Act does not contain a definition of 'article' (except in relation to an article in a journal) but section 22 states that the copyright in a work is infringed by a person who, without the licence of the copyright owner, imports into the United Kingdom, otherwise than for his private and domestic use, an article which is, and which he knows or has reason to believe is, an infringing copy of the work. If the work in question is an item of computer software which has been copied onto a magnetic disk which is being imported into the United Kingdom, it must be the computer software and not the disk which is the article. The reason being that the tangible item, the disk, is not itself an infringing copy of the work.

If a person is encouraged to make copies of software for sale, a criminal prosecution for incitement is possible. However, the person must be incited to commit a criminal offence and it is not sufficient if the encouragement is to perform an act which gives rise to civil liability only.

The above difficulties show that, despite their efforts to pass copyright legislation which is up to date and flexible in terms of technological development, the draftsmen behind the 1988 Act were still focused on older forms of works. It is a pity that the sort of activity described above was not specifically provided for and definitions of 'distribution' and 'article' included in the Act so as to cover electronic transmission of software. Even if we accept that placing software on the Internet without permission could fall within the criminal offences under copyright law, the prosecution would have one further difficulty. The person charged would have to be shown to have known or have had reason to believe that he or she had distributed an infringing copy. It seems strange that there is no problem under civil law (even if the person responsible did not know and had no reason to believe that he or she was carrying out an unauthorised act in relation to a work of copyright) yet the criminal offences are fraught with difficulties.

Other issues

Moral rights may also be adversely affected by use of the Internet. Even if a copyright owner has placed his work on the Internet and does not mind anyone freely taking copies, he or she might be very unhappy if a copy later turns up without any acknowledgement of authorship or, perhaps worse still, another name appears as the author of the work.

Someone might download a copy and place their own copyright notice on it and start selling copies commercially. Someone else might modify the work in such a way as to subject it to a derogatory treatment.

A number of other difficulties present themselves. For example if there is an infringement of copyright, which country's laws are applicable? There is no law of Cyberspace. As many organisations now allow employees access to the Internet, great care must be taken to educate employees not to download anything which could infringe copyright (or anything that could contain a virus) and not to place confidential documents on the Internet or otherwise compromise the organisation's intellectual property rights.

It has been argued by some commentators that copyright is no longer able to cope with such technology and that a new, *sui generis*, right is needed such as a transmission right. The United States' White Paper of 1996 on Intellectual Property and the National Information Infrastructure suggested that such a new right would be appropriate. There is certainly a need to make it clear that transmission of a copyright work infringes copyright if done without the express permission of the copyright owner. This should include multiple transmissions of different insubstantial parts of a work to an extent to prejudice the copyright owner's exploitation of his or her work. One possible way forward is for the growth of encryption coupled with licence agreements as the only means of access to works over networks. This has many implications. For instance, most of the permitted acts under copyright will no longer be relevant (it will not be possible to gain access to *any part* of the work without payment) and the Internet, which has been seen as a great liberator of information, promoting free speech, will become the restrictive domain of right owners.

COPYRIGHT IN THE INFORMATION SOCIETY

A Copyright Treaty was adopted by the World Intellectual Property Organisation (WIPO) on 20 December 1996, following a diplomatic conference. Another Treaty on Performance and

Phonograms was also adopted on that date. The Treaties focus on some of the issues relating to the use and dissemination of copyright materials on the Internet and other aspects of digitisation, the 'digital agenda'.

The main features of the Copyright Treaty of interest in the context of electronic publishing are set out below.

1. The Member States failed to agree to make it explicit in the Treaty that the reproduction right in the Berne Copyright Convention applies also to temporary reproduction. It was considered that existing international norms would suffice. In the United Kingdom, this should not be a problem in any case as copying includes copies that are transient and it has been held that displaying a work on a screen is reproducing the work in a material form.

2. Article 2 of the Treaty states that copyright extends to expression and not to ideas, procedures, *methods of operation* (note the influence of the United States here and the case of *Lotus v Borland* discussed in Chapter 3), or mathematical concepts as such.

3. Authors of literary and artistic works will have an exclusive right to authorise any communication to the public of their works by wire or wireless means, including the making available to the public of their works in such a way that members of the public may access them from a place and at a time individually chosen by them; Article 8. This covers, *inter alia*, the placing of material on the Internet or bulletin boards.

4. Protection will be afforded in relation to 'electronic rights management information'; Article 12. It will be an offence (in some cases, a civil matter only) to remove or alter such information without permission or to distribute copies of works knowing such information has been removed or altered. 'Rights management information' is that which identifies a work, its author, the owner of the relevant right and any information about the terms or conditions of use of the work whether attached to the work or appearing in connection with the communication of the work to the public. This is a very important measure and controls the dissemination of works where the copyright information

has been removed or modified. If not controlled by strong measures it would be too easy to place works on the Internet in such a way that persons accessing those works were not aware of the fact of copyright subsistence and the extent to which they could make use of those works.

Other provisions deal with the circumvention of technological measures adopted to restrict the use of works and confirming authors' rights to authorise making works available to the public and providing rental rights in relation to certain works embodied in phonograms.

Following the Treaties, there was a proposal for a European Parliament and Council Directive on the harmonisation of certain aspects of copyright and related rights in the Information Society (OJ C108, 7.4.98, p 6) which is intended to implement a significant number of the new international obligations flowing from the WIPO Treaties. In the explanatory memorandum to the proposal, it is estimated that electronic publishing in the 'off-line' market (DVD, CD and VHS) will, by the year 2000, account for between five and fifteen per cent of the publishing market and be worth between 8.8 and 12.4 billion ECU (very approximately around £5.5 to £8 billion) at that time. We have all seen how the 'on-line' market is increasing exponentially.

Particular rights provided for in the proposed Directive are:

- a reproduction right;
- a right of communication to the public (the doctrine of exhaustion of rights will not apply in respect of communication by wire or wireless means);
- a distribution right (the normal rules on exhaustion of rights applies here, thus, where a copy of a work is sold within the European Community by or with the consent of the rightholder, he or she may not exercise their right to prevent the subsequent resale of importation of that copy).

The right of reproduction and communication will be subject to a number of exceptions, for example, for private and non-commercial means or for the purpose of illustration for teaching or scientific research subject to an indication of the source.

There are provisions in respect of devices, etc, used for the purpose of circumventing copy-protection which are similar to those already in place in the United Kingdom. However, this will also apply to the database right which the present United Kingdom provisions do not. The Directive also includes provisions on electronic rights management information similar to those in the Copyright Treaty and, again, these provisions will apply to the database right.

The date mentioned for compliance with the Directive is 30 June 2000. At the time of writing, the Directive has not been fully adopted and this date now looks premature.

Chapter 8

Authorship and ownership of computer programs, databases and other computer works

INTRODUCTION

In the first two chapters, the distinction between the author and the owner of a work of copyright was drawn. This distinction is very important because the author (generally, the creator) will not always automatically enjoy the ownership of the copyright in the work he or she has created. The fact that the distinction is not appreciated by many people can lead to considerable difficulties later when it comes to exploiting the work. The purpose of this chapter is to examine ownership of copyright and the way it is exploited commercially, in addition to looking at the problems that may occur, how the law deals with them, and to suggest how they can best be avoided. Before this, the meanings and implications of authorship and ownership are discussed.

COPYRIGHT AUTHORS

The author of a literary, dramatic, musical or artistic work is the person who creates the work. Computer programs and databases (if copyright) are literary works. The author of a computer program is the programmer who wrote it. The author of a database is the person who inputs the intellectual creativity into its making. In practice, a computer program will be the result of the efforts of several people: systems analysts, designers and programmers. In terms of copyright, if the contribution of each is distinct, then each will be the author of the copyright subsisting in their own contributions but this will rarely be so, and usually a computer program which results from the efforts of several persons will be considered to be a work of joint authorship. This has implications for the duration of the copyright. The basic rule for the 'original' works of copyright (that is, literary, dramatic, musical and artistic works) is that copyright expires 70 years after the end of the calendar year during which the author dies. If the work is one of joint authorship, the 70 years is calculated from the end of the calendar year during which the last surviving author dies. The same rules apply to preparatory design material for computer programs.

A person may make a contribution to the creation of a work but fail to be considered to be a joint author. The contribution must be an act of authorship and the person must have a creative input in the work.

Case

Fylde Microsystems Ltd v Key Radio Systems Ltd [1998] FSR 449, Chancery Division

> The plaintiff developed telecommunications equipment and software for such equipment and the defendant made and sold mobile and portable telephones for use by security guards, for example. At one time, the plaintiff and defendant co-operated in the design of software for new radios to be sold by the defendant. The plaintiff developed PCBs (printed circuit boards) for the defendant's radios and these boards contained EPROMs (erasable programmable memory). Initially, the plaintiff supplied the defendant with PCBs on which were EPROMs loaded with the plaintiff's software. Eventually, as a more efficient way of working, the plaintiff supplied PCBs with blank EPROMs which were then loaded with the plaintiff's software by the defendant. Initially, the software was made available by the plaintiff on disk but it was later made available on-line. Although there was no formal contract, the relationship worked in both parties' interests. However, eventually, it appeared that the defendant was loading the plaintiff's software onto EPROMs

and PCBs obtained from a third party. The plaintiff sued for infringement of its copyright by the defendant making unlicensed copies. The defendant argued, *inter alia*, that it was a co-author of the software and, hence, a joint owner of the copyright, because of the work it had done during the development of the software such as setting the specification for the software, error fixing, reporting errors and bugs and making suggestions as to the cause of some of the faults which it detected.

It was held that the work done by the defendant, although requiring the expenditure of time, skill and effort was not such as to make it a joint author of the software. Mr Justice Laddie considered that the work of testing the software carried out by the defendant was analogous to that of a proof reader. Where faults and errors were reported, the defendant did not propose software solutions even though it may have suggested what was causing the fault. The contribution to the specification and other functional aspects was more to do with specifying what the software should do and settings for the parameters rather than how the software should do it. Although the defendant made valuable contributions to the software, his efforts did not amount to an act of authoring the software. The plaintiff was entirely responsible for the skill and labour involved as author of the software.

Drawing up a detailed functional specification for a new item of software does not, of itself, make the person doing so an author of the completed software. Such a specification tells the person writing the software what it is to do. However, if the specification goes further and includes operational aspects, for example, by specifying algorithms to be used in the software, then that may be sufficient to make the person drawing up the specification a joint author. It is a fine line between the programmer being a sole author and the programmer and person specifying the software being joint authors. If program structure, sequence and algorithms are precisely defined by the person specifying the software, it could be argued that his or her contribution as an author is even more than that of the programmer who has simply the drudgery of coding the detailed concepts. Indeed, given the right development software, the person writing such a specification could create the program himself by submitting the details to the development software which would then automatically create the relevant programs.

Copyright law accepts that there will be some works where the identity of the authors cannot be reasonably ascertained, in which case, the duration is limited to 70 years from the end of the calendar year in which it was made, or if made available to the public during that period, 70 years from the end of the calendar year during which the work was first made available to the public. Although a work may be one of unknown authorship, it will still have an owner. The identity of the author may be genuinely not known, or the author may wish to keep his or her identity secret.

If a literary, dramatic, musical or artistic work is computer-generated, that is, it is generated by a computer in circumstances such that there is no human author, for copyright purposes the author is the person by whom the arrangements necessary for the creation of the work are undertaken. (The duration of copyright in a computer-generated work is 50 years from the end of the calendar year during which the work was created.) As a computer program is a literary work, a computer-generated computer program is a theoretical possibility. (Computer-generated works are discussed in detail in Chapter 9.)

Computer software can include types of work other than literary or artistic works. Software may contain sound recordings and films, for example, in the case of a multimedia product. The author of a sound recording is the person by whom the arrangements necessary for the making of the sound recording are undertaken, now known as the 'producer'. The author of a film was the person making the arrangements necessary for its making, also now known as the "producer" but now (from 1 December 1996) the author of a film is the producer *and* the principal director; section 9(2)(ab) of the Copyright, Designs and Patents Act 1988 as amended by the Copyright and Related Rights Regulations 1996. The basic rule is that a film is now deemed to be a work of joint authorship unless the producer and director are one and the same.

In copyright law, a distinction can be made between moral rights and economic rights. Moral rights are the rights an author has over the work irrespective of the identity of the owner of the copyright and include the right to be identified as the author and the right to object to a derogatory treatment of the work. They apply, with exceptions, to authors of literary, dramatic, musical or artistic works and directors of films. The copyright owner has economic rights, the rights associated with the commercial exploitation of the work which are effected by giving the owner the exclusive right to do the acts restricted by the copyright, such as copying the work.

Moral rights do not apply in the case of computer programs or computer-generated works at all nor do they apply to employee authors in relation to things done by or with the authority of the copyright owner. However, they do apply in the case of works created with the aid of a computer, for example a document produced using a word processor or a copyright computer database. Therefore, self-employed persons using a programmed computer to produce literary works (other than computer programs), dramatic, musical or artistic works have these moral rights which they can enforce even if the works they created were commissioned and paid for, and even if the copyright in them now belongs to someone else. However, authors cannot complain if they consented, expressly or impliedly, to the infringement of the moral right in question, or if they had agreed to waive the moral right concerned. Furthermore, the right to be identified as author must be asserted, for example, by including an appropriate term in an assignment of copyright or licence agreement.

COPYRIGHT OWNERS

Because there are no formalities required for copyright to subsist in a work, ownership coincides with the creation of the work. The first owner of a work of copyright is the author of the work, except when the author is an employee who has created the work in the course of his or her employment, in which case the employer will be the first owner of the copyright subject to agreement to the contrary. There are other exceptions in the case of Crown copyright and parliamentary copyright and copyright belonging to certain international organisations such as the United Nations. Her Majesty the Queen is the first owner of the copyright in works produced by an officer or servant of the Crown in the course of his duties and of the copyright subsisting in Acts of Parliament and Measures of the General Synod of the Church of England. If a work is made by or under the direction or control of either or both Houses of Parliament, the first owner of the copyright is the appropriate House or Houses.

The fact that, normally, a self-employed author will be the first owner of the copyright in the work created is not widely recognised. Many persons think that the commissioner of a work will automatically own the copyright subsisting in it. They are mistaken. Unless the person creating the work can be considered to be an employee who has created the work in the course of his or her employment, the author will be the first owner of the copyright. Frequently, it will be obvious that the work has been made by an employee in the course of his employment, for example, an employed computer programmer who writes a computer program at the request of his employer during normal working hours. Difficulties can arise if the employee has created the work in his own time, whether or not using his employer's facilities or if the nature of the work is not that which the employee is normally paid for.

Example

Helen is a purchasing clerk working for Zeta Fittings Ltd, a firm specialising in manufacturing spare parts for motor cars. Helen is interested in computers and has learnt some basic programming. Partly during her own time and partly during slack periods at work, Helen has written a computer program to store and retrieve details of suppliers. Helen has installed the program on her computer at work.

Because Helen is not employed as a computer programmer, it would appear that she has not written the computer program in the course of her employment and, consequently, Helen will be the first owner of the copyright subsisting in the program.

Two questions are important in these situations: whether the author is an employee (merely describing someone as an employee is not conclusive), and whether the work was carried out in the course of employment. The contract of employment (or engagement) is an important source of assistance in answering both these questions. In determining whether the person is an employee, important questions are: who controls the work, whether the person is entitled to sick pay, whether a pension is provided, what is the method of payment (for example, weekly or monthly or on the basis of a lump sum for an agreed item of work), whether tax is deducted on PAYE and who bears financial liability for faulty work. If the person is engaged on a permanent basis and is paid an annual salary with tax deducted at source, this would lead to the obvious conclusion that the person is an employee. However, if the person is hired to perform a particular task (for example, to write a specific computer program) for an agreed lump sum with no provision for redundancy, this would almost certainly suggest that the person is not an employee.

To decide whether the work concerned falls within the course of the person's employment, any express terms (written or oral) contained in the contract of employment will be all important. The job description and duties indicated will help to determine whether the work concerned falls within the normal course of employment. Sometimes, it will be necessary to imply new job descriptions, such as when the employee's normal duties have changed due to natural developments and changes in the company and in respect of the employee's responsibilities. A basic test is to consider whether the employee's efforts in creating the work are part of that employee's normal duties (express or implied), or within any special duties imposed by the employer and accepted by the employee. If this is answered in the negative the employee will be the first owner of the copyright even if he or she has had the benefit of the employer's facilities or other assistance.

Case

Stephenson Jordan & Harrison Ltd v MacDonald [1952] RPC 10

> An employed accountant gave some lectures on the subject of accountancy which he later incorporated into a book. His

employer had given assistance by providing secretarial help.

It was held that, even though his employer had provided assistance, the copyright in the lectures belonged to the accountant. He was employed as an accountant to advise clients and not to deliver public lectures. However, part of the book was based on a report that the accountant had written for one of his employer's clients and the copyright in this part belonged to his employer.

A wise employer will make sure that employees' job descriptions accurately reflect the nature of the employment and are modified in line with changing duties. Occasionally, a keen employee might produce a work which will be of assistance in the workplace and which falls outside the scope of the job description. For example, an employee, whose normal duties do not involve work with computers, might create a computer program or spreadsheet template or database for use by the employee and colleagues at work. If the program or whatever is genuinely useful to the employer's business the question of ownership of the copyright should be dealt with immediately. A reasonable approach would be to reward the employee whilst obtaining a signed written assignment of the copyright to the employer.

If there is any doubt concerning the status of a person engaged to perform some work, that is, whether he or she is an employee, it is important to make provision prospectively for the ownership of the copyright in any works created by that person. There is a good deal of confusion about the ownership of commissioned works, the commissioner often believing, quite wrongly, that he or she will automatically own the copyright subsisting in the work created. In these situations, the person commissioning the work should insist that the contract contains provisions for the future assignment to him or her of the copyright and is signed by the person commissioned to create the work.

The form of words used should include the phrase 'with full title guarantee' to take advantage of the implied covenants in sections 2 to 5 of the Law of Property (Miscellaneous Provisions) Act 1994. In this context, there are implied covenants to the effect that:

- the assignor has the right to make the assignment and will do all that is reasonable to give the title to the assignee; and
- the copyright is free from all charges and incumbrances and all other rights exercisable by third parties.

Previously, the form of words used would include the phrase 'as beneficial owner' as in 'Karen Cooper, as beneficial owner, hereby assigns the copyright in . . .'.

Special care should be taken when hiring freelance workers through an agency because it is possible that the freelance worker is an employee of the agency and, as such, and in the absence of agreement to the contrary, the agency will be the first owner of the copyright subsisting in any works created by the freelance worker.

The courts have developed techniques to overcome some of the difficulties arising from misunderstandings concerning the first ownership of copyright, and another factor which may help is that there will usually also be an obligation of confidence, to a greater or lesser degree, owed by the creator of the work to the person for whom the work was created.

There are two ways that the courts can deal with ownership difficulties, one is by using the concept of beneficial ownership (where the copyright has two owners, an owner at law and an owner in equity), the second being the use of the implied licence. The two cases below illustrate each of these methods.

Case

Warner v Gestetner Ltd [1988] EIPR D-89

Warner was an artist who specialised in the drawing of cats and he agreed verbally to produce some drawings to be used by Gestetner in the promotion of a new product at a trade fair. After the fair, Gestetner continued to use the drawings for its promotional literature and Warner sued arguing that this went beyond their agreement and infringed his copyright in the drawings. As Warner was not an employee and had not assigned the copyright to Gestetner, he remained the owner of the copyright.

Mr Justice Whitford decided that a term could be implied into the original verbal agreement granting beneficial ownership of the copyright to Gestetner. Thus, the copyright had two owners, one at law and one in equity and Gestetner, as the beneficial owner, could continue to use the drawings in their literature. The concept of beneficial ownership was also used in the 'look and feel' case of *Richardson v Flanders*, discussed in Chapter 4.

Factors which might influence a court to take this approach are:

• the fee paid under the agreement (does it suggest transfer of ownership or merely a temporary licence);
• whether the parties came to the court with 'clean hands' (that is, how well have the parties behaved); and
• whether beneficial ownership is workable in the circumstances.

The use of beneficial ownership in copyright law has been criticised on the basis that it ignores the clear words of the Copyright, Designs and Patents Act 1988 which makes no provision for such a device. However, it is firmly established in other areas of property law and there is no logical reason why it should not apply to copyright which is, itself, a form of property. Beneficial ownership has been used in a number of copyright cases to good effect.

There are some weaknesses in having beneficial ownership only, especially as regards the availability of legal remedies against copyright infringers; the legal owner is far better placed in this respect. Another approach which has the same practical effect without some of the drawbacks of beneficial ownership is for the court to imply a term to the effect that the person for whom the work was created has an implied licence to continue to use the work as in the following case. (An alternative approach is to use the concept of non-derogation from grant.)

Case

Blair v Osborne & Tomkins [1971] 2 WLR 503

An architect was commissioned to draw building plans for the purpose of obtaining planning permission for a pair of houses. The copyright remained with the architect. The site for which the plans had been drawn was sold with the benefit of the planning permission, and the plans were transferred to the purchaser who employed his own surveyors who modified the plans for building regulations approval and put their name on the plans. Eventually, houses were built to the plans and the architect sued for infringement of his copyright in the plans.

It was held that the copyright in the plans had been infringed by the surveyors who had submitted the plans to the council in their own name but nominal damages only were awarded because no harm was suffered by the architect as a result of this. On the issue of the construction of the house by the purchaser of the land in accordance with the architect's plans, it was held that the purchaser had an implied licence to use the plans. The person who had originally commissioned the architect had such an implied licence which extended to the making of copies of the plans to be used in respect of that site only, and not for any other purpose, and this implied licence extended to any purchaser of the site.

Where a self-employed person or freelance worker has been engaged to write or modify a computer program or prepare documentation for a computer program or create a database and there has been no explicit agreement as to the ownership of the copyright, the courts are likely to imply a licence to allow the client to continue using or exploiting the program, documentation, or database to the extent which is compatible with the original agreement and the circumstances. A court of law will have little sympathy with a person who has been paid a reasonable fee to create a work for a client and then later, realising the he or she still owns the copyright, that person tries to demand additional payment, or tries to interfere with the use of the work which was reasonably within the contemplation of both parties when the agreement was made. Nevertheless, it is considerably more satisfactory to deal with ownership of copyright at the outset rather than to rely on litigation to resolve future disputes which may be unpredictable and, potentially, very expensive.

DATABASE MAKERS AND OWNERS OF DATABASE RIGHT

For databases subject to the database right, the maker of the database is the person who takes the initiative in obtaining, verifying or presenting the contents of the database and assumes the risk of investment in relation to such obtaining, verifying or presenting. This is subject to rules for employee makers, Crown and parliamentary database right. If two or more persons act together in collaboration in respect of such initiative and risk, then each will be a joint maker of that database though there is no requirement for the contributions to be indistinct as there is with copyright.

We have seen that the duration of the database right is not calculated by reference to the maker but is fifteen years from the end of the calendar year during which its making was complete or, if released to the public during that period, fifteen years from the end of the calendar year when it was so made available. There is no infringement of the database right if it is not possible by reasonable inquiry to ascertain the identity of the maker and it is reasonable to assume that the right has expired. Unlike the case with a copyright database, there are no provisions for computer-generated databases to be subject to a database right although, presumably such a database could still be deemed to have a maker being the person who made the arrangements for its making by virtue of his or her initiative and assumption of risk.

The owner of the database right is simply the maker of the database. Unlike the case with copyright, because of the definition of the maker of the database, there is less likely to be problems with ownership and the use of beneficial ownership or implied licences. Nevertheless, as the provisions relating to dealing with copyright works are also applied to the database right, there seems no reason why beneficial ownership or implied licences might not be used in appropriate cases.

EXPLOITATION OF COPYRIGHT AND DATABASE RIGHT

Copyright is a form of property and, as such, it can be dealt with commercially. The same applies to a database right which is declared to be a property right by the Copyright and Rights in Databases Regulations 1997. The ownership of copyright or database right can be transferred to another in whole or in part. This is known as an *assignment*. Alternatively, the owner may decide to retain his or her ownership and grant permission to others allowing them to do certain specified acts in relation to the work. This is known as *licensing*. Both these devices, the assignment and the licence, are extremely common. There are other means of dealing with these rights. For example, they can be used to raise capital by granting a mortgage in respect of the right. Ownership of copyright or the database right may also pass under a will. Both rights may also be used for investment purposes. For example, an investor might acquire ownership of the copyright in an old film in the hope that there will be a revival of interest in the film or in the characters portrayed in it. Similarly, the musical copyright of certain old rock and roll tunes might be an attractive, if speculative, investment.

Assignment and licensing will be described before looking at how these particular methods may be employed in order to exploit computer software or other works stored on a computer.

Assignment of copyright

Ownership of the copyright is transferred from the previous owner (the assignor) to the new owner (the assignee). By section 90 of the Copyright, Designs and Patents Act 1988, to be effective at law, the assignment must be in writing and signed by or on behalf of the assignor.

Although beneficial ownership can arise from the circumstances under which the creation of a work is commissioned, by section 53(1)(c) of the Law of Property Act 1925, an assignment of an equitable title to copyright must be in writing and be signed by or on behalf of the person transferring beneficial ownership. Thus, whether the title to the copyright is legal or equitable, to be effective an assignment must accord with the basic formality of being in writing or signed by or on behalf of the assignor. Failure to comply with this requirement can, at best, result in the grant of a licence to carry out the relevant acts.

The mechanism of assignment is relatively simple and is shown in Figure 8.1.

Figure 8.1 Assignment of copyright

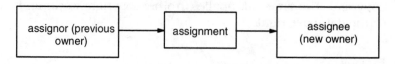

An assignment need not be in relation to the entire copyright or database right (or both). Because copyright comprises a set of rights according to the restricted acts, these can be dealt with separately (the same applies to a lesser extent to database right). For example, the owner of the copyright in a database may assign the copyright in so far as it relates to the electronic transmission rights to one person, whilst assigning the paper publication rights to another. The assignment can also be limited in terms of its geographical scope and the period of time for it can take effect. For example, the owner of the copyright in a computer program could assign the copyright in respect of Europe to one company and assign the copyright for the rest of the world to another company. Where the copyright is to be exploited by a group of companies operating throughout different regions of the world, this is a common thing to do. Normally, an assignment would be effective for the remainder of the duration of the copyright or database right but it is possible to limit it to a period of time, say ten years, after which the copyright or database right will revert back to the original owner.

Where a self-employed programmer is commissioned to write a new computer program, the original agreement should contain a term assigning the copyright in that program. Even though, at the time of the agreement, the program does not exist, section 91 of the Copyright, Designs and Patents Act 1988 contains the relevant provisions so that copyright in works to be created in the future can be assigned. When the work comes into existence, the copyright will automatically vest in the assignee. That person may also deal with that future copyright. The same rule applies to other copyright works and to the database right.

Example

Software Developments Ltd commissions Harvey, who is a programmer operating under the auspices of a limited company (Harvey & Co Ltd) of which he and his wife are co-directors. Harvey and his wife set up the company for tax purposes and Harvey is the only person actively engaged in writing programs on behalf of the company.

There is a formal agreement between Software Developments Ltd and Harvey & Co Ltd for the writing of the program (to be called X-Soft) which contains a term assigning the entire copyright in X-Soft to Software Developments Ltd. It is signed by Harvey and a director of Software Developments Ltd.

Whilst Harvey is still working on writing the program, Software Developments Ltd assigns the copyright to Truesoft Ltd which grants a licence in respect of X-Soft to James, an accountant.

When Harvey completes the X-Soft program, the copyright automatically vests in Software Developments Ltd and the assignment to Truesoft Ltd and licence to James take effect; see Figure 8.2.

If there had been no written assignment of the future copyright it would belong in the first instance to Harvey & Co Ltd as Harvey, albeit a director of the company, was an employee creating the program in the course of employment. Because of the circumstances, a court would be likely to decide that Software Developments Ltd was the beneficial owner of the copyright. This equitable title would have been transferred to Truesoft Ltd (because the formalities appear to have been complied with) and James's licence would be effective as against Truesoft Ltd. However, if a third party infringed the copyright, there would be little that Truesoft Ltd could do unless it joined Harvey & Co Ltd in the action. Of course, James would have contractual remedies against Truesoft Ltd, in accordance with the terms of the licence agreement.

Figure 8.2 Assignment of future copyright

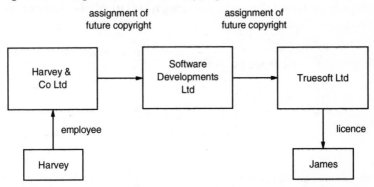

Assignment of copyright and, where it subsists, database right, in computer software is usual where a software house or individual programmer has been commissioned to write some new software for a client to the client's specification or requirements. This type of software is often referred to as 'bespoke' software; it is made specially for the client to meet his or her particular needs. A self-employed programmer who has written computer software may ask a software publisher to copy, market, distribute and sell (and, possibly, also maintain) the software. The software publisher will pay a royalty to the programmer and may require that the copyright in the software (and database right, if any) is assigned to the publisher. Alternatively, the publisher may seek an exclusive licence from the programmer who will retain the ownership of the rights. Licences are described next.

The licence

A licence is a permission granted by the copyright owner to another person, or persons, which allows that person, or persons, to do certain things in respect of the subject matter of the copyright or database right. The owner of the right, the *licensor*, grants a licence in favour of the *licensee*. Usually, licences are contractual, that is, they are based on a contractual agreement, binding both of the parties, and which is usually supported by consideration (the 'price' paid for the licence). However, consideration is not an express requirement of the Act. The mechanism of the licence is shown in Figure 8.3.

Figure 8.3   The basic licence

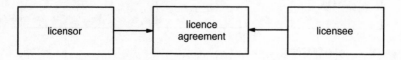

The licence agreement defines the
contractual relationship and what
the parties may or may not do
in relation to the software

Example

> Hugh owns the copyright in a computer program which is used to assist in stocktaking in supermarkets. Hugh grants a licence to Supermart Ltd allowing the use of the program on up to five personal computers. The licence allows the making of up to five copies of the program with the original copy supplied by Hugh to be retained as a back-up copy. Supermart Ltd is not allowed to transfer the program to anyone else. Supermart Ltd has agreed to pay Hugh £5,700 for the program. Hugh did not assign the copyright to Supermart Ltd as he intends to license the program to other supermarkets.

The licence in the above example is a contractual licence. Both parties have supplied consideration. Hugh has granted Supermart the right to perform some of the acts restricted by copyright (for example, copying the program) and Supermart have agreed to pay £5,700. This is known as the licence fee. If the licence is informal and unsupported by consideration it is described as a bare licence. For example, Hugh might have told Supermart that he does not mind if they use his program for a while, perhaps to assist in testing it. A bare licence does not bind the parties and either party can unilaterally release themselves from it unless it is an exclusive licence and the formalities are complied with (that is, that the licence is in writing and signed by or on behalf of the copyright owner).

A licence may be exclusive or non-exclusive. In the above example, Hugh has granted a non-exclusive licence. He is free to grant licences to other supermarkets. If it was important to Supermart Ltd that it was the only company allowed to use the program, it could have asked for an exclusive licence. This would mean that Hugh would not grant other licences in respect of the program. In fact, Hugh himself would not be allowed to use the software himself even if he had a supermarket of his own. Like an assignment, an exclusive licence must be in writing and signed by, or on behalf of, the copyright owner (section 92 of the Copyright, Designs and Patents Act 1988). An exclusive licence is binding on the parties even if one of them has not supplied consideration, although this would be extremely rare. As with assignments, licences can be restricted to part of the rights associated with the copyright or database right and be limited geographically and in duration.

Ready-made or 'off-the-shelf' software is licensed using non-exclusive licences. Off-the-shelf software includes the popular word processing, spreadsheet, database and other packages available from computer dealers and retail outlets. An item of software may include several copyrights and database rights, for example, in the program, databases, the documentation, diagrams and text on the packaging, and even the licence agreement itself. The person acquiring the software package does not obtain ownership of the various copyrights and other rights subsisting in the software but, instead, obtains a licence (a permission) to use the software. A licence agreement will accompany the software detailing the acts which may be done with the software. The following terms which relate to copyright law are commonly included:

- nature of the contract; that is, a licence agreement;
- whether the licence can be transferred to another;
- what use can be made of the software;
- whether the licensee can modify the programs or databases;
- an indemnity in favour of the licensee should the software infringe a third party's rights; and
- termination for breach of the terms of the licence including an infringement of copyright and database right.

The precise nature of a contract for off-the-shelf software is not always easy to determine. Several possibilities exist. First, it is a licence agreement between the person acquiring the software and the owner of the copyrights and other rights subsisting in the software (not the dealer who is acting as an agent). Second, it is a sale of goods contract between the person acquiring the software and the dealer. Third, it is a hybrid contract comprising a licence agreement in respect of the programs and a sale of goods contract in respect of the disks, packaging, etc – the tangible items.

A fourth approach, which has much to commend it, has been suggested by Lord Penrose, a judge of the Court of Session, Outer House, in Scotland. The case involved a 'shrink-wrap licence'. Such licences were commonly displayed on the outside of the package containing the disks and manuals for the software. Nowadays, they are likely to be found inside the package where the disks are in a sealed envelope or case which bears a statement to the effect that opening the envelope or case signifies acceptance of the terms of the licence. Usually, the person acquiring the software is given the opportunity to return the software and obtain a refund if not happy with the licence agreement providing the seal is unbroken.

Case

Beta Computers (Europe) Ltd v Adobe Systems (Europe) Ltd [1996]
FSR 367, Court of Session, Outer House

> The defender (defendant) had obtained from the pursuer
> (plaintiff) an off-the-shelf software package produced by a
> third party, Informix Software Inc. It came with a 'shrink-
> wrap' licence and carried the statement 'Opening the
> Informix S.I. Software Package indicates your acceptance
> of these terms and conditions'. The defender tried to return
> the software before using it. The pursuer refused to accept
> its return and sued for the price of the software.
>
> Lord Penrose held that the supply of software off-the-shelf
> for a price was a *sui generis* contract rather than a sale of goods
> contract or a hybrid contract. He said that the time the contract
> was made was when the conditions imposed by the copyright
> owner (Informix) were tendered to the purchaser and were
> accepted by the purchaser. Looking at the Copyright, Designs
> and Patents Act 1988, Lord Penrose concluded that the supply
> of the medium on which the software is stored must be
> accompanied by a licence between the copyright owner and
> the person acquiring the software.

On the basis of this case (and there are United States
authorities to similar effect) we can say that the sale of an
off-the-shelf software package exhibits the following
characteristics:

- the contract is not made until the person acquiring the
  software signifies his or her acceptance of the terms in the
  licence agreement by the act of opening the relevant
  packet, envelope or case;
- until the person acquiring the software accepts in this
  manner, he or she is free to return the software and is
  entitled to a refund of the price; and
- the contract is not a sale of goods contract otherwise the
  dominant purpose of the contract (to acquire the right to
  use the software) is subordinated to the medium on which
  the software is stored.

Of course, this is a Scots case, although it is likely to be
followed in the rest of the United Kingdom. It should be noted

that there are some differences between Scots and English contract law. The decision does reflect commercial reality and adapts quite easily to the acquisition of software without any physical medium, such as where it is made available by downloading from the Internet.

Typical mechanisms for the commercial exploitation of software

The owner of the copyright or database right in computer software may exploit it by simply assigning it to another or by granting exclusive or non-exclusive licences in respect of it. For example, the owner of the copyright in respect of a computer program can assign it or grant an exclusive licence to the ultimate user of the program. However, the matter does not stop there, because an assignee or licensee may then decide not to exploit the work directly but to allow others to do so instead. Another factor is that copyright consists of a number of rights associated with the acts restricted by the copyright, and each of these can be dealt with separately as the examples below indicate.

Example

A freelance programmer, Sarah, has written a computer game. Rather than try to 'sell' copies herself, she has agreed with a mail order software publisher, MEGA Ltd, that it will make copies of the game, advertise and sell them. Sarah has agreed to assign the entire copyright to MEGA for the remainder of its duration, and MEGA will grant non-exclusive licences to the ultimate purchasers of the game. Sarah will be paid a royalty of seven per cent of the net receipts obtained by MEGA from sales of the game. The arrangement is shown in Figure 8.4.

The agreement between Sarah and MEGA will contain provisions such as the timing of the royalty payments, which of the parties will be responsible for the correction of errors, and for producing the instructions for use, warranties as to title, indemnities against infringement of third party rights, etc.

Figure 8.4 Computer program transaction

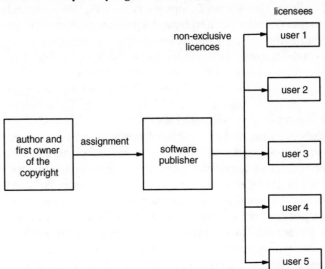

The rights granted in respect of computer programs will either be those associated with the use of the programs or publishing them, granting licences or sub-licences in respect of them. But other forms of works may be stored on a computer and, here, dealing with the rights separately may be more appropriate. Materials which are published traditionally on paper can also be made available in a computer database which may be accessed remotely and which may be subject to copyright and/or the database right. The advantage of this is that the material can be more easily kept up to date and relevant parts can be retrieved easily, for example, by using a query language.

Example

Weevil and Muggins publish a book of legal precedents (sample terms for legal agreements) and a new edition is printed approximately every four years. They decide to diversify in two ways. First, by granting an exclusive licence to an Australian publishing house, Koala Pty Ltd allowing it to print, publish and sell copies of the precedents in Australia,

New Zealand and Hong Kong. Second, in the United Kingdom and some European countries, Weevil and Muggins, under an agreement with the provider of an established on-line database system, have made their precedents available in a computer full text retrieval system. Figure 8.5 shows the contractual arrangements.

Weevil and Muggins will be paid an agreed royalty based on sales by the Australian publishing company. The provider of the on-line system, DATA ON-LINE has an exclusive licence to store and transmit the precedents to its customers who are charged a fee of £7 every time they access this service. The users have, in effect, non-exclusive sub-licences to use, search and inspect the precedents but they are not permitted to make permanent copies of more than five per cent of the entire precedent database in any three-month period. The provision of the precedents in the on-line system will be considered to be a cable programme service. The precedents themselves, whether stored on computer or printed on paper are literary works, individually and as a database.

Figure 8.5   Precedents transaction

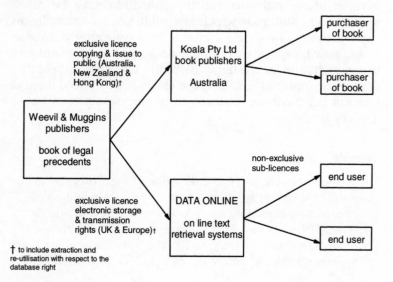

Of course, many other arrangements are possible. The agreements should fully state what rights under copyright law and other forms of intellectual property law are the subject matter of the transaction, together with details of any restrictions on the exercise of those rights. Copyright law must be seen through the perspective of the law of contract in this sense, and the nature of the interest in the copyright of a computer program or any other work is prescribed by the terms of the assignment or the licence agreement, as appropriate. Of course, a licence might impose restrictions on the use of the work which go beyond copyright. For example, a licence agreement might state that the licensee is not permitted to allow another to see the software in use. At the present time allowing others to see the software in operation, unless it falls within the scope of a public performance or showing is not an act restricted by copyright.

If one of the parties infringes the copyright or database right, there will probably also be remedies under the assignment or licence agreement on the basis of breach of contract. It is usual to find a term stating that copyright infringement, for example by making copies beyond the number permitted in the contract, will automatically terminate the agreement without prejudice to any other remedies the aggrieved party may have under the law of copyright. Similar considerations apply as regards the database right.

Chapter 9

Computer-generated works

INTRODUCTION

When the Copyright, Designs and Patents Bill was progressing through Parliament, some commentators (including the British Computer Society) became concerned about the question of copyright protection for works that were produced by a programmed computer, as opposed to works produced by a human who used a computer to assist him or her create the work. It was clear that the new legislation would deal with works created with the *aid* of a programmed computer, as it did with other copyright works, and the programmed computer would be equivalent to a tool which the creator used to fashion the work. However, and perhaps looking into the future, it is possible that the programmed computer itself might take on a creative role and produce new works with minimal direct human intervention.

As a result of these concerns, the Act contains provisions which are unique to the United Kingdom in that recognition is given to computer-generated works as a separate species of works. Because of this treatment, such works require different rules for determining the identity of the author and the duration of the copyright. (The Act also made modifications to design law to recognise the possibility of designs created by a programmed computer.) In principle, the concept of computer-generated works is plausible. It is only when the nature and existence of such works is examined that difficulties start to emerge. For example, where lies the dividing line separating computer-generated works from works which have been created by a person using the computer as a tool? Indeed, it can be argued that there can never be such a thing as a computer-generated work; that human expertise and skill lie at the root of all works created by, or with the aid of, a programmed computer. Case law prior to the 1988 Act adds weight to such arguments.

Case

Express Newspapers plc v Liverpool Daily Post & Echo plc [1985] 1 WLR 1089

The plaintiff ran a newspaper competition which involved the distribution to households of cards which contained grids of letters. Each day, in the plaintiff's newspapers, a table showing winning sequences of letters was published. The winning sequences were produced using a programmed computer (in much the same way that the Premium Bond winners are selected using 'Ernie'). The award of a prize was not dependent upon buying the plaintiff's newspaper and several evening newspapers copied the winning sequences. The plaintiff sued for infringement of the copyright in the tables of winning sequences of letters and the defendants claimed that these were not protected by copyright because they were not produced by a human being. In other words, the defendant's argument was that the tables had no human author.

The defendant's argument was rejected by Mr Justice Whitford, who said that the computer was no more than a tool with which the winning sequences of letters were produced using the instructions of a programmer. He said that the submission that there was no human author was as unrealistic as saying that a pen was the author of a work of literature. The tables of letters were therefore protected by copyright and the defendants were liable for infringing that copyright. (In an earlier case, concerning the creation of lists of runners and riders for horse races by a programmed computer, the same argument that there was no human author met with the same judicial response; *The Jockey Club v Rahim*, 22 July 1983, Chancery Division.)

Therefore, case law before the Copyright, Designs and Patents Act 1988 seemed to contradict the very existence of computer-generated works. If a sequence of letters selected at random by a programmed computer has a human author, being the person who wrote the computer program used to select the random numbers, then what type of work could be described as being created by a programmed computer? There are important implications tied up with this issue, especially concerning the ownership of works which have been produced by a process which has involved the operation of a programmed computer. Before looking at these implications, the way in which computer-generated works are defined and provided for by the 1988 Act is described.

WHAT IS A COMPUTER-GENERATED WORK?

The mystery surrounding the nature of a computer-generated work is not clarified by the Copyright, Designs and Patents Act 1988. At the outset, the Act contains an outrageous tautology; a real 'chicken and egg' situation. Section 178 of the Act (the interpretation section) defines a computer-generated work as being a work which is 'generated by computer in circumstances such that there is no human author'. However, every original work of copyright must have an author (which may be a living individual or a legal person such as a limited company or a corporation) and section 9(3) says that the author of a computer-generated literary, dramatic, musical or artistic work is 'the person by whom the arrangements necessary for the creation of the work are undertaken'. Therefore, a computer-generated work does have an author and that author will almost always be a human being. But if this is so it cannot be a computer-generated work, by definition. The only way around this conundrum is to say that authorship is determined immediately *after* the creation of the work, that is, at the time the work was generated by the (programmed) computer there was no human author but as soon as the work exists, we can assign authorship to the work on the basis of section 9(3). The difficulty here is that the person to whom authorship will be granted will have made the necessary arrangements before the creation of the work in question. The 'delayed authorship' approach is not a particularly satisfactory way around the problem and is certainly not suggested by taking a literal interpretation of the words in the statute. But, without taking this line, there can be no such thing as a computer-generated work for the purposes of copyright law.

Even if we assume that the 'delayed authorship' approach will be followed in the courts, there are other difficulties with regard to computer-generated works. First, it should be noted that in principle any type of work can be computer-generated for the purposes of copyright law. For some works such as sound recordings and films, there is no need for special treatment, the normal rules will suffice. However, with the original works of copyright (literary, dramatic, musical and artistic works) the issue of authorship and, hence, ownership must be provided for. Because literary works are defined by section 3(1) of the Act as including computer programs, it is possible to have a computer-generated computer program. This indeed seems, at first sight, to be a possibility. There are computer programs available which generate code, for example, to produce a screen display designed by a process of 'screen-painting'. The code to produce COBOL data entry and output screens may be produced in this way. The same applies to some fourth-generation languages. A copyright database is a literary work and, as such, the rules relating to computer-generated works ought to apply to such databases. However, the basic test for originality for a copyright database is that it is the author's own intellectual creation. That being so, can there ever be such a thing as a computer-generated database which is protected by copyright? If a database is generated in circumstances such that there is no human author, where does the intellectual creation come from for it to be deemed original? The only way around this is to take into account the creative skill of the person or persons who wrote the software which produced the database. But if we do this, the database cannot be computer-generated as there is, after all, one or more human authors. If this is so, there can never be any such thing as a computer-generated work, whichever of the 'original work' categories it

272 • *Computer-generated works*

appears to fall within. On the other hand, because the test of originality does not apply to other works such as sound recordings and cable programmes (and databases subject to the database right), such works can be computer-generated though there are no specific provisions for such works.

Can we reconcile the provisions in the Copyright, Designs and Patents Act 1988 with prior case law which suggested that even the most automated of processes must be the result of human effort and skill? One way would be to say that the Act has impliedly overruled this case law. However, a well-established presumption used in the interpretation of legislation is that 'in the absence of any clear indication to the contrary, Parliament can be presumed not to have altered the common law farther than was necessary to remedy the "mischief"' (Lord Reid in *Black-Clawson International Ltd v Papierwerke Waldhof-Aschaffenburg AG* [1975] 1 All ER 810 at 815). On this basis it is hard to say that the intention of Parliament was to overrule the *Express Newspapers* case otherwise it would have been explicit on this point in the Act. Another way at reconciling the case law and the Act would be to claim that the Act is not inconsistent with the prior case law, which merely gives an example of a work which is not computer-generated, because there is still some causal connection between the human being who wrote the program and the output. That is, the output was partly predetermined by the programmer. In the *Express Newspapers* case we could claim that the programmer decided on how many letters were to be drawn each time, whether any letters were excluded, what action should be taken if the same letter were selected more than once and what theory of random selection should be used. The programmer defined the basic rules for the *format* and *content* of the output. Although the Copyright, Designs and Patents Act 1988 contains rules of construction these are not particularly helpful (section 172). It was not intended that the Act would make sweeping changes to previous copyright law, and prior law may be used to determine whether there has been a departure from it. However, a mere change in expression does not, by itself, indicate that previous law has been departed from.

The following case concerns the giving of financial advice by computer software used by a customer who enters basic price information into the software to derive the advice. Although not a copyright case, it addresses the question of from whom the advice is generated. Nevertheless, the case is instructive and worth considering before looking at computer-generated works in more detail, especially as there is no direct case law on such works as yet.

Case

Re Market Wizard Systems (UK) Ltd (1998) Times, 31 July, Chancery Division

> A computer software package called Market Wizard Equity Options Trading System was used by customers to produce advice as to whether to buy, hold or sell certain stocks. The software was operated by the customer and linked to information such as daily prices downloaded via a telephone link. The company supplying the computer software claimed that it was not providing investment advice. The company was not licensed to give such advice and, under the Financial Services Act 1986, the court had jurisdiction to wind up the company in the public interest. The hearing was an application to wind up the company made by the Secretary of State for Trade and Industry.
>
> The court held that the company was providing investment advice. It had been argued on behalf of the company that it did nothing at the time the advice was produced. The sale of the software was to a customer who might use it in the future to generate advice. However, the judge said the essential question was whether the company was in the business of giving advice and that it was not necessary to identify a particular point in time when the advice was given. It was sufficient that the company had provided customers with a medium by which its purported expertise was communicated in the form of advice as to investments.

Although this is not a copyright case, it is interesting to note that once the software was sold to a customer, the company's contribution was over. That contribution was the rules and formulae which had been expressed in the software. Once the customer had a copy of the software he or she could be said to

274 • *Computer-generated works*

make the arrangements necessary for the creation of the advice by entering details relating to current prices. If we are prepared to accept the notion of computer-generated works, surely we could say that the advice in this case was computer-generated. Yet the court did not take that approach and still maintained that the advice flowed from the company providing the software. Although the advice derived may not have been such as to be a work of copyright, the court effectively said that the company was the 'author' of the advice. In other words, it had not been generated in circumstances such that there was no [human] author. Of course, in this case, the advice was deemed to be given by the company although, essentially, it was the company's employees or consultants who must have generated the rules and formulae in the software, their act of 'authorship' being attributable to the company.

TYPES OF WORKS CREATED BY OR WITH THE AID OF A COMPUTER

All types of works which are created by a process involving the use of a programmed computer owe their creation to human skill and judgment, although this human element may be indirect. A computer program may contain all the instructions necessary for the creation of a work and the direct human involvement consists of nothing more than switching on the computer and starting up the program. Looking into the future, the human element might be quite remote, involving the specification of basic rules which are used by the computer to generate programs which, in turn, generate other programs which produce some form of output, perhaps in response to some natural external phenomena or stimuli.

Example

A computer-generated work?

A team of experienced meteorologists specify a set of basic rules concerning the earth's weather system. These rules are entered into a computer system which is designed to accept information transmitted to it automatically by satellites, and to use this information, together with the basic rules, to develop and refine a model of the weather system. To do this, it may use another program which generates and refines the model, possibly by a process of induction. The computer system may also be able to make changes to the rules if they are later contradicted by the data collected by the computer. When the computer system has developed the basic model of the weather, it automatically generates weather forecasts which are printed out on paper. Are these forecasts computer-generated works?

The forecasts are obviously influenced by the formal representation of the meteorologists' expertise and the skill and knowledge of the persons who conceived of the system, and of those who designed the suite of programs containing rules about inductive techniques, and system development and refinement. Human creative processes may be quite remote, being several steps removed from the final computer output but, nevertheless, those creative processes are very much in evidence, and the computer system could not operate without them.

Even in this example, there is still a causal connection between human beings and the final computer output. Perhaps judges will take a less pedantic view and decide that the output generated by such a system is a computer-generated work. Even if this is so, this begs the question of how to draw a dividing line between computer-generated works and other works which have been created using a programmed computer as a tool. This question is of vital importance to persons and organisations using computers to create new works, because the identity of the owner or owners of the copyright in the new work is dependent upon the classification of the work as being either a computer-generated work or a work of human authorship. Another issue which depends upon this classification is the duration of copyright. For computer-generated works, copyright endures for 50 years from the end of the calendar year in which the work was made and not for 70 years from the end of the calendar year during which the author died (section 12). Therefore, in most cases, the duration of copyright in computer-generated works will be shorter than is the case with other literary, dramatic, musical and artistic works.

The difficulty in determining whether a work is or is not computer-generated may be eased if two characteristics relating to the finished work, *content* and *format*, are considered. These characteristics are discussed below in the context of four categories of works produced in a way which involves a programmed computer. Those categories of works are:

- works produced with the aid of a programmed computer;
- works produced by a programmed computer;
- intermediate works; and
- output derived from expert systems.

Works produced with the aid of a programmed computer

There are a great many examples of works which fall in this category. For example, a document produced using a word processing program, a table of calculations made with the aid of a spreadsheet program and an engineering drawing created with the assistance of a computer-aided design (CAD) system. Such works cannot be computer-generated works because the author is the person using the computer to produce the work. The computer is merely the tool with which the work is created. The person using the computer and the work are linked directly in a creative sense. The *content* of the work is governed entirely by the person using the programmed computer, as is the *format* of the work. The computer program may exert some minor control over elements of the format by imposing constraints but, nevertheless, the format is fundamentally a matter for the person creating the work.

Example

John Smith is an independent management consultant. He is commissioned by Delta Manufacturing Ltd to review the company's management structure and to prepare a report. John spends several weeks at Delta's premises to carry out this work and is permitted to use one of the company's computers. John uses a word processing program to write the report and a spreadsheet program to prepare tables of figures and bar-charts. The word processing program will not allow the report to be spaced at one-and-a-quarter line spacing as John would have preferred but he settles instead for one-and-a-half line spacing. The spreadsheet program imposes certain constraints on the format of the bar-charts.

For copyright purposes, John is the author of the report including the tables and charts. John has exerted total control over the content of these items, none of which is a computer-generated work. Although the programs have influenced the format of the finished works, this influence has been minor and of a negative nature, certainly not creative. In fact, the program limitations in this respect are simply obstacles to John's creative effort which John will overcome as best he can. The persons responsible for writing the word processing program and the spreadsheet program have had absolutely no creative influence on either the content or format of the finished report. (As John has been commissioned to produce the report rather than being an employee creating the report in the course of his employment, he will be the first owner of the copyright unless provision had been made for ownership. Delta asked John for a signed assignment of the copyright in the reports at the time he agreed to carry out the work.)

The use of a programmed computer to assist in the production of a work as in the above example is similar, in principle, to the case where a person uses a typewriter to produce a work of literature. It is clear that where the computer is used as a tool to create a work, the work is not a computer-generated work. Otherwise it would be as ridiculous as saying that a pen could be the author of a written work; a point made by Mr Justice Whitford in the *Express Newspapers* case.

Works produced by a programmed computer

Here, we are talking in terms of works which have been produced by a computer with very little direct human intervention. The work is largely the result of the operation of a programmed computer. The direct human intervention may comprise of little else than switching on the computer, loading the appropriate programs and making sure that the printer has a sufficient stock of paper. At the present time in the development of computer technology, it is not an easy matter to think of examples but possible candidates are:

- automatically generated weather forecasts produced by a computer receiving signals from weather satellites;
- lists of random numbers, for example, for the Premium Bond draw; and
- computer code automatically generated from screen layouts designed by the user.

In terms of the computer output, the finished work, all these systems operate with a minimum of direct human effort or skill. The person operating the system has very little or no control over either the *format* or the *content* of the output. Works produced in this way may be the computer-generated works provided for by the Copyright, Designs and Patents Act 1988. If this proposition is accepted, the skill and expertise of the persons who wrote the computer programs must be ignored in the act of creation and the *Express Newspapers* case must be considered to no longer represent the correct legal position. For literary, dramatic, musical and artistic works which are computer-generated, the author is the person who makes the arrangements necessary for the work to be created. That person will exercise very little, if any, skill or judgment but making him or her the author can be justified on two grounds:

1 It greatly simplifies questions of the ownership of the copyright in the work so produced. It is, therefore, a practical and expedient solution.
2 The person making the arrangements 'inherits' the skill of the original analysts and programmers. There must be some skill or judgment underpinning the work otherwise it cannot be 'original'. However, there is nothing in the Act to prevent the concept of adoptive skill being used to determine originality although this is an unusual approach.

Example

Rite, Bull and Partners are a firm of stockbrokers. They obtain a computer system from Fastbuck Co Ltd, a company developing computer systems for dealing with shares, monitoring the stock market and analysing trends. Fastbuck has just developed a set of computer programs which contain some rules and algorithms enabling the programs to develop and apply a model of the stock market. The programs are available to trusted clients of Fastbuck who can connect their computers to databases of share prices which the programs use automatically to develop the model. Once the model is working it produces reports at hourly intervals making recommendations regarding the sale and purchase of shares, set out in a table of shares, current prices and risk factors.

Eventually, the programs produce the reports specified above. All that Rite, Bull & Partners have to do is switch on the computer and load the programs and, occasionally, attend to the printer. The reports will probably be deemed to be computer-generated works, and the copyright in them will belong to Rite, Bull & Partners. It is they, or their employees, who make the arrangements necessary for the creation of the reports.

If such works were not deemed to be computer-generated, it would mean that others would have rights in the computer output. For example, in the above situation, Fastbuck would own the copyright in the reports. This could be inconvenient, especially if it is intended to make copies of the reports to pass on to clients. Although a court of law might be prepared to imply a licence in favour of the person or company obtaining the programs (or use the concept of non-derogation from grant), this could be both uncertain and inconvenient.

The approach in the United States seems to be to treat such works as being created by the author of the program, and this is used as a means of determining ownership of computer output. In other words, the user of the programmed computer (the person making the arrangements for the creation of the work) does not have rights in the output because he or she does not provide anything to the content of the output.

Case

Midway Manufacturing Inc v Artic international Inc (1983) 464 US 823

It was held that the copyright in a video game (particularly the screen displays) lies with the game's creator and not with the person playing the game. The latter may make some contribution to the final output, but he or she is constrained by the instructions in the program for the game.

Intermediate works

Even if the existence of computer-generated works is accepted without reservation, a third category of works will still be a source of problems as regards the identity of the author of the work. Intermediate works are those which lie between the two categories discussed above; they are works in connection with which the human expertise required to produce the work flows from more than one source and is partly direct, partly indirect. The *content* of the output produced using the programmed computer is the result of the skill of the person operating it combined with the skill of the person or persons responsible for the designing and writing of the computer programs. The operator may, however, have only a limited effect on the *format* of the finished work. There are many examples of intermediate works, for example, output produced by a specialised accounting system for a particular type of business, music created by a music synthesiser, and price breakdowns produced using a system to assist with the production of estimates and quotations. Reports generated by using expert systems are a special form of intermediate work and are considered separately later in this chapter.

Example

Quickbuild plc, a building firm, obtains a licence to use a computer estimating system called Questor from Exodus Ltd, a software house specialising in developing computer systems for the construction industry. The system comprises a suite of computer programs, which include routines to provide analyses and breakdowns of the costs derived, and a database of standard prices, based on sets of resources and performances. Exodus engaged George Price, an experienced estimator, to produce the database. The person using the system to work out the cost of a building brings a substantial degree of skill by deciding whether the standard prices are applicable, and if not, by building up new prices and entering them into the database.

The resulting computer output, which could be a substantial printed document or a large computer file containing information concerning a particular project, has three sources of expertise, that of the analysts and programmers employed by Exodus, that of George Price who was responsible for developing the database of standard prices and, finally, the individual estimators using the system to produce a comprehensive estimate for a particular project. The problem here is to identify who the author is in respect of the computer output.

Because the person using the system will exercise a fair degree of skill and expertise in working up the estimate, it would not be unreasonable to suggest that he is the author. However, it could be argued that the finished work is a hybrid work being created in part by a human author (the estimator using the system), the remainder being computer-generated. Alternatively, the estimator using the system, the analysts and programmers and George, the database developer, could all be deemed to be joint authors. The ownership provisions of the Copyright, Designs and Patents Act 1988 can be strongly criticised for not dealing effectively with the ownership of the copyright in intermediate works.

Output from expert systems

The output derived from the use of an expert system can be considered to be a very special form of intermediate or hybrid work. The phrase 'expert system' is used to describe computer systems which have some special characteristics when compared to conventional computer systems. An expert system can be said to be one which is designed to provide advice at, or approaching, the level of an expert professional. For example, a junior doctor can use an expert system which will help him or her in making a preliminary diagnosis in respect of a patient complaining of abdominal pain. There are two ways in which expert systems can be distinguished from conventional computer systems. One way is to look to the how the system is constructed. In simple terms, expert systems comprise a knowledge-base, an inference engine and an explanation interface as shown in Figure 9.1. The knowledge-base contains the raw material of the expert system; the rules and facts and heuristics representing the expertise. The knowledge-base will have been developed using experts in the domain represented, who have worked with knowledge engineers to identify, structure and formalise the knowledge. The inference engine is a computer program (or set of programs) which attempts to resolve inquiries made by the user of the system by interacting with the knowledge-base. The inference engine may be either a ready-made program, often referred to as a shell, or a program specially written for the particular application. Finally, there will be a user interface to make the system easy to use, and to provide a means of inspecting the advice produced by the system, as well as supplying an explanation of that advice and the means of verifying it. Most expert systems include an explanation facility, allowing 'backtracking', going back from the final advice through the rules to see how the advice was derived. (There will usually be other parts to expert systems, such as a knowledge refining program, but they are not relevant to the discussion.)

Figure 9.1   Basic structure of an expert system

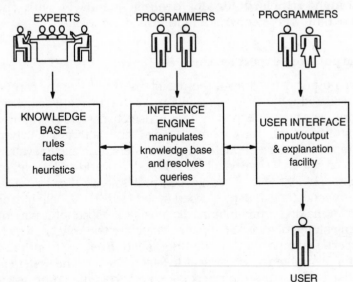

An alternative but complementary approach is to define an expert system in terms of its performance. Basically, to qualify as an expert system, it should perform at or near the level of an expert in a given domain. It should provide advice at that level and be able to justify and explain the reasoning leading to the advice. It is likely that the system will be used by persons who have a more than superficial knowledge of the domain in which the system operates. For example, a medical diagnostic system would be used by a general practitioner or junior doctor; it could not be used by a layperson who knows little or nothing of medical matters. This last point is really more to do with the current stage of development of expert systems rather than being a fundamental feature of them.

In terms of copyright issues, the point about expert systems is that the advice they produce is the result of the joint efforts of several persons. For example, the advice may flow from:

1) the experts who provided the knowledge contained in the knowledge-base;
2) the knowledge engineers who helped the experts to make the knowledge explicit and who refined and formalised the knowledge so that it could be represented and installed in the knowledge-base;
3) the persons who wrote the inference engine and, to a lesser extent, the user interface;
4) the person using the expert system.

The last person, the user of the system, provides expertise because he or she will have to understand, interpret and respond to questions asked during the operation of the system, and he or she will also have to know what the scope and limitations of the system are. At the present stage of development of expert systems, the user of an expert system must possess a reasonable general knowledge of the domain covered by the system to be able to use it successfully.

What will the law make of the output of expert systems when it comes to deciding the authorship and ownership of that output? If the computer-generated work concept is persevered with, it might be argued that the person who uses the system will be the author of the advice produced by using the system. But, to take this line runs counter to common sense. The person using the system makes a significant contribution, as do the persons who were involved in the development and construction of the system. An alternative approach, producing the same result, is to say that the user is the author, by treating the output as being created by using the programmed computer as a tool. This is unrealistic. To attribute authorship to the experts and knowledge engineers who developed the knowledge base is unsatisfactory because they cannot predict how the system will be used and what responses will be made by the user; they have no control over its use. Logically, all the persons described above should be the joint authors, in differing proportions, of the output resulting from the use of the system. For copyright purposes, a work of joint authorship is one in which the individual contributions of the joint authors are not distinct from each other.

The courts will have to face these problems in the future and it is unlikely that an easy solution will be found; judicial opinion may vary depending upon the individual judge's understanding of computer technology (and copyright law). Of course, in some cases, computer output will not attract copyright protection. For example, using a medical expert system might produce the following printed advice: 'Take two aspirins and go to bed'. Due to the *de minimis* principle discussed in Chapter 1, this will be considered to be too small for protection. But in many cases, the advice and the explanation may run to several printed pages. The explanation may contain significant extracts from the knowledge-base and the persons creating that knowledge-base may wish to restrain publication of the report and claim ownership rights in the computer output to do this. On the other hand, the output may be commercially valuable, for example, where an expert system has been used in the creation of a new piece of music and the persons who have been involved in the development of the system may claim joint ownership of the copyright in the music.

As mentioned above, the simplest solution is to say that output derived from an expert system (or any other intermediate work) is either a work produced with the aid of a programmed computer, where the programmed computer is little more than the tool with which the work is produced or, alternatively, the work is computer-generated. Both solutions give the same result. The person using the computer system is the author of the work and the ownership of the copyright will flow naturally from this fact. Any computer scientist will know, instinctively, that these approaches do not reflect the true position and the persons involved in the development and making of expert systems, and other intermediate systems, play a vital role in the creative process *vis-à-vis* the finished work. Nevertheless, if the courts are brave enough to follow this logical conclusion, it could lead to all manner of complications regarding the commercial use of expert systems and other 'intermediate' systems.

PRACTICAL IMPLICATIONS

Several options are available to judges faced with authorship and ownership issues relating to works produced by, or with, the aid of a programmed computer. One is to imply a licence in favour of the person lawfully acquiring the computer program which is used to create the work. That licence would allow that person to use, copy or publish the work depending on the circumstances. The terms of the implied licence would be based on what the parties would have agreed if, at the time of the agreement to acquire the program, they had directed their minds towards the question of ownership of copyright or the right to perform certain acts in relation to the output. An alternative approach would be to use the doctrine of non-derogation from grant. That is, a person may not give something with one hand only to take it away with the other. In other words, the person who allows his computer programs to be used by another may not use his rights in copyright law to prevent that other person making full use of the output derived from using the programs. A final but messy solution is to use the notion of beneficial ownership. That is, the computer output would have two owners, a legal owner and an owner in equity. The latter would be able to make use of the output despite any wishes of the legal owner to the contrary. This method might be appropriate where the legal owner has not acted in good faith. It is, however, far better to be aware of the difficulties surrounding works produced using a programmed computer and to make suitable arrangements at the outset.

The normal way to overcome any potential dispute as to the ownership of computer output is to make contractual provision dealing with this matter at the time the computer programs are obtained. If the programs are licensed, the licence agreement should contain terms dealing with who owns what in terms of the output produced after running the programs. (Of course, this will not be necessary in the case of straightforward word processing and spreadsheet programs.) In some cases, because all the persons involved are employees of the company developing and using the software, there will be little difficulty, but if outsiders are involved at any stage, terms should be inserted in contractual agreements dealing with ownership and use of the computer output.

As a footnote, it is interesting to note that the European Community, in its Directives affecting computer software, has steadfastly chosen to ignore the concept of computer-generated works. This adds fuel to arguments that these provisions of the Copyright, Designs and Patents Act 1988 should be repealed and replaced with new rules to deal with the authorship of intermediate works and the output of expert systems.

Chapter 10

Maintenance of computer software

INTRODUCTION

Computer software is rarely a static entity. It is continually being improved and developed. Even a software system written for a particular client will need amending and augmenting as the client's business develops and changes and as the client's demands on the information which can be obtained from computer systems increase and become more sophisticated. In addition to the need to modify and enhance software there will be, from time to time, a need to correct errors detected in the software. It is indeed a brave (and foolish) software producer who argues that his or her software is completely error-free. Because of the enormous number of paths possible in many computer programs, absolute testing is often a practical impossibility. The documentation and computer databases may also contain errors. Whether for error correction, development or enhancement, there is a continuing need for the maintenance and modification of computer software and anyone acquiring computer software must take this issue into account and provide for it in one way or another. An organisation which acquires an item of computer software might wish to be allowed to correct errors and modify the software itself whereas another acquiring organisation might be happy with a maintenance agreement with the supplier of the software. The owner of the copyright in the software may or may not be prepared to allow others to modify the software. The fact of ownership of copyright gives the owner the ability to control the use and modification of the software but this control is not absolute and may be compromised by law. Even if the copyright owner does not want anyone else to alter the software, the law might defeat his or her wishes in the interests of those who have lawfully obtained copies of the software. In terms of maintenance and modification what is feasible depends largely upon the type of software involved. Different factors apply to off-the-shelf software compared to specially written, bespoke software.

OFF-THE-SHELF SOFTWARE

The standard of off-the-shelf software is generally very high and companies producing such software usually include terms in their licence agreements to the effect that the software may not be modified in any way whatsoever, except in accordance with the 'decompilation' permitted act within section 50B of the Copyright, Designs and Patents Act 1988. The presumption that a lawful user may modify a computer program for error correction purposes under section 50C appears to be vulnerable to terms in the licence agreement to the contrary. Persons acquiring off-the-shelf software would rarely want to modify it (most would not even contemplate doing so) and so this should not present too much of a problem. Indeed, it would be extremely difficult to modify the programs, if not impossible, as only the object code is made available. However, the presence of errors or 'bugs' is always a possibility, and the person or organisation obtaining the software should check to see whether there are any arrangements for error correction, and whether enhancements are likely to be made available to present users at a reasonable price.

The software company's past record in terms of new versions and their compatibility with earlier versions of their software should be questioned. Normal practice is for software to be upwardly compatible. That is, files created using earlier versions can be used with later versions of the software but not *vice versa*. Some software companies allow existing users to upgrade to new versions at very reasonable prices.

Computer software has to be able to interface with various peripheral devices and other items of software. A typical problem is that a person who has bought a new printer finds that there is no interface in the software for the new printer. Will the software company provide a printer file for the new printer? If the user upgrades his or her computer or the operating system, what effect does this have on the software package? Does the software company provide any form of user support, either through the dealer or direct? These are the sort of questions that a person about to acquire an off-the-shelf software package ought to ask, bearing in mind that he or she will not be allowed to modify the software. Even if the licence agreement does not prohibit modification by the licensee or a third party, as the programs will be in object code form, the vast majority of licensees will not have the technical competence to be able to modify the software.

BESPOKE SOFTWARE

With software that is specially written (or adapted) at the client's request, the emphasis changes, and it is more likely that both the client and the software producer will have considered in detail the importance of maintenance and modification, and made some specific and appropriate provisions for this. If the client is a company or other organisation it may well have its own computer professionals on its staff, or freelance consultants who are used from time to time. The client's staff will probably have been involved in the specification, installation and testing of the software and they will, consequently, have some knowledge of the software. In these circumstances, the client may well wish to take over total control of the software and may obtain the copyright in the software by way of an assignment, or obtain an exclusive licence which allows for modification by or on behalf of the client. However, this is not necessarily the wisest approach and there are disadvantages as well as advantages.

Advantages of modification by client

- Modification can be made very quickly and errors corrected almost instantly.
- Flexibility – the client should be able to develop and enhance the software in line with changing requirements and priorities.
- It should be possible to 'tweak' the software enabling one-off reports to be produced.
- It should be easier for the client to develop interfaces and bridges between the software in question and the client's other computer systems.

Disadvantages to modification by client

- The client's staff or consultants will probably not have the depth of understanding of the system that the software producer has, at least, initially.
- Modifications by the client inevitably cloud liability issues should the software prove defective; by permitting modification by the client, the software producer is almost washing his hands of the software and its standard of performance.
- Enhancements developed by the software producer (for example, for other clients) would be very difficult to incorporate in the modified software.

Where the client or a third party is allowed to modify the software, the question of ownership of the copyright in the modified version must be addressed in the agreement governing the writing and delivery of the software. This is particularly important as Mr Justice Jacob in the *Ibcos* case (discussed in Chapter 3) recognised that modifying a computer program can give rise to a new copyright. It may be that the software company which wrote the original software requires the 'grant-back' of rights in modified versions, perhaps in the form of a licence.

Other issues are that the software producer might be reluctant to allow the client to modify the software in case this is not done correctly or skilfully, and the software gets a bad name which reflects on the software producer. The software producer may wish to continue to maintain the software because of the ongoing work and revenue that this will generate. Another related aspect is that the software producer has a creative link with the software and has an interest (not only a legal or economic interest) in its continued use and improvement. However, unlike other forms of literary works, persons writing computer programs do not have the moral rights of identification and integrity, and have no automatic right to control (or object to) the subsequent modification of the program. This results in the anomalous situation that a person who writes a computer program and the documentation for it can have moral rights in relation to the documentation but not the program. Moral rights may also subsist in any databases or non-program files or other works in digital form included in the software.

In many cases, the software producer, if the software is licensed, will agree with the client to maintain the software, usually by way of a renewable annual maintenance agreement, which may also provide for making enhancements available as and when they are produced. Under the licence, the client will receive only the object code version of any of the programs. If the terms are reasonable, this is probably the most satisfactory of arrangements, as the software is maintained by the persons who know it best. However, there is a danger that the producer of the software may be no longer able or willing to maintain the software. There are two ways around this difficulty. One is to make contractual provision for this occurrence by using an 'escrow' arrangement; the other, less satisfactory, approach is to rely on the courts and, in particular, policy over maintenance and repair.

Escrow

If the software producer has supplied only the object code version of the programs, continuing maintenance and modification of the software will be very difficult, if not impossible, should the software producer go out of business. If a receiver is appointed, he or she may be prepared to allow the client to have a copy of the source code and other materials such as the specification and flowcharts but will require payment for these items. The receiver might sell them to a third party or dispose of them in some other way. The receiver's duties lie to those owed money by the company in receivership, and the receiver will have no special responsibility to those who had obtained software from the company in the past. In this and other ways, the user of the software could find that he or she is left high and dry without the source code. Hence, where a licence agreement for the writing of computer software does not provide the client with a copy of the source code of the programs and other design materials, there should be a term detailing an escrow arrangement.

Escrow is an arrangement whereby the software producer deposits, with an independent third party, a copy of the source code of the programs together with copies of all the documentation and flowcharts relevant to the design and development of the software. These materials will enable the client (either directly or by engaging the necessary consultants) to take over the maintenance and further development of the software. Under the escrow arrangement, the independent person holding the materials (the stakeholder) is instructed not to allow access to them except after the occurrence of a specified event such as the software producer going out of business or being unable or unwilling to continue to support the software, for example, by entering into liquidation, having a receiver appointed or ceasing to trade. It may be that the software producer simply fails to respond to a request for maintenance work within a specified time. If any of these things happen, the stakeholder will give the materials to the client, who will then have all the information he needs to arrange for the software to be supported. Escrow is, therefore, like a form of guarantee or insurance should the software producer no longer be in a position to continue the maintenance of the software. Normally, the licensor will pay an initial fee at the commencement of the escrow and the licensee will then pay an annual fee to the escrow organisation and, if the licensor goes out of business or fails to maintain the software, the release fee to obtain the source code and other materials.

Organisations such as the National Computing Centre Ltd provide an escrow service. Its address is: Oxford House, Oxford Road, Manchester, M1 7ED. Without an escrow, the client may have to rely on legal policy which might permit reverse analysis of the object code programs in order to maintain the software. However, even if this is allowed, the client will not have access to other important materials such as flowcharts and detailed design specifications.

Policy controls

There is a danger that the manufacturer of a product can abuse the rights in the product to the detriment of the consumer, especially if the nature of the product is such that it will probably need repairing and replacement parts fitting during its life. The manufacturer might be tempted to charge exorbitant prices for spare parts if he or she has monopoly control of the making of such spares. The law has traditionally disliked attempts to control or interfere with the use of something after it has been sold, and the implied licence has been used to excuse what would otherwise be an infringement of an intellectual property right, for example, where an article requires repairing.

Case

Solar Thompson Engineering Co Ltd v Barton [1977] RPC 537

The plaintiff sold a conveyer system which included pulley wheels having elastomeric (rubber) rings in peripheral grooves (these were the subject of a patent). The plaintiff also claimed copyright in drawings of the system. A purchaser of the conveyer system from the plaintiff instructed the defendant (who was a repairer) to make and fit new steel rings to the pulleys and the plaintiff sued the defendant on the basis of infringement of both the patent and the copyright.

The Court of Appeal held that there was an implied licence under the patent to repair the pulleys by replacing the worn rings, and also an implied licence in respect of the copyright in the drawings to the extent necessary to carry out the repairs. (It had previously long been accepted that the purchaser of a patented article could carry out repairs without infringing the patent.)

This concept of the implied licence can be similar in effect to another legal principle which derives from land law known as the principle of non-derogation from grant. For example, if a landlord lets a shop to a tenant, the tenant will be able to obtain legal redress if the landlord then erects scaffolding making it very difficult for persons to enter and exit from the shop. The landlord will not be permitted to take away with one hand what he has given with the other.

Case

British Leyland Motor Corpn Ltd v Armstrong Patents Co Ltd
[1986] 2 WLR 400 (also discussed in Chapter 4)

The plaintiff made motor vehicles including the Morris Marina car and also made spare parts for these cars. The plaintiff also granted licences to spare part manufacturers permitting them to make spare parts for the plaintiff's cars. The defendant refused to obtain such a licence and made exhaust pipes for cars manufactured by the plaintiff after obtaining an exhaust pipe and measuring it to discover its shape and dimensions. The plaintiff sued for indirect infringement of the copyright subsisting in the drawings of the exhaust pipes.

The House of Lords held that the defendant had infringed the plaintiff's copyright in the drawings of the exhaust pipes but that the copyright could not be enforced. The reason given was that car owners had an inherent right to repair their cars as economically as possible and, therefore, they had a right to have access to a free market in spare parts. The plaintiff could not interfere with that right by controlling the market by means of its copyright. Although there was no difficulty in accepting that the principle of non-derogation from grant allowed purchasers to repair articles, this case extended that principle to manufacturers who make replacement spare parts.

Note that, since this case, the Copyright, Designs and

Patents Act 1988 has introduced certain changes in connection with artistic copyright and designs. In essence, the owner of a design right cannot rely on artistic copyright subsisting in the drawings of articles made to the design nor in other design documents such as photographs and data stored in a computer. However, it does not appear that the Act has prevented the further application of non-derogation from grant to copyright cases. Indeed, section 171(3) states that nothing in the part of the Act relating to copyright affects any rule of law preventing or restricting the enforcement of copyright, on grounds of public interest or otherwise.

In the *British Leyland* case, Lord Templeman saw no reason why the non-derogation from grant principle, traditionally associated with land law, should not be applied to the sale of motor cars. There would seem to be no logical reason why it could not also be extended to an agreement for the acquisition of computer software. The principle would mean, in this context, that the lawful acquirer of computer software would be able to disassemble, modify and reassemble the program code without infringing the copyright even if these actions were expressly prohibited by the agreement if the purpose was to correct errors. In the absence of terms to the contrary, this is now permitted for error correction by section 50C of the Act but the *British Leyland* principle is potentially wider and could even override express terms in a licence agreement, if applicable.

There have been a number of unreported cases in which it has been accepted that it is, at least, arguable that the *British Leyland* defence applies to computer software. For example, in *Digital Equipment Corpn v LCE* (unreported) 22 May 1992 and *Intergraph Corpn v Solid Systems CAD Services Ltd* (unreported) 20 March 1992, both cases involving third parties providing maintenance of software, the principle of non-derogation from grant was accepted to provide an arguable defence to copyright infringement. However, as both of these cases were at the interlocutory stage only, the matter is not beyond doubt.

Where the software company is a major concern, a refusal to allow maintenance by the client or third parties offering maintenance services might well fall foul of European

Community competition law or the United Kingdom Competition Act 1998 when it comes into force.

It is more difficult to predict whether the above principles would apply not just to error correction but to enhancements being written into the program. Where the software company provides the client with a copy of the source code it was held, in *Saphena Computing v Allied Collection Agencies* [1995] FSR 616 (decided in 1989), that there is an implied licence that the client can use the source code for error correction but not for adding improvements to the program. This would seem to limit the application of the *British Leyland* principle to error correction, the software equivalent of mechanical repair of a vehicle.

Example

Apex Toys make furry toys. They have acquired from Pitware Ltd, a software house, a non-exclusive licence in respect of computer programs to control an automated assembly line for the manufacture of teddy bears. The licence is silent on the matter of modification of the programs. Apex Toys have subsequently made some changes to the design of their teddy bears, necessitating a few minor modifications to the programs controlling the assembly line. Pitware have said that it can modify the programs but that they cannot start the work for two months and that it will cost £3,000. Apex's information technology manager has approached a freelance programmer who has said that he can carry out the necessary modifications immediately, that the work will take only two days and he will charge £500 for the work.

As the licence agreement does not expressly prohibit the carrying out of modifications to the programs by the licensee or a person acting on the licensee's behalf, section 50C allows error correction and, for work in excess of this, a court would almost certainly imply a term in the licence permitting this should Pitware object. However, if the licence does carry a term prohibiting modification by the licensee the point becomes less predictable. The Copyright, Designs and Patents Act 1988 does not help and it is a matter of relying on the principle of non-derogation from grant.

Whether this would apply would depend on a number of factors such as whether the licensor was willing to carry out the modifications at a reasonable cost and whether it was reasonable to assume, at the outset, that the program would require frequent modification as production methods change and different designs of soft toys are introduced.

The *British Leyland* 'right to repair' principle is probably more limited than may have been thought, following a veiled attack on the principle in a case before the Privy Council on appeal from Hong Kong.

Case

Canon Kabushiki Kaisha v Green Cartridge Co (Hong Kong) Ltd
[1997] FSR 817

The plaintiff manufactured laser printers and photocopying machines. These had toner cartridges which needed replacement from time to time. The cost of the cartridges was a significant portion of the plaintiff's aftermarket. Over the life of a machine, the cost of replacement cartridges cost more than the original purchase price of the machine.

There was a thriving business in making toner cartridges. The defendant, who was originally a refiller of old cartridges, decided to manufacture new cartridges for the plaintiff's machines. The plaintiff commenced proceedings for infringement of patents held in parts of the cartridges and infringement of copyright subsisting in drawings of the cartridges. The defendant claimed that the manufacture and supply of its cartridges fell within the right to 'repair' exception in *British Leyland*.

The appeal by the plaintiff from the Hong Kong Court of Appeal was allowed. Lord Hoffmann in the Judicial Committee of the Privy Council said that *British Leyland* addressed the concern that enforcing copyright in drawings would permit manufacturers of complex products to control the aftermarket. The defendant had argued that, on the basis of *British Leyland*, there should be a free market in toner cartridges as these were necessary to keep a photocopier or laser printer working.

Lord Hoffmann, giving the judgment of the Privy Council, differed. He suggested that the *British Leyland* principle had been applied too rigidly in the past and that economic patterns should be recognised and taken into consideration. In contrast with the position with motor vehicles, in the present case, the prudent buyer of a copier or printer would take into account the cost of replacement cartridges. If a manufacturer priced his cartridges too highly, he would sell fewer machines. He could not, therefore, be considered to abuse his dominant position. The thriving refill market already had increased competition and this kept a reign on the plaintiff's prices of his toner cartridges.

The general tenor of the judgment in *Canon* shows that the *British Leyland* principle is to be used sparingly and in quite limited circumstances. Lord Hoffmann questioned whether it was proper for judges to make law in an area which Parliament had legislated in considerable detail. Although, strictly speaking, decisions of the Judicial Committee of the Privy Council are not of binding authority, it is almost certain that *Canon* will be followed in future. That being so, it would be unwise to rely on *British Leyland* except in very limited circumstances.

To summarise the situation with respect to bespoke software, it is in the interests of both parties that the question of maintenance and modification is clearly addressed and dealt with, and that a reasonable mechanism is achieved. The ideal situation is where the software producer remains responsible for the maintenance and future development of the software package including the programs and documentation, providing this service is furnished at a reasonable cost, and with reasonable speed and efficiency. If the client has a large computer department with a number of proficient computer analysts and programmers, the client may feel that his or her interests are best served by taking over responsibility for maintenance and modification after the expiry of the initial maintenance period. If this is so, the client must ensure that the source code and all preparatory design materials are handed over. In all cases, software maintenance is an issue that must be given careful thought and be fully provided for rather than relying on the uncertain scope of the error correction provisions and common law controls over the exploitation of works of copyright.

Chapter 11

Semiconductor products protection

INTRODUCTION

Semiconductor products, in particular integrated circuits, are at the heart of modern technology. The revolution in miniaturisation made possible by the development of the silicon chip has transformed computer technology, and the technology has been applied to a wide variety of areas such as motor vehicle electronic ignition systems, video and audio equipment, weapon guidance systems, and even the humble washing machine. Integrated circuits include a computer's central processing unit, permanent computer read only memory, random access memory, and micro-electronic circuits (for example, amplifying, rectifying and switching circuits including logical gates). They may contain programs and/or data. These integrated circuits are of tremendous commercial importance, and the design and manufacture of them often entails very large financial investment.

Integrated circuits are usually made from layers of materials by a process which includes etching using various 'masks' (templates) which are made photographically. The simplest integrated circuit consists of three layers, one of which is of semiconductor material. A wafer of semiconductor material is coated with a layer of silicon oxide (an insulator), and the electronic components, such as transistors, are formed by a process of diffusion (chemically doping the semiconductor material with impurities through holes etched through the oxide). Finally, an aluminium coating is applied which is partly evaporated using a mask, leaving behind the interconnections between components formed in the semiconductor layer. Figure 11.1 shows, diagrammatically, a minute part of an integrated circuit.

Figure 11.1 Part of an integrated circuit (greatly magnified)

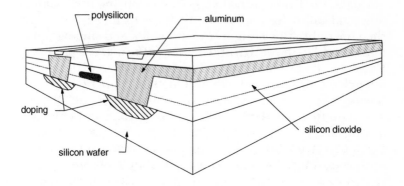

As one of the purposes of intellectual property law is to stimulate investment by offering the prospect of a reward on capital, effort and time invested in the creation of new works and products, it is only fitting that integrated circuits are given some form of protection, by providing legal remedies against others who are prepared to copy them without permission or licence of the originator of a particular design of integrated circuit. Although, in some cases, integrated circuits (referred to in the legislation as semiconductor products) may be protected indirectly through copyright law, it was considered appropriate that they should be given their own *sui generis* form of protection. Some semiconductor products contain computer programs, and copying them might infringe the copyright in the computer program but copyright protection of the computer programs contained in some integrated circuits might be denied because they are considered to be part of the defining elements of the hardware in which they are installed, and thus are deemed to be ideas. Hence the apparent need for separate protection of semiconductor products.

Previously, copyright protection for the layout and arrangement of the circuitry in integrated circuits was very strong in the United Kingdom because copying the layout of any semiconductor product would have infringed, indirectly, the copyright subsisting in the drawings and photographic masks used in the design and manufacture of these products. However, the law has changed and a new form of protection is available for semiconductor products. Copyright protection has been suppressed by section 51 of the Copyright, Designs and Patents Act 1988 which states that it is not an infringement of the copyright in a design document (which is defined to mean drawings, written descriptions, photographs and computer data) to make an article to the design represented in the document or to copy such an article. Thus, copying a silicon chip no longer infringes the copyright in the drawings and photographs used in its manufacture.

Largely as a result of pressure from the United States which enacted its own protection for semiconductor products in 1984, the Semiconductor Chip Protection Act, the European Community issued a Directive which led to the Semiconductor Products (Protection of Topography) Regulations 1987 which came into force on 7 November 1987. These regulations gave a right (called a 'topography right') in the layout of an integrated circuit. However, with the advent of the Copyright, Designs and Patents Act 1988, it was decided to replace these regulations with an amended version of the design right by the Design Right (Semiconductor Regulations) 1989, which came into force on 1 August 1989. The new right, referred to below as the 'semiconductor design right' draws heavily from Part III of the Copyright, Designs and Patents Act 1988 which deals with the unregistered design right, but with some differences as far as semiconductor topographies are concerned. Before considering how semiconductor products are dealt with, a brief description of the unregistered design right will be helpful.

THE DESIGN RIGHT

Before the Copyright, Designs and Patents Act 1988 came into force, the law concerning the protection of designs was in a mess. A design could be protected by registration if it had eye-appeal. If such a design was not registered, it could be protected through the artistic copyright subsisting in any drawings from which articles to the design were made. However, if the design was potentially registrable, this protection was limited to fifteen years. A ridiculous anomaly was that a design which was purely functional and which was not registrable could be protected through its drawings for the full period of copyright provided a layperson could recognise articles made to the design from the drawing (that is, the drawing looked like the articles). The *British Leyland* case is an example of the difficulty faced by judges in dealing with design law and artistic copyright (bearing in mind a drawing does not have to display any artistic merit to be protected by copyright and even drawings of purely functional items were protected).

The Copyright, Designs and Patents Act 1988 set out to correct the anomaly and to remove copyright protection via the medium of drawings (and other design documents including data stored in a computer) from designs. The registered system of designs was retained, with certain amendments which included extending the maximum period of protection from 15 to 25 years and changing the requirement for aesthetic quality. However, in addition, a new design right was created by the Act which gives protection to designs which are primarily functional in character. This design right is not subject to registration and has many similarities to copyright. It is not a monopoly right but a right to prevent copying.

The design right is a property right which subsists in an original design. A 'design' is, by section 213(2), 'the design of any aspect of the shape or configuration (whether internal or external) of the whole or part of an article'. As noted above, there are some similarities between the design right and copyright and, like copyright, the design right is automatic, does not depend on registration but requires some form of tangible expression. There are qualification requirements, and the design must be 'original' for the right to subsist. However, there are differences.

Original designs

A design is not original if it is commonplace in the relevant design field at the time of its creation. This is probably a more stringent test than is the case with copyright (where originality means that the work should have originated from the author, be the result of skill and judgment and have not been copied from another work). Indeed, in a case on the design right, *C & H Engineering v F Klucznik & Sons Ltd* [1992] FSR 421, the judge considered a two-stage test for originality should be used. First, was the design original in a copyright sense, and second, was the design not commonplace at the time of its creation? The overall result seemed not far removed from the novelty requirement for registered designs though perhaps slightly less stringent. However, subsequent cases show that novelty is not required.

The meaning of 'commonplace' has been considered in a number of other cases on the design right. In *Ocular Sciences Ltd v Aspect Vision Care Ltd* [1997] RPC 289, in the Patents Court, Mr Justice Laddie pointed out that the word is not one previously used in United Kingdom law but derives from the European Directive on the legal protection of semiconductor topographies. Whilst not wanting to paraphrase a word used in a statute, Laddie J liked counsel's submission that any design which is 'trite, trivial, common-or-garden, hackneyed or of the type which would excite no peculiar attention in those in the relevant art is likely to be commonplace'. However, and in line with the semiconductor Directive, he confirmed that a design which is made up of a number of such features need not necessarily itself be commonplace. For protection, the combination must itself not be commonplace and this could be so even if the constituent parts are trivial or mundane.

In *Farmers Build Ltd v Carier Bulk Materials Handling Ltd* [1999] RPC 461, the Court of Appeal held that Laddie J was correct in not trying to formulate a precise definition of 'commonplace'. Lord Justice Mummery said that the word ought to be interpreted narrowly rather than broadly, given the relatively short life of the design right (the same sentiment must apply to semiconductors). He said that Parliament cannot have intended the test to be one of novelty otherwise it would have used a test such as that which applies to registered designs. Furthermore, other concepts from the law of registered designs such as 'variants commonly used in the trade' should not be used when judging whether a design is commonplace.

Mummery LJ considered the purposes underlying the design right which are equally applicable to semiconductor protection. One purpose was to guard against situations were even a short-term protection would create practical difficulties, for example, where substantial similarity of designs could give rise to a suspicion of copying even though the similarity was an inevitable consequence of the functional nature of the article for which the design was intended to be applied. He said that, as well as originating from the designer, the design must, in some respects, be different from other designs applied to similar articles. This required an objective comparative exercise which would including hearing evidence from experts pointing out similarities and differences between designs and explaining their significance.

The more similar designs, the more likely the one under scrutiny was commonplace and this was especially so if there was a causal link such as copying. If a number of designers working independently produce very similar designs by coincidence, the most likely explanation is that there is only one way of designing the article and the design can fairly and reasonably be said to be commonplace. However, if there are aspects of the plaintiff's design not found in other designs in the design field in question but which are found in the defendant's design, the court would be entitled to conclude that design was not commonplace.

Thus, in terms of semiconductor products, by their very nature, many independently created designs may have some similarities. Also, such designs are likely to have some distinguishing features not found in other topographies. Furthermore, a new topography may be the result of a combination of commonplace elements which have not been combined in precisely the same way before. The presence of distinguishing features, even though they may not account for a large proportion of the design, may be sufficient to satisfy the test that the design of the topography is not commonplace. If the narrow approach to 'commonplace' is taken as suggested by Mummery LJ, it is likely that most new designs of semiconductor topographies will be original and not commonplace if they are independently designed, and even if the design has some familiarity (which is almost inevitable) compared with designs which have already been put into circulation.

The design right applies to any aspect of the shape or configuration of the whole or part of an article; it does not apply to the article itself. Basically, for the design right to apply to a shape or configuration, it must be original (not commonplace) and it must be in some tangible form, that is, recorded in a design document (alternatively, an article must have been made to the design) and the qualification requirements must be satisfied. A design document includes data stored in a computer. The exceptions are similar to, but not identical with, those which apply to registered designs, and can be justified on the basis that they prevent the right from becoming too strong or from working to the disadvantage of consumers requiring spare parts (compare to the *British Leyland* case discussed in Chapter 10). A further exception is surface decoration which lies firmly within the scope of registered designs. The qualification requirements may be satisfied in one of three ways, first by reference to the designer (the term 'designer' is used here rather than 'author'; basically the two terms are equivalent) or, if the design is created under a commission or in the course of employment, by reference to the commissioner or employer and, finally, by reference to the person by whom and country in which articles made to the design are first marketed.

Other aspects of design right

The ownership provisions for the design right do not exactly mirror those for copyright and it is important that designers (including designers of semiconductor products), employers and commissioners are aware of the disparities. The designer is the first owner, subject to exceptions relating to employees and commissioned designs. A commissioned design must be created under a commission for money or money's worth. A further provision applies to designs which qualify for the right by reference to the first marketing of articles made to the design. In this case, the person who first markets the articles is the first owner of the right. That person must be a qualifying person exclusively authorised to put articles made to the design on the market in the United Kingdom but it does not matter if the place where the first marketing occurs is in the United Kingdom or any other member state of the European Community.

Table 11.1 shows the identity of potential first owners of the new design right (and also the equivalent right in respect of semiconductors) and copyright. For copyright, the first owner only can be either the author or his employer (ignoring Crown and parliamentary copyright). Of course, the first owner may assign the right to another immediately upon its coming into existence or may agree to do so in respect of a future design.

Table 11.1 Potential first owner of copyright and design right

Type of Right	Creator of Right Known as	Potential Identity of First Owner from Amongst			
		Creator	Employer	Comr	1st Marketer
Copyright	Author	Yes	Yes	No	No
Design right	Designer	Yes	Yes	Yes	Yes

In Table 11.1, the order of priority runs from left to right. Thus, the first owner of the design right will be the designer, unless he is an employee, in which case the employer will be the first owner, and unless the design is commissioned, in which case the commissioner will be the first owner. If the right fails to accrue because none of these persons qualifies (that is, none are citizens of, or resident in, the European Community), the design can still qualify by means of the person who first markets the design in the European Community, and, in this case, the marketer will be the first owner of the design right.

The design right provisions are not retrospective, and anything which would have qualified and which was recorded in a design document, or if an article had been to the design, before the commencement of the design right provisions (1 August 1989) is excluded. That does not prevent the design right applying to a design which was thought of before 1 August 1989 but which was not recorded until after that date, providing no articles were made to the design in the meantime. Designs created prior to 1 August 1989 are protected by the copyright subsisting in any drawings or other design documents although, under the transitional provisions, such copyright expires no later than 1 August 1999, that is, ten years after the commencement of the 1988 Act.

If there is an overlap between copyright and the design right, the design right is suppressed, leaving protection by copyright only. However, it is not an infringement of copyright in a design document (for example, a drawing, photograph or data stored in a computer) to make an article to the design, unless the article is itself an artistic work. Therefore, copying a functional article (like an exhaust pipe) does not infringe the copyright in a drawing of the article, nor in the set of co-ordinates stored in a computer describing the three-dimensional shape or configuration of the article.

SEMICONDUCTOR REGULATIONS

These regulations adopt a modified version of the design right to protect semiconductor products. The 1989 regulations, following the precedent of the 1987 regulations, protect the topography of a semiconductor being, by regulation 2(1), a design which is either:

(a) the pattern fixed, or intended to be fixed, in or upon –
   (i) a layer of a semiconductor product, or
   (ii) a layer of material in the course of and for the purpose of the manufacture of a semiconductor product, or

(b) the arrangement of the patterns fixed, or intended to be fixed, in or upon the layers of a semiconductor product in relation to one another.

'Semiconductor product' is also defined in regulation 2(1) and is:

'an article the purpose, or one of the purposes, of which is the performance of an electronic function and which consists of two or more layers, at least one of which is composed of semiconducting material and in or upon one or more of which is fixed a pattern appertaining to that or another function.'

These definitions are very technical but this should not cause any difficulties, and it is fairly plain that all integrated circuits will be covered by the regulations. Basically, the semiconductor product must have at least two layers, one of which must be of a semiconducting material such as silicon. The patterns protected can be two-dimensional or three-dimensional, and patterns used in the manufacturing process are also protected. Therefore, intermediate patterns are protected as well as the final pattern fixed in the semiconductor product. It is interesting to note that it is the patterns that are protected and not their function or purpose, although the pattern must have some function, not necessarily an electronic one. This demonstrates that the right is more akin to a copyright rather than a patent, and that the ideas and principles of which the patterns are part of their tangible expression, are not protected.

The question of originality also requires consideration of whether the semiconductor topography is commonplace at the time of its creation as discussed above. The chances are that any newly designed topography which is not simply a copy of an existing design will have at least some features or combination of features which are dissimilar to features already well-known in respect of semiconductor products. That being so, it should not be too difficult for the owner to adduce appropriate evidence to indicate that his or her design is not commonplace. Even where an independently designed topography is very similar to an existing one, it is likely to be the defendant in any infringement action that has the uphill task of proving that the differences, although slight, are not such as to encourage the court to take the view that the design is not commonplace. The Court of Appeal, in *Farmers Build v Carier*, discussed earlier, strengthens the view that most new designs of semiconductor topographies will be protected. Of course, it is likely that, given the international nature of computer technology and chip design, that the need for a topography not to be commonplace will be construed in a global context.

For semiconductor topographies, the qualification requirements are very similar to those for other forms of designs, with some minor differences. In terms of the first marketing qualification rule, normally no account is to be taken of any sale or hire, or any offer or exposure for sale or hire, which is subject to an obligation of confidence. On the international scene, there are reciprocity arrangements with several non-European Community countries such as the United States, Switzerland and Japan. Indeed, the implementation of semiconductor protection throughout Europe was largely the result of pressure from the United States, and threats from there not to offer reciprocal protection for European topographies if the protection granted did not measure up to the United States standard.

The ownership provisions are very similar to those for the normal design right, and the right given is as with normal designs and, on the whole, infringement (primary and secondary) is similarly defined. However, reproduction of the design privately for non-commercial aims is specifically excluded from the scope of the right, as is an equivalent to some of the permitted acts, including fair dealing, in copyright. An important provision introduced by the regulations allows reproduction for the purpose of analysing or evaluating the design or analysing, evaluating or teaching the concepts, processes, systems or techniques embodied in the semiconductor product. This paves the way for reverse analysis of existing semiconductors as a step in the development of new, non-competing, products. This is reinforced by regulation 8(4) which states that it is not an infringement of the semiconductor design right to create another *original* topography as a result of such analysis or evaluation, or to reproduce that other topography. At first sight, this seems to defeat the whole object of the regulations but, although reproducing the topography is permitted, reproducing by making articles is not. As regards reverse analysis, a limiting factor will be the requirement for the resultant topography to be original; that is, originating from the designer and not commonplace. Regulation 8(5) retains the substantiality test for infringement and we must assume that this will be interpreted in line with copyright law, that is, whether an important part has been copied, irrespective of its physical proportion to the whole. Secondary infringement does not apply if the article in question has previously been sold or hired within the United Kingdom by or with the licence of the owner of the right, or within the European Community or Gibraltar by or with the consent of the person who, at the time, was entitled to import it or sell it within the appropriate territory.

The duration of the semiconductor design right depends on if and when the topography is commercially exploited. Normally, the right endures for ten years from the end of the year in which it was first commercially exploited (anywhere in the world). However, if the right is not commercially exploited within the first five years of the creation of the topography, the right expires fifteen years from the time the topography was first recorded in a design document, or the time when an article was first made to the design, whichever is the earlier. Contrary to the position with other designs in which the design right subsists, licences as of right are not generally available during the last five years of the semiconductor design right. However, licences may be declared available as of right, as with other designs, as a result of a report from the Monopolies and Mergers Commission (now renamed the 'Competition Commission'). Remedies for infringement are as for the design right generally. At the time of writing, the author is not aware of any cases concerning the semiconductor topography right in the United Kingdom.

Chapter 12

Summary

Items of computer software such as user manuals and other documentation, flowcharts, specifications and the like have always been protected by copyright law and, in some circumstances, by the law of confidence. Databases too have been well protected by copyright law in the United Kingdom although the form of protection law has changed recently and a new database right has been introduced. The protection of computer programs has, however, been the subject of more controversy. We have seen that from a period when there were serious doubts as to whether computer programs were protected by copyright law from unauthorised copying, we have now reached a stage where the protection afforded to computer programs by copyright law is very strong. New or improved computer software is often the result of massive commitment in terms of skill, time and finance and without strong and effective protection there is a significant danger that the development of better and more powerful software in the future would be severely limited.

The computer software industry has often alluded to the fact that it loses considerable income because of unauthorised copying of its products. Organisation such as the Business Software Alliance, representing some of the largest software producers, point to the fact that considerably more computers are sold than software packages, leading to the only logical conclusion that many of these computers are being used to run applications programs that must have been 'pirated', otherwise their only use would be as expensive paperweights.

This disregards the fact that many computers are now sold complete with applications software (the so-called 'bundled software'). In terms of pure software piracy, that is, where popular software packages are copied and the copies sold for gain as the genuine article, the software industry has been relatively successful in stamping out this activity with the assistance of trading standards officers and organisations such as the Federation Against Software Theft (FAST). No one would argue that this form of unauthorised copying should be tolerated. Even the argument that software has been too highly priced and that reductions in prices would lead to greatly increased sales is no justification for out and out piracy, 'stealing' the fruits of another's efforts and investment.

Attention has more recently been focused on the use of computer software by business organisations and other bodies such as local authorities. The danger here is that a single-user licence will be obtained for a software package which will then be copied, and those copies used simultaneously on dozens of computers throughout the organisation. The industry has obtained Anton Piller Orders (search orders) permitting 'raids' on several corporate software users throughout the United Kingdom and Europe. Claims that some companies running several hundreds of copies of software have licences in respect of only a handful of those copies are rife. Allegedly, some very large settlements have been agreed. Again, there is no real excuse for this internal unauthorised copying by firms and businesses and the same companies would not hesitate to take action if they thought that someone was interfering with their property rights.

There has been a popular attitude that copying computer software without permission is not serious, that it is fair game. This attitude has not been helped by the computer game industry and the disproportionate charges made for some items of computer software. In many respects, the problems faced by the computer software industry mirror those which have been faced by the music industry ever since the introduction of inexpensive copying equipment. Nevertheless, copying software without permission and in the absence of a defence, is a clear infringement of a legal right and, as such, must be taken seriously. In some circumstances it can give rise to criminal penalties. The fact that, in some cases, the copyist would not have bought a legitimate copy anyway does not lessen the infringement. To a large extent the solution lies in educating computer software users and by adopting more sensible licence agreements, particularly for networked software and multiple-user situations. The benefits of using legitimate software should be spelt out, such as support (this could be vastly improved in some cases) and the availability of updates and enhancements at reasonable prices. However, threats made by pressure groups representing software copyright owners, 'requiring' organisations to carry out software audits to prevent a suspicion of unauthorised copying or use are very questionable and, possibly, counter-productive.

Now that the piracy problem has been contained (subject to the growing threat of copying over the Internet) and the internal copying in businesses is being tackled, the future will see a shift in attention from straightforward duplication of software to the scope and extent of copyright protection. Several issues are becoming of increasing importance, as evidenced by recent case law, being:

- the position regarding ex-employee computer analysts and programmers, and what use they can make of their knowledge of their previous employer's computer programs either for themselves or for new employers;
- whether non-literal elements of computer programs such as program structure and user interfaces are protected by copyright law;
- to what extent copyright protects ancillary items such as screen displays and computer output; and
- under what circumstances is reverse analysis of computer programs permitted in order to discover the ideas and principles underlying a computer program, or for the purposes of achieving interoperability?

Other points of note concern the question of modification by the lawful user of a computer program, and whether the body of legal principle associated with non-derogation from grant and implied licences will be extended to computer software in the face of non-modification clauses in licence agreements or whether, in line with recent developments, this body of law will be severely curtailed.

Changes to copyright law as a result of the implementation of the Directive on the legal protection of computer programs and the cases of *Richardson v Flanders* and *Ibcos Computers v Barclays Mercantile* have gone some way to resolving a number of these issues. Even so, considerable doubt remains and further case law is needed to provide greater clarification of the interaction between copyright law and computer software. For example, some parts of the judgments in the cases above are difficult to reconcile, particularly in respect of the views of the respective judges as to the applicability of United States case law. The one thing that the software industry wants above anything else is certainty and predictability. Software companies must be able to assess whether their intended actions will infringe the rights of others. Judges must bear this in mind: an uncertain law is a bad law.

The copyright protection of databases may have been prejudiced as far as some databases are concerned following implementation of the Directive on the legal protection of databases. Even so, the new database right should help to boost protection and provide, in many cases, an ancillary and alternative form of protection.

Whilst intellectual property rights circumscribe and define the property owned, it is a perfectly legitimate aim of commercial enterprise to get as near as is legally possible to a successful product belonging to a competing business. If a patented invention is very successful, competitors will scrutinise the patent specification and claims to see if they can make a rival product which is as close to the invention as possible but without infringing the patent.

Case

Improver Corpn v Raymond Industries Ltd [1991] FSR 223

The plaintiff was the proprietor of a patent for a device, called the 'Epilady', which was used for removing hair from arms and legs. The patent specification and claims referred to a helical spring which was rotated to pluck hairs. The defendant imported and distributed a device which operated in a similar way called 'Smooth & Silky'.

It was held that the helical spring was an essential element of the patent and the fact the defendant's device used an elastomeric rod instead, even though this had no material effect on how the invention worked, indicated that the defendant's device did not infringe the patent. The skilled man reading the patent specification and claim would have considered that the patentee had not intended to include such a variant. (However, a different result was achieved in Germany in respect of the same invention.)

This is also the case with works of copyright. Unless copyright law prohibits the doing of an act, anyone may perform the act, even a rival, and make use of the information gained to make another work even if it competes with the original work, providing that the copyright in the original has not been infringed in the process. Even if the copyright appears, at first sight, to have been infringed, it may be that an exception to infringement applies, such as the fair dealing exceptions or the decompilation exception now added to United Kingdom copyright law. Of course, care must also be taken not to infringe any rights other than copyright which may subsist in the program.

Copyright law now more clearly recognises the rights of competitors and producers of comparable products by effectively removing protection from interfaces and allowing access to them by virtue of the decompilation exception to infringement. However, the exception is tightly drawn and would-be decompilers must be careful not to step outside its tight confines. Other problems now loom on the horizon such as how to deal with intellectual property rights in products that have become industry standards. Copyright owners of software such as operating systems like Windows are put in a very powerful position if their system becomes the *de facto* standard, far more powerful than should be the case for a non-monopoly right such as copyright. The opportunities for abuse of the right are manifold. There remain many challenges ahead for copyright law. The decision of the European Court of Justice in the TV listings case indicates how the law is likely to develop in this area. Abuses of intellectual property rights are unlikely to go unchecked and competition law in the

United Kingdom will be significantly strengthened soon when the Competition Act 1998 comes into force.

SOFTWARE LICENCES

Most software is obtained and used under a licence agreement, and a consideration of the copyright protection of computer software is important in analysing and interpreting the terms in the licence agreement. Where the licence agreement is negotiable, both parties should be aware of the copyright implications of what they agree to include in their formal agreement. Particular attention should be given to the following terms in software licences.

- The nature of the agreement. Is the agreement a licence or an assignment of the copyright? Is it a hybrid agreement, being part licence, part sale of goods? Is it covered by the Sale of Goods Act 1979, the Supply of Goods and Service Act 1982 and/or the Unfair Contract Terms Act 1977 or is it really an agreement *sui generis*?
- If the agreement is in the form of a licence is it an exclusive or non-exclusive licence? What is its duration and what is the scope of the acts which can be performed in respect of the software?
- What is the position regarding liability for loss or damage caused by defective software? Since the cases of *The Salvage Association v CAP Financial Services Ltd* [1995] FSR 654 and *St Albans & District Council v International Computers Ltd* [1995] FSR 686 (confirmed in the Court of Appeal as regards the question of liability [1997] FSR 251); it is clear that clauses limiting liability for defective software must be reasonable to be effective. The 'Millennium Bug' has focused attention on the dangers of software 'bugs'.
- If the software is to be specially written or modified for the client, to whom will the copyright in the software belong? Does provision need to be made to alter the basic rules of copyright ownership?
- What is to be provided under the agreement? How many copies of the programs and documentation are to be

delivered? Is any training provided? Will the programs be provided in object code form only or will the source code and other material also be provided?

- Can the person acquiring the software maintain and modify it personally or by using a third party? If this is not permitted, are the arrangements for maintenance, modifications and enhancements reasonable?
- If the person acquiring the software can maintain and modify it, to whom does the copyright in any modifications belong?
- If the source code is not provided, are there any arrangements for escrow in respect of the source code and other materials essential for the future maintenance and modification of the software?
- Is there an indemnity in favour of the person acquiring the software should it be found that the software or its use infringes a third party's intellectual property rights?
- Is there an arbitration clause in case of a dispute under the agreement? It is usual for provision to be made for the appointment of an arbitrator by the President, for the time being, of the British Computer Society should the parties be unable to agree upon an arbitrator. The advantage of having a dispute referred to arbitration is that the arbitrator will have legal knowledge as well as being well versed in computer technology.
- As an alternative to an arbitration clause is there provision for using alternative dispute resolution (ADR)? This form of dealing with disputes is particularly suited to the software industry. A number of techniques may be used, the most common being mediation. The Centre for Dispute Resolution, Princes House, 95 Gresham Street, London EC2V 7NA supplies standard ADR clauses.
- What is the applicable law? Is the agreement subject to the law of England and Wales or some other jurisdiction? Do the courts in England and Wales have sole jurisdiction over disputes?

Of course, other terms will also be found in agreements for the acquisition of computer software, for example, terms dealing with liability for defects and consequential 'down-time' loss. As far as copyright law is concerned, it is important that the precise nature and subject matter of the agreement is clearly dealt with, and that both parties know their relative duties and responsibilities under the agreement. Terms which are vague or unreasonable must be avoided at all costs. A basic legal principle adhered to by the courts is that an ambiguous term will be construed in the way which is least favourable to the party seeking to rely on it. It is not uncommon for terms to contradict other terms, and for there to be inconsistencies in such agreements. The basic rule must be to determine the precise nature of the right or interest in the copyright materials which stands at the root of the contract and to construct the agreement from that. If the agreement includes a licence to use the programs, it should specify the duration of the licence agreement (even if it be for the duration of the copyright), and which of the acts restricted by the copyright can be performed by the other party, for example, whether modification can be carried out by the person obtaining the software under the agreement. Care must be taken not to include terms that are void by the operation of copyright law or otherwise. In particular, the effect of section 296A of the Copyright, Designs and Patents Act 1988 must be taken account of. The same applies to section 296B in relation to databases.

Finally, it must be noted that a contractual agreement is not limited to the acts restricted by the copyright, and other restrictions can be imposed upon the use of the software, for example the number of computers the software can be used upon concurrently.

SOLUTION TO SAMPLE PROBLEM FROM CHAPTER 1

In Chapter 1 an example was given of an estimator, Betty Bliss, who through an interest in computer technology, ended up being involved in the development of a computer system to assist in the preparation of estimates for construction schemes. Betty later decided to set up in business on her own account and to write software for the construction industry, performing similar functions to those performed by the programs she was involved with when she was employed by Zenith Construction plc. In view of the various discussions throughout this book on the scope of copyright protection (and also considering the law of confidence where appropriate) the advice to Betty must be along the following lines.

Advice to Betty Bliss

Let us deal first with the small programs written in BASIC which were converted by Betty to operate on the company's computers. The copyright in the original version of these programs rests with Betty. They were written in her own time and not in the course of her duties as an estimator. As regards the modifications Betty made so that the programs would operate on Zenith's computers, the copyright (if any) in the modifications would probably belong to Zenith as it is at least arguable that Betty's contract of employment had been varied orally by Zenith, giving her time off her normal duties, which Betty accepted. However, it would seem that Betty can use the original programs as she likes, including improving them and licensing the improved versions to others. The only possible proviso would be if the programs contained confidential information belonging to Zenith, such as a secret technique or formula used in the calculations performed by the programs. The technique or formula would have to be special in some way, and not merely part and parcel of an estimator's skill and experience.

As regards the main estimating programs and the database files, it is unlikely that the functions performed by the programs were extraordinary in any way, and it is probable that the system simply reflected the traditional and normal techniques used manually. That being so, the law of confidence is unlikely to prevent Betty making use of the ideas contained in the system. However, as far as copyright is concerned, Betty is in a much more difficult situation. Zenith will own the copyright in all the programs, including Betty's prototype programs, and the databases together with the 'database rights'. Again the basis for holding that Zenith own the copyright in the prototype programs is that there was a implied variation in Betty's contract of employment (it would have been better if the change in Betty's work had been expressly agreed, and a varied contract of employment with a new job description issued instead).

If Betty disassembles the COBOL programs, she will infringe copyright. Even if she wishes only to obtain details of interfaces so that she can make an interoperable program, she cannot rely on the decompilation exception to infringement as she is no longer a lawful user of the programs, having left the employment of Zenith. If Betty uses the object code program this will infringe, because a copy will be made in the computer's volatile memory whilst the program is running, and making a transient copy can still fall within the restricted act of copying. The databases are probably protected by copyright and by the database right. Although Betty only has print-outs of these, if she enters the information into her computer, either by typing it in or by using an optical character reader, and saving the information to disk, this will be making a copy and hence will infringe any copyright in the databases and any database right. Betty's retention of these files is also a breach of confidence.

The best advice to Betty is that there is nothing to prevent her making use of the ideas and principles underlying the computer estimating system, and she can develop a new program from these ideas and principles to perform the same function (providing there is nothing about the function which could be considered to be a trade secret). Betty should be advised that, as an ex-employee, if her new software bears an objective similarity to that belonging to Zenith, if she was sued for infringement of copyright and database right because of the causal connection (Betty was involved in the development of both software systems) she could bear the burden of proof. Instead of Zenith having to prove that Betty infringed their copyright and database right, Betty might have to prove that she did not, in fact, copy from the Zenith software. This could be very onerous. To reduce the possibility of this, Betty should make positive effort to make her new software look different to that produced for Zenith. In particular, if this is feasible, Betty should use a different program structure and algorithm and make sure that the screen displays are different. She should also be careful not to use the same user interface. This is because copyright extends to program structure, screen displays and, probably in the United Kingdom at least, user interfaces; the non-literal elements of the program.

Betty may face a conundrum if alternative structures, screen displays and the like are unsatisfactory when compared with the original system. For example, where the Zenith system makes use of all the best techniques. If this is so, Betty should go back to the basic ideas, and specify the system she requires to her programmer without referring to any of the details of the Zenith system and leave it up to her programmer to devise the system as he or she thinks fit, not even allowing him or her to see the Zenith system. In this way, the programmer will develop the new system independently. If there are similarities, these will be the result of chance, although Betty could still face difficulties in proof. Of course, Betty should ensure that she obtains an assignment of copyright and, if applicable, database right from the programmer. Even though she specifies the software, this may not be sufficient to make her a joint author. In any case, she will want the entire rights.

A final piece of advice to Betty would be to destroy all materials she has retained from her past employment. If Zenith obtained an Anton Piller Order (search order) and discovered these materials this would do little, in practice, to help Betty's case.

CONCLUDING REMARK

It is hoped that this book has illuminated some of the problems associated with the protection of computer software and that some helpful answers have been provided. Of course, not all the answers can be given with absolute certainty. Some can only remain speculative because of the relative newness of some of the legislation in this area, the speed of development of computer software technology and the paucity of case law in the United Kingdom though this is steadily being built up. The two major cases of *Richardson v Flanders* and *Ibcos Computers v Barclays Highland Mercantile Finance* have gone some way to clarifying the law but large, grey areas remain to be resolved. Developments in the United States give us some idea of how things may develop here, although it must be noted that things are far from settled there and that, at the end of the day, the basic keystone principle of copyright law is that it does not protect ideas (despite one judge's dislike of aphorisms such as 'copyright does not protect ideas') and, consequently, ideas and principles cannot be monopolised by rights under copyright law. It is to be hoped that judges in the United Kingdom bear this in mind when dealing with copyright disputes concerning computer software and retain a sensible balance between the copyright owner's rights, the rights of competitors and the general public interest in having a vibrant and competitive software industry.

Appendix 1

European Directive on the legal protection of computer programs

COUNCIL DIRECTIVE
of 14 May 1991
on the legal protection of computer programs

(91/250/EEC)

THE COUNCIL OF THE EUROPEAN COMMUNITIES

Having regard to the Treaty establishing the European Economic Community and in particular Article 100a thereof,

Having regard to the proposal from the Commission([1]),

In co-operation with the European Parliament([2]),

Having regard to the opinion of the Economic and Social Committee([3]).

Whereas computer programs are at present not clearly protected in all Member States by existing legislation and such protection, where it exists, has different attributes;

Whereas the development of computer programs requires the investment of considerable human, technical and financial resources while computer programs can be copied at a fraction of the cost needed to develop them independently;

Whereas computer programs are playing an increasingly important role in a broad range of industries and computer program technology can accordingly be considered as being of fundamental importance for the Community's industrial development;

(1) OJ No C 91, 12. 4. 1989, p 4 and OJ No C 320, 20. 12. 1990, p 22.
(2) OJ No C 231, 17. 9. 1990, p 78; and Decision of 17 April 1991, yet to be published in the Official Journal).
(3) OJ No C 329, 30. 12. 1989, p 4.

Whereas certain differences in the legal protection of computer programs offered by the laws of the Member States have direct and negative effects on the functioning of the common market as regards computer programs and such differences could well become greater as Member States introduce new legislation on this subject;

Whereas existing differences having such effects need to be removed and new ones prevented from arising, while differences not adversely affecting the functioning of the common market to a substantial degree need not be removed or prevented from arising;

Whereas the Community's legal framework on the protection of computer programs can accordingly in the first instance be limited to establishing that Member States should accord protection to computer programs under copyright law as literary works and, further, establishing who and what should be protected, the exclusive rights on which protected persons should be able to rely in order to authorise or prohibit certain acts and for how long the protection should apply;

Whereas, for the purpose of this Directive, the term 'computer program' shall include programs in any form, including those which are incorporated into hardware; whereas this term also includes preparatory design work leading to the development of a computer program provided that the nature of the preparatory work is such that a computer program can result from it at a later stage;

Whereas, in respect of the criteria to be applied in determining whether or not a computer program is an original work, no tests as to the qualitative or aesthetic merits of the program should be applied;

Whereas the Community is fully committed to the promotion of international standardisation;

Whereas the function of a computer program is to communicate and work together with other components of a computer system and with users and, for this purpose, a logical and, where appropriate, physical interconnection and interaction is required to permit all elements of software and hardware to work with other software and hardware and with users in all the ways in which they are intended to function;

Whereas the parts of the program which provide for such interconnection and interaction between elements of software and hardware are generally known as 'interfaces';

Whereas this functional interconnection and interaction is generally known as 'interoperability'; whereas such interoperability can be defined as the ability to exchange information and mutually to use the information which has been exchanged;

Whereas, for the avoidance of doubt, it has to be made clear that only the expression of a computer program is protected and that ideas and principles which underlie any element of a program, including those which underlie its interfaces, are not protected by copyright under this Directive;

Whereas, in accordance with this principle of copyright, to the extent that logic, algorithms and programming languages comprise ideas and principles, those ideas and principles are not protected under this Directive;

Whereas, in accordance with the legislation and jurisprudence of the Member States and the international copyright conventions, the expression of those ideas and principles is to be protected by copyright;

Whereas, for the purposes of this Directive, the term 'rental' means the making available for use, for a limited period of time and for profit-making purposes, of a computer program or a copy thereof; whereas this term does not include public lending, which, accordingly, remains outside the scope of this Directive;

Whereas, the exclusive rights of the author to prevent the unauthorised reproduction of his work have to be subject to a limited exception in the case of a computer program to allow the reproduction technically necessary for the use of that program by the lawful acquirer;

Whereas this means that the acts of loading and running necessary for the use of a copy of a program which has been lawfully acquired, and the act of correction of its errors, may not be prohibited by contract; whereas, in the absence of specific contractual provisions, including when a copy of the program has been sold, any other act necessary for the use of the copy of a program may be performed in accordance with its intended purpose by a lawful acquirer of that copy;

Whereas a person having a right to use a computer program should not be prevented from performing acts necessary to observe, study or test the functioning of the program, provided that these acts do not infringe the copyright in the program;

Whereas the unauthorised reproduction, translation, adaptation or transformation of the form of the code in which a copy of a computer program has been made available constitutes an infringement of the exclusive rights of the author;

Whereas, nevertheless, circumstances may exist when such a reproduction of the code and translation of its form within the meaning of Article 4(a) and (b) are indispensable to obtain the necessary information to achieve the interoperability of an independently created program with other programs;

Whereas it has therefore to be considered that in these limited circumstances only, performance of the acts of reproduction and translation by or on behalf of a person having a right to use a copy of the program is legitimate and compatible with fair practice and must therefore be deemed not to require the authorisation of the rightholder;

Whereas an objective of this exception is to make it possible to connect all components of a computer system, including those of different manufacturers, so that they can work together;

Whereas such an exception to the author's exclusive rights may not be used in a way which prejudices the legitimate interests of the rightholder or which conflicts with a normal exploitation of the program;

Whereas, in order to remain in accordance with the provisions of the Berne Convention for the Protection of Literary and Artistic Works, the term of protection should be the life of the author and fifty years from the first of January of the year following the year of his death, or in the case of an anonymous or pseudonymous work, 50 years from the first of January of the year following the year in which the work is first published;

Whereas protection of computer programs under copyright laws should be without prejudice to the application, in appropriate cases, of other forms of protection; whereas, however, any contractual provisions contrary to Article 6 or to the exceptions provided for in Article 5(2) and (3) should be null and void;

Whereas the provisions of this Directive are without prejudice to the application of the competition rules under Articles 85 and 86 of the Treaty if a dominant supplier refuses to make information available which is necessary for interoperability as defined in this Directive;

Whereas the provisions of this Directive should be without prejudice to specific requirements of Community law already enacted in respect of the publication of interfaces in the telecommunications sector or Council Decisions relating to standardisation in the field of information technology and telecommunications;

Whereas this Directive does not affect derogations provided for under national legislation in accordance with the Berne Convention on points not covered by this Directive.

HAS ADOPTED THIS DIRECTIVE:

Article 1

Object of protection

1.   In accordance with the provisions of this Directive, Member States shall protect computer programs, by copyright, as literary works within the meaning of the Berne Convention for the Protection of Literary and Artistic Works. For the purposes of this Directive, the term 'computer programs' shall include their preparatory design material.

2.   Protection in accordance with this Directive shall apply to the expression in any form of a computer program. Ideas and principles which underlie any element of a computer program, including those which underlie its interfaces, are not protected by copyright under this Directive.

3.   A computer program shall be protected if it is original in the sense that it is the author's own intellectual creation. No other criteria shall be applied to determine its eligibility for protection.

Article 2

Authorship of computer programs

1.   The author of a computer program shall be the natural person or group of natural persons who has created the program or, where the legislation of the Member State permits, the legal person designated as the rightholder by that legislation. Where collective works are recognised by the legislation of a Member State, the person considered by the legislation of the Member State to have created the work shall be deemed to be its author.

2.   In respect of a computer program created by a group of natural persons jointly, the exclusive rights shall be owned jointly.

3.   Where a computer program is created by an employee in the execution of his duties or following the instructions given by his employer, the employer exclusively shall be entitled to exercise all economic rights in the program so created, unless otherwise provided by contract.

Article 3

Beneficiaries of protection

Protection shall be granted to all natural or legal persons eligible under national copyright legislation as applied to literary works.

Article 4

Restricted acts

Subject to the provisions of Articles 5 and 6, the exclusive rights of the rightholder within the meaning of Article 2, shall include the right to do or to authorise:

(a) the permanent or temporary reproduction of a computer program by any means and in any form, in part or in whole. Insofar as loading, displaying, running, transmission or storage of the computer program necessitate such reproduction, such acts shall be subject to authorisation by the rightholder;

(b) the translation, adaptation, arrangement and any other alteration of a computer program and the reproduction of the results thereof, without prejudice to the rights of the person who alters the program;

(c) any form of distribution to the public, including the rental of the original computer program or of copies thereof. The first sale in the Community of a copy of a program by the rightholder or with his consent shall exhaust the distribution right within the Community of that copy, with the exception of the right to control further rental of the program or a copy thereof.

Article 5

Exceptions to the restricted acts

1.   In the absence of specific contractual provisions, the acts referred to in Article 4(a) and (b) shall not require authorisation by the rightholder where they are necessary for the use of the computer program by the lawful acquirer in accordance with its intended purpose, including for error correction.

2.   The making of a back-up copy by a person having a right to use the computer program may not be prevented by contract insofar as it is necessary for that use.

3.   The person having a right to use a copy of a computer program shall be entitled, without the authorisation of the rightholder, to observe, study or test the functioning of the program in order to determine the ideas and principles which underlie any element of the program if he does so while performing any of the acts of loading, displaying, running, transmitting or storing the program which he is entitled to do.

Article 6

Decompilation

1.   The authorisation of the rightholder shall not be required where reproduction of the code and translation of its form within the meaning of Article 4(a) and (b) are indispensable to obtain the information necessary to achieve the interoperability of an independently created computer program with other programs, provided that the following conditions are met:

(a) these acts are performed by the licensee or by another person having a right to use a copy of a program, or on their behalf by a person authorised to do so;
(b) the information necessary to achieve interoperability has not previously been readily available to the persons referred to in subparagraph (a); and
(c) these acts are confined to the parts of the original program which are necessary to achieve interoperability.

2.   The provisions of paragraph 1 shall not permit the information obtained through its application:

(a) to be used for goals other than to achieve the interoperability of the independently created computer program;
(b) to be given to others, except when necessary for the interoperability of the independently created computer program; or
(c) to be used for the development, production or marketing of a computer program substantially similar in its expression, or for any other act which infringes copyright.

3.   In accordance with the provisions of the Berne Convention for the protection of Literary and Artistic Works, the provisions of this Article may not be interpreted in such a way as to allow its application to be used in a manner which unreasonably prejudices the rightholder's legitimate interests or conflicts with a normal exploitation of the computer program.

Article 7

Special measures of protection

1.   Without prejudice to the provisions of Articles 4, 5 and 6, Member States shall provide, in accordance with their national legislation, appropriate remedies against a person committing any of the acts listed in subparagraphs (a), (b) and (c) below:

(a) any act of putting into circulation a copy of a computer program knowing, or having reason to believe, that it is an infringing copy;

(b) the possession, for commercial purposes, of a copy of a computer program knowing, or having reason to believe, that it is an infringing copy;

(c) any act of putting into circulation, or the possession for commercial purposes of, any means the sole intended purpose of which is to facilitate the unauthorised removal or circumvention of any technical device which may have been applied to protect a computer program.

2.   Any infringing copy of a computer program shall be liable to seizure in accordance with the legislation of the Member State concerned.

3.   Member States may provide for the seizure of any means referred to in paragraph 1(c).

Article 8

Term of protection

1.   Protection shall be granted for the life of the author and for fifty years after his death or after the death of the last surviving author; where the computer program is an anonymous, or pseudonymous work, or where a legal person is designated as the author by national legislation in accordance with Article 1(1), the term of protection shall be fifty years from the time that the computer program is first lawfully made available to the public. The term of protection shall be deemed to begin on the first of January of the year following the above-mentioned events.

2.   Member States which already have a term of protection longer than that provided for in paragraph 1 are allowed to maintain their present term until such time as the term of protection for copyright works is harmonised by Community law in a more general way.

Article 9

Continued application of other legal provisions

1.   The provisions of this Directive shall be without prejudice to any other legal provisions such as those concerning patent rights, trade-marks, unfair competition, trade secrets, protection of semi-conductor products or the law of contract. Any contractual provisions contrary to Article 6 or to the exceptions provided for in Article 5(2) and (3) shall be null and void.

2.   The provisions of this Directive shall apply also to programs created before 1 January 1993 without prejudice to any acts concluded and rights acquired before that date.

Article 10

Final provisions

1.   Member States shall bring into force the laws, regulations and administrative provisions necessary to comply with this Directive before 1 January 1993.

When Member States adopt these measures the latter shall contain a reference to this Directive or shall be accompanied by such reference on the occasion of their official publication. The methods of making such a reference shall be laid down by the Member States.

2.   Member States shall communicate to the Commission the provisions of national law, which they adopt in the field governed by this Directive.

Article 11

This Directive is addressed to the Member States.

Done at Brussels, 14 May 1991.

For the Council

The President

J.F. POOS

Appendix 2

European Directive on the legal protection of databases

COUNCIL DIRECTIVE
of 11 March 1996
on the legal protection of databases
(96/9/EC)

THE EUROPEAN PARLIAMENT AND THE COUNCIL OF THE EUROPEAN UNION,

Having regard to the Treaty establishing the European Community, and in particular Article 57(2), 66 and 100a thereof,

Having regard to the proposal from the Commission[1],

Having regard to the opinion of the Economic and Social Committee[2],

Acting in accordance with the procedure laid down in Article 189b of the Treaty[3],

1. Whereas databases are at present not sufficiently protected in all Member States by existing legislation; whereas such protection, where it exists, has different attributes;

2. Whereas such differences in the legal protection of databases offered by the legislation of the Member States have direct negative effects on the functioning of the internal market as regards databases and in particular on the freedom of natural and legal persons

---

(1) OJ No C 156, 23. 6. 1992, p 4 and OJ No C 308, 15.11. 1993, p 1.
(2) OJ No C 19, 25. 1. 1993, p 3.
(3) Opinion of the European Parliament of 23 June 1993 (OJ No C 194, 19. 7. 1993, p 144), Common Position of the Council of 10 July 1995 (OJ No C 288, 30. 10. 1995, p 14), Decision of the European Parliament of 14 December 1995 (OJ No C 17, 22. 1. 1996) and Council Decision of 26 February 1996.

to provide on-line database goods and services on the basis of harmonized legal arrangements throughout the Community; whereas such differences could well become more pronounced as Member States introduce new legislation in this field, which is now taking on an increasingly international dimension;

3.   Whereas existing differences distorting the functioning of the internal market need to be removed and new ones prevented from arising, while differences not adversely affecting the functioning of the internal market or the development of an information market within the Community need not be removed or prevented from arising:

4.   Whereas copyright protection for databases exists in varying forms in the Member States according to legislation or case-law, and whereas, if differences in legislation in the scope and conditions of protection remain between the Member States, such unharmonized intellectual property rights can have the effect of preventing the free movement of goods or services within the Community;

5.   Whereas copyright remains an appropriate form of exclusive right for authors who have created databases;

6.   Whereas, nevertheless, in the absence of a harmonized system of unfair-competition legislation or of case-law, other measures are required in addition to prevent the unauthorized extraction and/ or re-utilization of the contents of a database;

7.   Whereas the making of databases requires the investment of considerable human, technical and financial resources while such databases can be copied or accessed at a fraction of the cost needed to design them independently;

8.   Whereas the unauthorized extraction and/or re-utilization of the contents of a database constitute acts which can have serious economic and technical consequences;

9.   Whereas databases are a vital tool in the development of an information market within the Community; whereas this tool will also be of use in many other fields;

10.   Whereas the exponential growth, in the Community and world-wide, in the amount of information generated and processed annually in all sectors of commerce and industry calls for investment in all the Member States in advanced information processing systems;

11.   Whereas there is at present a very great imbalance in the level of investment in the database sector both as between the Member States and between the Community and the world's largest database-producing third countries;

12. Whereas such an investment in modern information storage and processing systems will not take place within the Community unless a stable and uniform legal protection regime is introduced for the protection of the rights of makers of databases;

13. Whereas this Directive protects collections, sometimes called 'compilations', of works, data or other materials which are arranged, stored and accessed by means which include electronic, electro-magnetic or electro-optical processes or analogous processes;

14. Whereas protection under this Directive should be extended to cover non-electronic databases;

15. Whereas the criteria used to determine whether a database should be protected by copyright should be defined to the fact that the selection or the arrangement of the contents of the database is the author's own intellectual creation; whereas such protection should cover the structure of the database;

16. Whereas no criterion other than originality in the sense of the author's intellectual creation should be applied to determine the eligibility of the database for copyright protection, and in particular no aesthetic or qualitative criteria should be applied;

17. Whereas the term 'database' should be understood to include literary, artistic, musical or other collections of works or collections of other material such as texts, sound, images, numbers, facts, and data; whereas it should cover collections of independent works, data or other materials which are systematically or methodically arranged and can be individually accessed; whereas this means that a recording or an audiovisual, cinematographic, literary or musical work as such does not fall within the scope of this Directive;

18. Whereas this Directive is without prejudice to the freedom of authors to decide whether, or in what manner, they will allow their works to be included in a database, in particular whether or not the authorization given is exclusive; whereas the protection of databases by the *sui generis* right is without prejudice to existing rights over their contents, and whereas in particular where an author or the holder of a related right permits some of his works or subject matter to be included in a database pursuant to a non-exclusive agreement, a third party may make use of those works or subject matter subject to the required consent of the author or of the holder of the related right without the *sui generis* right of the maker of the database being invoked to prevent him doing so, on condition that those works or subject matter are neither extracted from the database nor re-utilized on the basis thereof;

19.   Whereas, as a rule, the compilation of several recordings of musical performances on a CD does not come within the scope of this Directive, both because, as a compilation, it does not meet the conditions for copyright protection and because it does not represent a substantial enough investment to be eligible under the *sui generis* right;

20.   Whereas protection under this Directive may also apply to the materials necessary for the operation or consultation of certain databases such as thesaurus and indexation systems;

21.   Whereas the protection provided for in this Directive relates to databases in which works, data or other materials have been arranged systematically or methodically; whereas it is not necessary for those materials to have been physically stored in an organized manner;

22.   Whereas electronic databases within the meaning of this Directive may also include devices such as CD-ROM and CD-i;

23.   Whereas the term 'database' should not be taken to extend to computer programs used in the making or operation of a database, which are protected by Council Directive 91/250/EEC of 14 May 1991 on the legal protection of computer programs[1];

24.   Whereas the rental and lending of databases in the field of copyright and related rights are governed exclusively by Council Directive 92/100/EEC of 19 November 1992 on rental right and lending right and on certain rights related to copyright in the field of intellectual property[2];

25.   Whereas the term of copyright is already governed by Council Directive 93/98/EEC of 29 October 1993 harmonizing the term of protection of copyright and certain related rights[3];

26.   Whereas works protected by copyright and subject matter protected by related rights, which are incorporated into a database, remain nevertheless protected by the respective exclusive rights and may not be incorporated into, or extracted from, the database without the permission of the rightholder or his successors in title;

27.   Whereas copyright in such works and related rights in subject matter thus incorporated into a database are in no way affected by the existence of a separate right in the selection or arrangement of these works and subject matter in a database;

---

(1)   OJ No L122, 17. 5. 1991, p 42. Directive as last amended by Directive 93/98/EEC (OJ No L 290, 24. 11. 1993, p 9.)
(2)   OJ No L 346, 27. 11. 1992, p 61.
(3)   OJ No L 290, 24. 11. 1993, p 9.

28. Whereas the moral rights of the natural person who created the database belong to the author and should be exercised according to the legislation of the Member States and the provisions of the Berne Convention for the protection of Literary and Artistic Works; whereas such moral rights remain outside the scope of this Directive;

29. Whereas the arrangements applicable to databases created by employees are left to the discretion of the Member States; whereas, therefore nothing in this Directive prevents Member States from stipulating in their legislation that where a database is created by an employee in the execution of his duties or following the instructions given by his employer, the employer exclusively shall be entitled to exercise all economic rights in the database so created, unless otherwise provided by contract;

30. Whereas the author's exclusive rights should include the right to determine the way in which his work is exploited and by whom, and in particular to control the distribution of his work to unauthorized persons;

31. Whereas the copyright protection of databases includes making databases available by means other than the distribution of copies;

32. Whereas Member States are required to ensure that their national provisions are at least materially equivalent in the case of such acts subject to restrictions as are provided for by this Directive;

33. Whereas the question of exhaustion of the right of distribution does not arise in the case of on-line databases, which come within the field of provision of services; whereas this also applies with regard to a material copy of such a database made by the user of such a service with the consent of the rightholder; whereas, unlike CD-ROM or CD-i, where the intellectual property is incorporated in a material medium, namely an item of goods, every on-line service is in fact an act which will have to be subject to authorization where the copyright so provides;

34. Whereas, nevertheless, once the rightholder has chosen to make available a copy of the database to a user, whether by an on-line service or by other means of distribution, that lawful user must be able to access and use the database for the purposes and in the way set out in the agreement with the rightholder, even if such access and use necessitate performance of otherwise restricted acts;

35. Whereas a list should be drawn up of exceptions to restricted acts, taking into account the fact that copyright as covered by this

Directive applies only to the selection or arrangements of the contents of a database; whereas Member States should be given the option of providing for such exceptions in certain cases; whereas, however, this option should be exercised in accordance with the Berne Convention and to the extent that the exceptions relate to the structure of the database; whereas a distinction should be drawn between exceptions for private use and exceptions for reproduction for private purposes, which concerns provisions under national legislation of some Member States on levies on blank media or recording equipment;

36.   Whereas the term 'scientific research' within the meaning of this Directive covers both the natural sciences and the human sciences;

37.   Whereas Article 10(1) of the Berne Convention is not affected by this Directive;

38.   Whereas the increasing use of digital recording technology exposes the database maker to the risk that the contents of his database may be copied and rearranged electronically, without his authorization, to produce a database of identical content which, however, does not infringe any copyright in the arrangement of his database;

39.   Whereas, in addition to aiming to protect the copyright in the original selection or arrangement of the contents of a database, this Directive seeks to safeguard the position of makers of databases against misappropriation of the results of the financial and professional investment made in obtaining and collecting the contents by protecting the whole or substantial parts of a database against certain acts by a user or competitor;

40.   Whereas the object of this *sui generis* right is to ensure protection of any investment in obtaining, verifying or presenting the contents of a database for the limited duration of the right; whereas such investment may consist in the deployment of financial resources and/or the expending of time, effort and energy.

41.   Whereas the objective of the *sui generis* right is to give the maker of a database the option of preventing the unauthorized extraction and/or re-utilization of all or a substantial part of the contents of that database; whereas the maker of a database is the person who takes the initiative and the risk of investing, whereas this excludes subcontractors in particular from the definition of maker;

42.   Whereas the special right to prevent unauthorized extraction and/or re-utilization relates to acts by the user which go beyond

his legitimate rights and thereby harm the investment; whereas the right to prohibit extraction and/or re-utilization of all or a substantial part of the contents relates not only to the manufacture of a parasitical competing product but also to any user who, through his acts, causes significant detriment, evaluated qualitatively or quantitatively, to the investment;

43.   Whereas, in the case of on-line transmission, the right to prohibit re-utilization is not exhausted either as regards the database or as regards a material copy of the database or of part thereof made by the addressee of the transmission with the consent of the rightholder;

44.   Whereas, when on-screen display of the contents of a database necessitates the permanent or temporary transfer of all or a substantial part of such contents to another medium, that act should be subject to authorization by the rightholder;

45.   Whereas the right to prevent unauthorized extraction and/or re-utilization does not in any way constitute an extension of copyright protection to mere facts or data;

46.   Whereas the existence of a right to prevent the unauthorized extraction and/or re-utilization of the whole or a substantial part of works, data or materials from a database should not give rise to the creation of a new right in the works, data or materials themselves;

47.   Whereas, in the interests of competition between suppliers of information products and services, protection by the *sui generis* right must not be afforded in such a way as to facilitate abuses of a dominant position, in particular as regards the creation and distribution of new products and services which have an intellectual, documentary, technical, economic or commercial added value; whereas, therefore, the provisions of this Directive are without prejudice to the application of Community or national competition rules;

48.   Whereas the objective of this Directive, which is to afford an appropriate and uniform level of protection of databases as a means to secure the remuneration of the maker of the database, is different from the aim of Directive 95/46/EC of the European Parliament and of the Council of 24 October 1995 on the protection of individuals in regard to the processing of personal data and on the free movement of such data([1]), which is to guarantee free circulation of personal data on the basis of harmonized rules designed to protect fundamental rights, notably the right to privacy which is recognized

(1)   OJ NO l 281, 23. 11. 1995, p 31.

in Article 8 of the European Convention for the Protection of Human Rights and Fundamental Freedoms; whereas the provisions of this Directive are without prejudice to data protection legislation;

49. Whereas, notwithstanding the right to prevent extraction and/ or re-utilization of all or a substantial part of a database, it should be laid down that the maker of a database or rightholder may not prevent a lawful user of the database from extracting and re-utilizing insubstantial parts; whereas, however, that user may not unreasonably prejudice either the legitimate interests of the holder of the *sui generis* right or the holder of copyright or a related right in respect of the works or subject matter contained in the database;

50. Whereas the Member States should be given the option of providing for exceptions to the right to prevent the unauthorized extraction and/or re-utilization of a substantial part of the contents of a database in the case of extraction for private purposes, for the purposes of illustration or teaching or scientific research, or where extraction and/or re-utilization are/is carried out in the interests of public security or for the purposes of an administrative or judicial procedure; whereas such operations must not prejudice the exclusive rights of the maker to exploit the database and their purpose must not be commercial;

51. Whereas the Member States, where they avail themselves of the option to permit a lawful user of a database to extract a substantial part of the contents for the purposes of illustration for teaching or scientific research, may limit that permission to certain categories of teaching or scientific research institution;

52. Whereas those Member States which have specific rules provided for a right comparable to the *sui generis* right provided for in this Directive should be permitted to retain, as far as the new right is concerned, the exceptions traditionally specified by such rules;

53. Whereas the burden of proof regarding the date of completion of the making of a database lies with the maker of the database;

54. Whereas the burden of proof that the criteria exist for concluding that a substantial modification of the contents of a database is to be regarded as a substantial new investment lies with the maker of the database resulting from such investment;

55. Whereas a substantial new investment involving a new term of protection may include a substantial verification of the contents of the database;

56. Whereas the right to prevent unauthorized extraction and/or re-utilization in respect of a database should apply to databases

whose makers are national or habitual residents of third countries or to those produced by legal persons not established in a Member State, within the meaning of the Treaty, only if such third countries offer comparable protection to databases produced by nationals of a Member State or persons who have their habitual residence in the territory of the Community;

57.   Whereas, in addition to remedies provided under the legislation of the Member States for infringements of copyright or other rights, Member States should provide for appropriate remedies against unauthorized extraction and/or re-utilization of the contents of a database;

58.   Whereas, in addition to the protection given under this Directive to the structure of the database by copyright, and to its contents against unauthorized extraction and/or re-utilization under the *sui generis* right, other legal provisions in the Member States relevant to the supply of database goods and services continue to apply;

59.   Whereas this Directive is without prejudice to the application to databases composed of audiovisual works of any rules recognized by a Member State's legislation concerning the broadcasting of audio-visual programmes;

60.   Whereas some Member States currently protect under copyright arrangements databases which do not meet the criteria for eligibility for copyright protection laid down in this Directive; whereas, even if the databases concerned are eligible for protection under the right laid down in this Directive to prevent unauthorized extraction and/or re-utilization of their contents, the term of protection under that right is considerably shorter than that which they enjoy under the national arrangements currently in force; whereas harmonization of the criteria for determining whether a database is to be protected by copyright may not have the effect of reducing the term of protection currently enjoyed by the rightholders concerned; whereas a derogation should be laid down to that effect; whereas the effects of such derogation must be confined to the territories of the Member States concerned,

HAVE ADOPTED THIS DIRECTIVE;

CHAPTER I

SCOPE

Article 1

Scope

1.   This Directive concerns the legal protection of databases in any form.

2. For the purposes of this Directive, 'database' shall mean a collection of independent works, data or other materials arranged in a systematic or methodical way and individually accessible by electronic or other means.

3. Protection under this Directive shall not apply to computer programs used in the making or operation of databases accessible by electronic means.

Article 2

Limitations on the scope

This Directive shall apply without prejudice to Community provisions relating to:

(a) the legal protection of computer programs;
(b) rental right, lending right and certain rights related to copyright in the field of intellectual property;
(c) the term of protection of copyright and certain related rights.

CHAPTER II

COPYRIGHT

Article 3

Object of protection

1. In accordance with this Directive, databases which, by reason of the selection or arrangement of their contents, constitute the author's own intellectual creation shall be protected as such by copyright. No other criteria shall be applied to determine their eligibility for that protection.

2. The copyright protection of databases provided for by this Directive shall not extend to their contents and shall be without prejudice to any rights subsisting in those contents themselves.

Article 4

Database authorship

1. The author of a database shall be the natural person or group of natural persons who created the base or, where the legislation of the Member States so permits, the legal person designated as the rightholder by that legislation.

2. Where collective works are recognized by the legislation of a Member State, the economic rights shall be owned by the person holding the copyright.

3. In respect of a database created by a group of natural persons jointly, the exclusive rights shall be owned jointly.

Article 5

Restricted acts

In respect of the expression of the database which is protectable by copyright, the author of a database shall have the exclusive right to carry out or to authorize:

(a) temporary or permanent reproduction by any means and in any form, in whole or in part;
(b) translation, adaptation, arrangement and any other alteration;
(c) any form of distribution to the public of the database or of copies thereof. The first sale in the Community of a copy of the database by the rightholder or with his consent shall exhaust the right to control resale of that copy within the Community;
(d) any communication, display or performance to the public;
(e) any reproduction, distribution, communication, display or performance to the public of the results of the acts referred to in (b).

Article 6

Exceptions to restricted acts

1. The performance by the lawful user of a database or of a copy thereof of any of the acts listed in Article 5 which is necessary for the purposes of access to the contents of the databases and normal use of the contents by the lawful user shall not require the authorization of the author of the database. Where the lawful user is authorized to use only part of the database, this provision shall apply only to that part.

2. Member States shall have the option of providing for limitations on the rights set out in Article 5 in the following cases:

(a) in the case of reproduction for private purposes of a non-electronic database;
(b) where there is use for the sole purpose of illustration for teaching or scientific research, as long as the source is indicated and to the extent justified by the non-commercial purpose to be achieved;
(c) where there is use for the purposes of public security or for the purposes of an administrative or judicial procedure;
(d) where other exceptions to copyright which are traditionally authorised under national law are involved, without prejudice to points (a), (b) and (c).

3. In accordance with the Berne Convention for the protection of Literary and Artistic Works, this Article may not be interpreted in such a way as to allow its application to be used in a manner which unreasonably prejudices the rightholder's legitimate interests or conflicts with normal exploitation of the database.

CHAPTER III

SUI GENERIS RIGHT

Article 7

Object of protection

1. Member States shall provide for a right for the maker of a database which shows that there has been qualitatively and/or quantitatively a substantial investment in either the obtaining, verification or presentation of the contents to prevent extraction and/or re-utilization of the whole or of a substantial part, evaluated qualitatively and/or quantitatively, of the contents of that database.

2. For the purposes of this Chapter:

(a) 'extraction' shall mean the permanent or temporary transfer of all or a substantial part of the contents of a database to another medium by any means or in any form;

(b) 're-utilization' shall mean any form of making available to the public all or a substantial part of the contents of a database by the distribution of copies, by renting, by on-line or other forms of transmission. The first sale of a copy of a database within the Community by the rightholder or with his consent shall exhaust the right to control resale of that copy within the Community;

Public lending is not an act of extraction or re-utilization.

3. The right referred to in paragraph 1 may be transferred, assigned or granted under contractual licence.

4. The right provided for in paragraph 1 shall apply irrespective of the eligibility of that database for protection by copyright or by other rights. Moreover, it shall apply irrespective of eligibility of the contents of that database for protection by copyright or by other rights. Protection of databases under the right provided for in paragraph 1 shall be without prejudice to rights existing in respect of their contents.

5. The repeated and systematic extraction and/or re-utilization of insubstantial parts of the contents of database implying acts which conflict with a normal exploitation of that database or which

unreasonably prejudice the legitimate interests of the maker of the database shall not be permitted.

Article 8

Rights and obligations of lawful users

1.   The maker of a database which is made available to the public in whatever manner may not prevent a lawful user of the database from extracting and/or re-utilizing insubstantial parts of its contents, evaluated qualitatively and/or quantitatively, for any purposes whatsover. Where the lawful user is authorized to extract and/or re-utilize only part of the database, this paragraph shall apply only to that part.

2.   A lawful user of a database which is made available to the public in whatever manner may not perform acts which conflict with normal exploitation of the database or unreasonably prejudice the legitimate interests of the maker of the database.

3.   A lawful user of a database which is made available to the public in any manner may not cause prejudice to the holder of a copyright or related right in respect of the works or subject matter contained in the database.

Article 9

Exceptions to the *sui generis* right

Member States may stipulate that lawful users of a database which is made available to the public in whatever manner may, without the authorization of its maker, extract or re-utilize a substantial part of its contents;

(a) in the case of extraction for private purposes of the contents of a non-electronic database;

(b) in the case of extraction for the purposes of illustration for teaching or scientific research, as long as the source is indicated and to the extent justified by the non-commercial purpose to be achieved;

(c) in the case of extraction and/or re-utilization for the purposes of public security or an administrative or judicial procedure.

Article 10

Term of protection

1. The right provided for in Article 7 shall run from the date of completion of the making of the database. It shall expire fifteen years

from the first of January of the year following the date of completion.

2.   In the case of a database which is made available to the public in whatever manner before expiry of the period provided for in paragraph 1, the term of protection by that right shall expire fifteen years from the first of January of the year following the date when the database was first made available to the public.

3.   Any substantial change, evaluated qualitatively or quantitatively, to the contents of a database, including any substantial change resulting from the accumulation of successive additions, deletions or alterations, which would result in the database being considered to be a substantial new investment, evaluated qualitatively or quantitatively, shall qualify the database resulting from that investment for its own term of protection.

Article 11

Beneficiaries of protection under the *sui generis* right

1.   The right provided for in Article 7 shall apply to databases whose makers or rightholders are nationals of a Member State or who have their habitual residence in the territory of the Community.

2.   Paragraph 1 shall also apply to companies and firms formed in accordance with the law of a Member State and having their registered office, central administration or principal place of business within the Community; however, where such a company or firm has only its registered office in the territory of the Community, its operations must be genuinely linked on an ongoing basis with the economy of a Member State.

3.   Agreements extending the right provided for in Article 7 to databases made in third countries and falling outside the provisions of paragraphs 1 and 2 shall be concluded by the Council acting on a proposal from the Commission. The term of any protection extended to databases by virtue of that procedure shall not exceed that available pursuant to Article 10.

CHAPTER IV

COMMON PROVISIONS

Article 12

Remedies

Member States shall provide appropriate remedies in respect of infringements of the rights provided for in this Directive.

Article 13

Continued application of other legal provisions

This Directive shall be without prejudice to provisions concerning in particular copyright, rights related to copyright or any other rights or obligations subsisting in the data, works or other materials incorporated into a database, patent rights, trade marks, design rights, the protection of national treasures, laws on restrictive practices and unfair competition, trade secrets, security, confidentiality, data protection and privacy, access to public documents, and the law of contract.

Article 14

Application over time

1.   Protection pursuant to this Directive as regards copyright shall also be available in respect of databases created prior to the date referred to Article 16 (1) which on that date fulfil the requirements laid down in this Directive as regards copyright protection of databases.

2.   Notwithstanding paragraph 1, where a database protected under copyright arrangements in a Member State on the date of publication of this Directive does not fulfil the eligibility criteria for copyright protection laid down in Article 3(1), this Directive shall not result in any curtailing in that Member State of the remaining term of protection afforded under those arrangements.

3.   Protection pursuant to the provisions of this Directive as regards the right provided for in Article 7 shall also be available in respect of databases the making of which was completed not more than fifteen years prior to the date referred to in Article 16 (1) and which on that date fulfil the requirements laid down in Article 7.

4.   The protection provided for in paragraphs 1 and 3 shall be without prejudice to any acts concluded and rights acquired before the date referred to in those paragraphs.

5.   In the case of a database the making of which was completed not more than fifteen years prior to the date referred to in Article 16(1), the term of protection by the right provided for in Article 7 shall expire fifteen years from the first of January following that date.

Article 15

Binding nature of certain provisions

Any contractual provision contrary to Articles 6(1) and 8 shall be null and void.

Article 16

Final provisions

1.   Member States shall bring into force the laws, regulations and administrative provisions necessary to comply with this Directive before 1 January 1998.

When Member States adopt these provisions, they shall contain a reference to this Directive or shall be accompanied by such reference on the occasion of their official publication. The methods of making such reference shall be laid down by Member States.

2.   Member States shall communicate to the Commission the text of the provisions of domestic law which they adopt in the field governed by this Directive.

3.   Not later than at the end of the third year after the date referred to in paragraph 1, and every three years thereafter, the Commission shall submit to the European Parliament, the Council and the Economic and Social Committee a report on the application of this Directive, in which, *inter alia*, on the basis of specific information supplied by the Member States, it shall examine in particular the application of the *sui generis* right, including Articles 8 and 9, and shall verify especially whether the application of this right has led to abuse of a dominant position or other interference with free competition which would justify appropriate measures being taken, including the establishment of non-voluntary licensing arrangements. Where necessary, it shall submit proposals for adjustment of this Directive in line with developments in the area of databases.

Article 17

This Directive is addressed to the Member States.

Done at Strasbourg, 11 March 1996.

For the European Parliament	*For the Council*
The President	*The President*
K. HÄNSCH	L. DINI

Appendix 3

Annotated Extracts from the Copyright, Designs and Patents Act 1988 (as amended) and Annotated Extracts from the Copyright and Rights in Databases Regulations 1997

COPYRIGHT, DESIGNS AND PATENTS ACT 1988 (AS AMENDED)

SUBSISTENCE, OWNERSHIP AND DURATION OF COPYRIGHT

Descriptions of work and related provisions

Section 3 – literary, dramatic and musical works

(1) In this Part—

'literary work' means any work, other than a dramatic or musical work, which is written spoken or sung, and accordingly includes-

  (a) a table or compilation other than a database,
  (b) a computer program,
  (c) preparatory design material for a computer program and
  (d) a database;

  ...

(2) Copyright does not subsist in a literary, dramatic or musical work unless and until it is recorded, in writing or otherwise; and references in this Part to the time at which such a work is made are to the time at which it is so recorded.

  ...

Note: preparatory design material for a computer program was added by the Copyright (Computer Programs) Regulations 1992 which came in force 1 January 1993 and databases were specifically added by the Copyright and Rights in Databases Regulations which came into force on 1 January 1998. Previously databases would generally have been protected as compilations but now the section makes it clear that databases are excluded from the meaning of compilation.

Section 3A – databases

(1) In this Part 'database' means a collection of independent works, data or other materials which—

    (a) are arranged in a systematic or methodical way, and

    (b) are individually accessible by electronic or other means.

(2) For the purposes of this Part a literary work consisting of a database is original if, and only if, by reason of the selection or arrangement of the contents of the database the database constitutes the author's own intellectual creation.

Note: this section inserted by the Copyright and Rights in Databases Regulations 1997 which came in force 1 January 1998. It takes the definition of database from the EC Directive on the legal protection of databases. Notice that it is not limited to electronic databases ('accessible by electronic or other means') and should also apply to paper databases such as a card index system.

To be protected by copyright, a database must be the author's own intellectual creation. This derives from the German test for copyright subsistence and is, arguably, a higher standard than that which applies generally for copyright works in the UK which is that the work originated from the author and was the result of skill, effort or judgment. The requirement for intellectual creation was also stated in the EC Directive on the legal protection of computer programs but the implementing regulations ignored this test and, for a computer program, it is required that it is original without further qualification of that word.

There is also a right in databases which will apply to many databases, whether or not they are protected by copyright.

Authorship and ownership of copyright

Section 9 – authorship of work

(1) In this Part 'author', in relation to a work, means the person who creates it.

…

(3) In the case of a literary, dramatic, musical or artistic work which is computer-generated, the author shall be taken to be the person by whom the arrangements necessary for the creation of the work are undertaken.

…

Note: for the original works, authorship is self-evident except for computer-generated works which are defined in section 178 as being generated in circumstances such that there is no human author.

ACTS PERMITTED IN RELATION TO COPYRIGHT WORKS

General

Section 29 – research and private study

(1) Fair dealing with a literary [work, other than a database, or a] dramatic, musical or artistic work for the purposes of research or private study does not infringe any copyright in the work or, in the case of a published edition, in the typographical arrangement.

[(1A) Fair dealing with a database for the purposes of research or private study does not infringe any copyright in the database provided that the source is indicated.]

...

[(4) It is not fair dealing—

  (a) to convert a computer program expressed in a low level language into a version expressed in a higher level language, or
  (b) incidentally in the course of so converting the program to copy it, these acts being permitted if done in accordance with section 50B (decompilation).]

[(5) The doing of anything in relation to a database for the purposes of research for a commercial purpose is not fair dealing with the database.]

Note: fair dealing cannot now apply to the act of decompilation of a computer program. Otherwise, fair dealing may be available, for example, if a sub-routine is reproduced for research or private study providing this does not involve decompilation. Also fair dealing will be available for other items of software such as conventional works stored digitally.

Also note that fair dealing with a database must have an indication of the source and that, unlike the other works covered by this section, fair dealing for a commercial purpose is excluded.

ACTS PERMITTED IN RELATION TO COPYRIGHT WORKS

Computer Programs: Lawful Users

[Section 50A – back-up copies]

[(1) It is not an infringement of copyright for a lawful user of a copy of a computer program to make any back up copy of it which it is necessary for him to have for the purposes of his lawful use.

(2) For the purposes of this section and sections 50B and 50C a person is a lawful user of a computer program if (whether under a

licence to do any acts restricted by the copyright in the program or otherwise), he has a right to use the program.

(3) Where an act is permitted under this section, it is irrelevant whether or not there exists any term or condition in an agreement which purports to prohibit or restrict the act (such terms being, by virtue of section 296A, void).]

Note: this and the following two permitted acts apply to lawful users only, however, this is not restricted to licensees. Prior to this provision it would have been likely that, in most circumstances, and in the absence of an express term to the contrary, the courts would have implied a right to make back up copies of computer programs (and probably also other items of software such as a thesaurus or database). The meaning of the word 'necessary' is probably not to be taken in a strong sense.

[Section 50B – decompilation]

[(1) it is not an infringement of copyright for a lawful user of a copy of a computer program expressed in a low level language—

(a) to convert it into a version expressed in a higher level language, or
(b) incidentally in the course of so converting the program, to copy it, (that is, to 'decompile' it), provided that the conditions in subsection (2) are met.

(2) The conditions are that—

(a) it is necessary to decompile the program to obtain the information necessary to create an independent program which can be operated with the program decompiled or with another program ('the permitted objective'), and
(b) the information so obtained is not used for any purpose other than the permitted objective.

(3) In particular, the conditions in subsection (2) are not met if the lawful user—

(a) has readily available to him the information necessary to achieve the permitted objective;
(b) does not confine the decompiling to such acts as are necessary to achieve the permitted objective;
(c) supplies the information obtained by the decompiling to any person to whom it is not necessary to supply it in order to achieve the permitted objective; or
(d) uses the information to create a program which is substantially similar in its expression to the program decompiled or to do any act restricted by copyright.

354 • *Annotated extracts*

(4) Where an act is permitted under this section, it is irrelevant whether or not there exists any term or condition in an agreement which purports to prohibit or restrict the act (such terms being, by virtue of section 296A, void).]

Note: decompilation of computer programs is not permitted except in accordance with this act. In particular, fair dealing has been restricted to exclude decompilation (section 29(4)). It is important to note that the act is not restricted to achieving interoperability with the program decompiled but may be done to achieve interoperability with another program. As with section 50A, the word 'necessary' is likely to be taken in a weak sense. In practice, because of the limitation in subsections 2 and 3 and because decompilation is very difficult to perform effectively and successfully, this particular permitted act, which caused so much controversy whilst being formulated in the European Commission, is unlikely to be relied on very often.

[Section 50C – other acts permitted to lawful users]

[(1) It is not an infringement of copyright for a lawful user of a copy of a computer program to copy or adapt it, provided that the copying or adapting—

  (a) is necessary for his lawful use, and
  (b) is not prohibited under any term or condition of an agreement regulating the circumstances in which his use is lawful.

(2) It may, in particular, be necessary for the lawful use of a computer program to copy it or adapt it for the purpose of correcting errors in it.

(3) This section does not apply to any copying or adapting permitted under section 50A or 50B.]

Note: in essence, this is an example of non-derogation from grant. The owner of the copyright in a program may not limit the acts that may be done in a way inconsistent with the grant of the right to perform acts, for example, in a licence agreement. Error correction is given as a particular example allowing the making of copies or adaptations but the wording of section 50C(1)(b) appears to permit the exclusion of this and other particular forms of copying and making adaptations. The Directive is itself ambiguous on this point. *Saphena Computing v Allied Collection Agencies* [1995] FSR 605 is authority for the fact that a licensee need not hand over the source code of a program unless the agreement provides for this. Error correction without the source code version is well nigh impossible.

Databases: permitted acts

[Section 50D – acts permitted in relation to databases]

[(1) It is not an infringement of copyright in a database for a person who has a right to use the database or any part of the database, (whether under a licence to do any of the acts restricted by the copyright in the database or otherwise) to do, in the exercise of that right, anything which is necessary for the purposes of access to and use of the contents of the database or of that part of the database.

(2) Where an act which would otherwise infringe copyright in a database is permitted under this section, it is irrelevant whether or not there exists any term or condition in any agreement which purports to prohibit or restrict the act (such terms being, by virtue of section 296B, void).]

Note: this section was inserted by the Copyright and Rights in Databases Regulations 1997 which came into force on 1 January 1998. It is, fundamentally, a non-derogation from grant provision. In other words and for example, a licensor cannot use terms in the licence to prohibit or restrict the rights granted by the licence in relation to access and use of the contents.

Section 296B makes any term or condition in such a licence void to the extent that it is inconsistent with the rights of access and use granted by the licence.

MISCELLANEOUS AND GENERAL

Computer Programs

[Section 296A – avoidance of certain terms]

[(1) Where a person has the use of a computer program under an agreement, any term or condition in the agreement shall be void in so far as it purports to prohibit or restrict—

(a) the making of any back up copy of the program which is necessary for him to have for the purpose of the agreed use;

(b) where the conditions in section 50B(2) are met, the decompiling of the program; or

(c) the use of any device or means to observe, study or test the functioning of the program in order to understand the ideas and principles which underlie any element of the program.

(2) In this section, decompile, in relation to a computer program, has the same meaning as in section 50B.]

Note: apart from making terms and conditions void in so far as they attempt to prohibit or restrict the making of back up copies under section 50A or the decompilation permitted act under section 50C, this provision contains an important and potentially wide-ranging exception to infringement allowing the use of devices or means to observe, study or test the functioning of a program as a way to gain access to the underlying ideas and principles. This is required because, unlike other works of copyright, ideas and principles underlying computer programs are not readily transparent. However, this is restricted to persons 'having the use of a program under an agreement' (such as a licence agreement) and not to 'lawful users'. 'Device or means' should include computer software, such as a program monitoring and logging the flow and output of the program being studied. Another example is where an electric meter detects and records the electronic output of a computer program to, say, a peripheral device such as a printer or other item of hardware.

Databases

[Section 296B – avoidance of certain terms relating to databases]

[Where under an agreement a person has a right to use a database or part of a database, any term or condition in the agreement shall be void in so far as it purports to prohibit or restrict the performance of any act which would but for section 50D infringe the copyright in the database.]

Note: this section inserted by the Copyright and Rights in Databases Regulations 1997, which came into force on 1 January 1998. It protects the 'non-derogation from grant' provision in section 50D.

THE COPYRIGHT AND RIGHTS IN DATABASES REGULATIONS 1997
PART III DATABASE RIGHT

Regulation 12 – interpretation

(1) In this Part—

'database' has the meaning given by section 3A(1) of the 1988 Act

'extraction', in relation to any contents of a database, means the permanent or temporary transfer of those contents to another medium by any means or in any form;

...

'investment' includes any investment, whether of financial, human or technical resources;

...

'lawful user', in relation to a database, means any person who (whether under a licence to do any of the acts restricted by any database right in the database or otherwise) has a right to use the database;

're-utilisation', in relation to any contents of a database, means making those contents available to the public by any means;

'substantial', in relation to any investment, extraction or re-utilisation, means substantial in terms of quantity or quality or a combination of both.

...

(5) Where a copy of a database has been sold within the EEA by, or with the consent of, the owner of the database right in the database, the further sale within the EEA of that copy shall not be taken for the purposes of this Part to constitute extraction or re-utilisation of the contents of the database.

Note: 'investment' is defined in relation to financial, human or technical resources, unlike any test required for copyright, showing the commercial nature of this right. The meaning of re-utilisation is deceptive. It does not mean re-using but making the contents of the database available to the public by any means. Substantiality, in copyright terms, tends to be concerned with quality rather than quantity but here they appear to be of equal weight.

Regulation 13 – database right

(1) A property right ('database right') subsists, in accordance with this Part, in a database if there has been a substantial investment in obtaining, verifying or presenting the contents of the database.

(2) For the purposes of paragraph (1) it is immaterial whether or not the database or any of its contents is a copyright work, within the meaning of Part 1 of the 1988 Act.

(3) This Regulation has effect subject to Regulation 18.

Note: the database right subsists irrespective of whether the database or its contents are protected by copyright. This is subject to regulation 18 which deals with qualification for the right. Qualification comes about if the maker is a national of an EEA state, a person habitually resident within the EEA or if the maker is an incorporated body or a partnership or other unincorporated body.

Where a database was created on or before 27 March 1996 (the date the EC Directive on the legal protection of databases was published) and is protected by copyright immediately before 1 January 1998, copyright will continue to subsist for its full term (regulation 29). Thus an existing database which was protected by copyright before the introduction of the database right will not have that copyright prejudiced notwithstanding that the database would not qualify for copyright because of the new requirement for it to be the author's own intellectual creation.

Regulation 14 – the maker of a database

(1) Subject to paragraphs (2) to (4), the person who takes the initiative in obtaining, verifying or presenting the contents of a database and assumes the risk of investing in that obtaining, verification or presentation shall be regarded as the maker of, and as having made, the database.

(2) Where a database is made by an employee in the course of his employment, his employer shall be regarded as the maker of the database, subject to any agreement to the contrary.

...

(5) For the purposes of this Part a database is made jointly if two or more persons acting together in collaboration take the initiative in obtaining, verifying or presenting the contents of the database and assume the risk of investing in that obtaining, verification or presentation.

(6) References in this Part to the maker of a database shall, except as otherwise provided, be construed, in relation to a database which is made jointly, as references to all the makers.

Note: paragraphs 3 and 4 deal with Crown database right and parliamentary database right. The maker of a database is the first owner of the database right, under regulation 15, and the rules to determine the identity of the maker are broadly similar to those applying in relation to the original works of copyright. Especially note the provision for employees which also mirrors that for copyright. However, for copyright, an employee making a work in the course of employment is still the author of the work even though the employer will normally be the first owner. For database right, the employer is the maker and first owner.

Regulation 15 – first ownership of database right

The maker of a database is the first owner of database right in it.

Note: see the commentary on regulation 14.

Regulation 16 – acts infringing database right

(1) Subject to the provisions of this Part, a person infringes database right in a database if, without the consent of the owner of the right, he extracts or re-utilises all or a substantial part of the contents of the database.

(2) For the purposes of this Part, the repeated and systematic extraction or re-utilisation of insubstantial parts of the contents of a database may amount to the extraction or re-utilisation of a substantial part of those contents.

Note: infringement is of two types. The first is expressed in terms of a substantial part of the database. The second is a reflection of the danger of persistent extraction or re-utilisation of insubstantial parts. The EC Directive on the legal protection of databases contains an additional qualification in that insubstantial taking on a repeated and systematic basis implies acts which conflict with the normal exploitation of the database or which unreasonably prejudice the legitimate interests of the maker of the database.

Although copyright is expressed in terms of taking a substantial part of the work, it has been held that repeated insubstantial taking can infringe copyright.

Regulation 17 – term of protection

(1) Database right in a database expires at the end of the period of fifteen years from the end of the calendar year in which the making of the database was completed.

(2) Where a database is made available to the public before the end of the period referred to in paragraph (1), database right in the database shall expire fifteen years from the end of the calendar year in which the database was first made available to the public.

(3) Any substantial change to the contents of a database, including a substantial change resulting from the accumulation of successive additions, deletions or alterations, which would result in the database being considered to be a substantial new investment shall qualify the database resulting from that investment for its own term of protection.

(4) This Regulation has effect subject to Regulation 30.

Note: the basic period of protection is 15 years from the end of the calendar year when the making of the database was completed. However, if it is made available to the public during that period, the 15 years is calculated from the end of the calendar year during which it was so made available.

As databases are often subject to continual change, there is provision for a new term of protection where there is a substantial change including one resulting from an accumulation of successive changes which would mean that the database would fall to be considered a substantial new investment.

The rules on duration of the database right are subject to regulation 30 which provides that where the making of the database was completed on or after 1 January 1983 and, on 1 January 1998 the database right begins to subsist in the database, the database right shall subsist for a period of 15 years starting from 1 January 1998.

Regulation 19 – avoidance of certain terms affecting lawful users

(1) A lawful user of a database which has been made available to the public in any manner shall be entitled to extract or re-utilise insubstantial parts of the contents of the database for any purpose.

(2) Where under an agreement a person has a right to use a database, or part of a database, which has been made available to the public in any manner, any term or condition in the agreement shall be void in so far as it purports to prevent that person from extracting or re-utilising insubstantial parts of the contents of the database, or of that part of the database, for any purpose.

Note: basically, this is a non-derogation from grant provision.

Regulation 20 – exceptions to database right

(1) Database right in a database which has been made available to the public in any manner is not infringed by fair dealing with a substantial part of its contents if-

    (a) that part is extracted from the database by a person who is apart from this paragraph a lawful user of the database,

(b) it is extracted for the purpose of illustration for teaching or research and not for any commercial purpose, and

(c) the source is indicated.

...

Note: fair dealing by lawful users is permitted. However, this is limited to illustration for teaching or research (but not commercial research). The source must be indicated. Further exceptions are contained in Schedule 1 to the Regulations and include exceptions for public administration similar to the equivalent permitted acts for copyright.

APPENDIX 4

Navigator's guide to important computer software provisions of The Copyright, Designs and Patents Act 1988

General layout of the Act (copyright provisions–Part I)

Section Nos	Provisions
1–8	Subsistence of copyright and types of works
9–11	Authorship and ownership
12–15	Duration of copyright
15A	Meaning of country of origin
16–21	Rights of copyright owner and infringement
22–27	Secondary infringement ('dealing' with infringing copies)
28–76	The permitted acts (exceptions to infringement)
77–89	Moral rights
90–95	Copyright dealing (eg assignment, and licences)
96–103	Remedies for infringement
104–106	Evidential presumptions
107–115	Offences and supplemental
116–144A	Licensing schemes
145–152	The Copyright Tribunal
153–162	Qualification for copyright protection
163–169	Crown & Parliamentary copyright, etc
170–171	Transitional provisions (also see Schedule 1)
172–179	Interpretation, including definitions and useful index of defined expressions
(180–295)	Parts of Act on rights in performances, design right, registered designs, patent agents and trade mark agents and patents
296–306	Miscellaneous and general
Schedules	Including Schedule 1 – Copyright: transitional provisions and savings

Particular provisions for computer software

(Normal copyright provisions apply otherwise)

Section Nos	Provisions
3(1)	Confirms that a computer program and preparatory design material for a computer program are literary works. Databases are now also specifically defined as literary works
3A	Definition of 'database' and of the requirement for originality required for databases
9(3)	Identifies the author of a computer-generated work as the person making the arrangements necessary for the creation of the work
12(7)	States the duration of copyright subsisting in a computer-generated work (being 50 years from the end of the calendar year during which it was made) (previously section 12(3))
17(2)	Copying literary dramatic, musical or artistic works includes storage in any medium by electronic means
18(3)	The restricted act of issuing copies to the public includes rental of computer programs (note: new section 18A details restricted acts of rental or lending to the public for most literary, dramatic, musical or artistic works, films or sound recordings)
21(3)(ab) & (ac) & 21(4)	An adaptation of a computer program means an arrangement, altered version or translation. Similarly, an adaptation of a database means an arrangement or altered version of the database or a translation of it. A translation of a computer program includes a version of a program in which it is converted into or out of a computer language or code or into a different computer language or code
27(3A)	A copy of a computer program which has previously been sold in any other Member State (of the European Community), by or with the consent of the copyright owner, is not an infringing copy
29(1A), (4) & (5)	Fair dealing with a database for research or private study (but not for the purposes of research for a commercial purpose) does not infringe copyright in the database providing the source is indicated. It is not fair dealing to decompile a computer program, however, this may be permitted under section 50B

50A	A lawful user of a computer program may make a back up copy if necessary for his lawful use
50B	A lawful user may decompile a computer program for the permitted objective of achieving interoperability with that or another program, subject to conditions
50C	A lawful user may copy or adapt a computer program if necessary for his lawful use (including error correction) providing this is not prohibited or restricted in an agreement governing the use of the program
50D	A person having the right to use a database or any part of a database may do, in exercising that right, anything necessary for the purposes of access to and use of the contents of the database or part thereof
56	Provisions for transfer of copies of works stored in electronic form
79(2)	The moral right to be identified as author does not apply in relation to computer programs
81(2)	The moral right to object to a derogatory treatment of a work does not apply in relation to computer programs or computer-generated works
105(3)	Evidential presumptions as to ownership of copyright in a computer program issued to the public in electronic form and as to the country of first publication (that the person named as owner on a copy is the owner and that the named country of first publication is correct)
175	Meaning of publication and commercial publication includes making available by means of an electronic retrieval system
178	Definitions, including: 'computer-generated' 'electronic' 'reprographic process'
296	Devices designed to circumvent copy-protection of works issued in an electronic form which is copy protected (copyright owners' rights against persons making, importing, selling, etc such devices, etc)
296A	Avoidance of terms in agreements – terms or conditions prohibiting or restricting the permitted acts under sections 50A and 50B or the use of a device or means to observe, study or test the functioning of a program to understand the ideas and principles underlying any element of it are void

296B   Avoidance of terms in agreements in relation to databases – a term or condition purporting to prohibit or restrict the performance of any act which would infringe copyright but for section 50D shall be void to that extent.

Glossary

A COMPUTER TERMS

CD-ROM

Read only memory on an optical disk, based on the CD music disk laser technology, which can hold up to around 600 megabytes of data. A great deal of software is now available in this format, including databases, dictionaries, operating systems and applications programs. This form of memory is sometimes referred to as WORM – write once read many. More expensive computers tend to have DVD-ROM drives which can also read CD-ROMs. DVD-ROMs are a denser version of CD-ROMs.

Computer hardware

Computer hardware comprises the physical pieces of equipment that make up a computer system including the computer and peripheral devices such as printers, monitors, disk drive, CD-ROM drives, optical character readers, etc. Many items of computer hardware also contain computer software, for example, a computer usually contains integrated circuits holding 'bootstrap' programs and some operating system programs. Sometimes computer hardware is sold 'bundled' with computer software. For example, a personal computer is likely to be sold in a transaction which includes a licence for the operating system software and, often, with applications software such as word processing or spreadsheet software.

Computer program

A series of instructions which control or condition the operation of a computer. There are a large number of languages in which computer programs may be written. Programs may be stored in several ways, for example, on magnetic or optical disks or tape, on punched cards or paper tape, or stored permanently in the computer on integrated circuits. Generally, it is a relatively easy matter to make a copy of a computer program.

Computer software

Computer software is a term lacking a precise definition but can be taken as including computer programs and information stored in or on a computer or computer media. Any form of work stored in digital form and intended to be accessed by a computer is within the definition. Software also includes associated documentation such as specifications, flowcharts, guides and manuals. Output produced by running a computer program such as screen displays, data files and printed reports are further examples of computer software.

Data and databases

Data comprises information which is stored in a computer or on computer storage media such as magnetic disks or CD-ROM disks. A database is a collection or compilation of computer data stored in a computer or on computer media such as a list of clients' names and addresses, a list of employees and their salary and pension details, or sets of co-ordinates defining the three-dimensional shape of new designs. Databases may be relational whereby a number of databases have a common link and are used together. An example is a database of customers which includes an identification number and a database of transactions, each having the appropriate customer identification number. The two databases can be used to create a report comprising a table of customers each with a list of all their transactions.

Databases are usually accessed, retrieved, modified and manipulated using a computer program but following the European Directive on the legal protection of databases protection is also afforded to paper databases also (for example, a card index). Many databases are of significant commercial value. Databases are protected by copyright (if the result of the author's intellectual creation) or by the database right (if the result of a substantial investment) or by both copyright and the database right. The protection of databases as databases does not compromise the copyright position relating to the individual items within a database. Thus, a database of digitised photographs may be protected by copyright and/or the database right and each photograph will have separate protection under copyright law.

Decompilation – see Reverse analysis

DVD-ROM

Digital Versatile Disk ROM – a form of CD-ROM that can hold about 6 times more data than a CD-ROM and which is particularly suited to films and moving images.

Firmware

Computer programs which are permanently 'wired' into a computer or other hardware device are sometimes referred to as firmware or as being 'hard-wired'. These programs are permanently stored on integrated circuits ('silicon chips'). In principle, the mode of storage should make no difference to legal protection but some judges have erred on this point in the past.

Fourth generation language

A software design/programming environment in which complicated and sophisticated handling of data is possible and which allows the system designer, or even the end-user, to write programs and routines for specific requirements. Typically, a fourth generation language (4GL) comprises a database management system permitting the specification, structuring and development of a database. Many features such as the generation of reports, display formats and the like are automated to a significant extent. The designer simply specifies his or her requirements and the 4GL produces the program code to perform the required functions. 4GLs usually have a query language which may be used to retrieve or modify data stored in the database. Some have a standard query language (SQL) originally developed by IBM. Most 4GLs may be used in different ways, by using a menu system, by entering queries direct or by running a program written using the 4GL programming language. Most can operate on several linked database files at any given time; such a database is known as a relational database.

Integrated circuit

Sometimes referred to as a silicon chip. An integrated circuit is a small piece of semiconducting material which together with layers of conducting and insulating materials make up a micro-electronic circuit incorporating numerous semiconductor devices (such as transistors, resistors and diodes). The contents of some integrated circuits are permanently fixed (called ROM chips – Read Only Memory) whilst the contents of others are volatile and can be changed (called RAM chips – Random Access Memory). Other forms of integrated circuits exist such as EPROMS (Erasable Programmable Read Only Memory – the programs and data on these can be electronically erased and re-used to store new programs and data). The central processing unit (CPU) of a computer is contained on an integrated circuit and carries out the machine language instructions emanating from computer programs.

Object code program

A computer program must be converted into machine language before it can be operated on by a computer. A source code computer program (the form in which it is written) is usually compiled or assembled to create a permanent version of the program in machine language which is used as the working version of the program. This is known as the object code and is the usual form in which the program will be distributed or licensed. It has several advantages over source code programs, for example, the object code programs operate much more quickly than interpreted source code programs and the know-how underlying the program is difficult to access. In many computer programming languages (such as COBOL), programs can only be run in object code form, the programs must be compiled first. In other languages (such as BASIC), programs may be compiled into object code or they may be run in interpreted mode in which an interpreter program converts a source code program line by line to temporary object code as the program is being run.

Reverse analysis

The process where information about the ideas, principles or design of a computer program is determined by an examination of the program code, usually after disassembly or decompilation of object code. Disassembly is a process where the object code form of a program is converted into a low level language form (assembly language). Decompilation is a similar process but this produces the original high level language source code – it is more difficult to perform than disassembly and comment or remark lines inserted into the original source code version will not be retrieved. The term 'decompilation' is used in the Copyright, Designs and Patents Act 1988 in a sense that includes disassembly also. In both cases, the program code is converted from a low-level language into a higher-level language which is more readily understood by programmers.

Source code program

Source code is the version of the program as it is written by the programmer. The programmer may use a high-level programming language such as FORTRAN or COBOL or C or he or she may use assembly language which is very close to the computer's machine language. To be executed on a computer, the source code program must be converted into object code form, either permanently using a compiler program or transiently using an interpreter program. Not all programming languages can be used in interpreted mode. It is relatively easy for programmers to understand source code programs and the ideas and methodology underlying them (especially if written in a high-level language). For this reason, the source code is not usually made available to persons acquiring software. Source code may be made available to a person commissioning the writing of particular software but the precise terms of the contract must be examined. Sometimes, a copy of the source code (and other materials such as flowcharts) is put into the possession of a third party who will make it available should the software company go out of business or refuse to maintain the software. This arrangement is known as source code escrow.

User interface

The means by which a computer program interacts with the user of the program. The interface may be accomplished simply by typing in responses as prompted, selecting from options on a menu or list or by using a 'Windows' (sometimes referred to as 'WIMPS') environment. Entry of the user's responses may be by keyboard, mouse, touch-screen, digitiser, etc or a combination of these methods.

Windows or WIMPS environment

The acronym 'WIMPS' stands for 'windows, icons, menus and pointers (or, alternatively, windows, icons, mice and pull-down menus)'. It is not used frequently nowadays, the term 'Windows' generally being preferred. A windows environment is one in which the screen can be divided up into different areas so that several files, applications or items of information can be displayed together. Icons are small symbols displayed on the screen representing various actions or items of software or hardware devices. For example, a tiny picture of a filing cabinet may be used representing files in a directory. Rather than typing in a command, the user may move the cursor over an icon and select the function or device it represents by using a mouse, an input device which can reduce the need to use a keyboard. A pull-down menu is a menu of commands from which the user can select which is not normally displayed but which can be called up by the user usually by clicking the mouse on the heading for the menu or entering an appropriate keystroke.

B LEGAL TERMS

On 26 April 1999, new Civil Procedure Rules came into force. These new rules resulted in some changes of terminology. Where this has occurred in the definitions below, the new term appears in square brackets after the old terminology.

Account of profits

This is often an alternative to damages, for example, in a case of copyright infringement. The copyright owner (or exclusive licensee) is entitled to a sum equal to the monetary gain (or profit) the infringer has made as a result of the infringement.

Anton Piller Order [Search Order]

An order of the High Court permitting the aggrieved party to enter the premises of a suspected infringer and remove evidence of the supposed infringement. The name derives from the case of *Anton Piller KG v Manufacturing Processes Ltd* [1976] 1 Ch 55. The order must be executed by a solicitor and its purpose is the preservation of evidence, that is, to prevent the destruction or concealment of evidence. An order will be granted only when the applicant can show a very strong *prima facie* case. There are now strict guidelines as to the form of the order and its execution; *Practice Direction: Mareva Injunctions and Anton Piller Orders* [1994] RPC 617.

Assignment

The transfer of ownership of a 'thing in action' (intangible personal property) such as a debt, shares in a company or a copyright. An assignment must be in writing and signed by or on behalf of the assignor (the person making the assignment) for it to be binding at law. Failure to observe this formality may result in the purported assignee only obtaining beneficial ownership. This is an unsatisfactory form of ownership and the legal owner must be joined in any court action if a permanent injunction or damages are asked for. Because persons and organisations commissioning an independent contractor to create computer software sometimes omit to obtain a signed and written assignment of copyright, beneficial ownership is not uncommon.

Copyright

Copyright is a property right associated with certain types of creative works such as literary, musical and artistic works. Computer programs, preparatory design material for computer programs and databases are literary works for copyright purposes. Databases are also protected by a *sui generis* form of protection known as the database right, in addition to or instead of copyright. Copyright is a right to do certain specified acts (such as making copies) in relation to the work in question and anyone else performing any of these acts (to the whole or a substantial part of the work) without the permission of the copyright owner will infringe the copyright and may be sued by the copyright owner or by an exclusive licensee of the copyright owner. In some cases, copyright law can give rise to criminal penalties, such as where a software pirate is making or selling infringing copies of software, knowing or having reason to believe that he is dealing with infringing copies.

Damages

A sum of money awarded by the court as compensation for a breach of contract or other civil wrong such as an infringement of copyright. Substantial damages are awarded when actual damage has been caused, for example, the copyright owner has lost 'sales' of his software as a result. Nominal damages (a small sum) may be awarded where there is no actual loss. There are other forms of damages such as aggravated damages, exemplary (or punitive) damages and conversion damages. Additional damages (a form of exemplary damages) are available under copyright law and may be awarded in rare cases, for example, where the infringement is flagrant and the infringer has derived significant benefit from the infringement. A recent example in which an order was granted for an inquiry into the amount payable under additional damages involved the infringement of copyright in architect's plans for houses is *Cala Homes (South) Ltd v Alfred McAlpine Homes East Ltd (No 2)* [1996] FSR 36. Apart from additional damages, the purpose of damages in copyright infringement cases is to put the plaintiff in the position he would have been in had the infringement not occurred as far as money can do this. For example, one way to do this would be to calculate how much the infringer would have had to pay for a licence to do the acts complained of. In terms of contract, the purpose of damages is to put the injured party in the position he or she would have been in had the other party performed his or her obligations under the contract in the required manner.

Database right

A new form of right, introduced on 1 January 1998, designed to give protection to databases which fail to reach the new standard for copyright protection as a database. The database right resulted from a European initiative in the form of a Directive on the legal protection of databases.

Injunction

An injunction is a court order addressed to a particular person which either prohibits him or her from doing or continuing to do some act (prohibiting injunction) or ordering him or her to carry out some act (mandatory injunction). In terms of computer software an injunction might be granted prohibiting a suspected copyright infringer from continuing to distribute or sell copies of the suspect software. As it can take some time for a case to come to court for the full trial, if the harm done to the copyright owner in the meantime is likely to be serious, the court may grant an interlocutory injunction (interim injunction) which is one which will last until the full trial of the case. Until recently, the applicant would simply have to show a serious issue to be tried but now, the court is likely to look at the relative strength of the parties' cases. Furthermore, the 'balance of convenience' must be satisfied, and an interlocutory injunction is unlikely to be granted if damages would be an adequate remedy and the alleged infringer will be in a position to pay should he lose the case at full trial. Nor is the order likely to be granted if to do so would put the alleged infringer out of business.

Lawful user

A lawful user of a computer program is defined in section 50A(2) of the Copyright, Designs and Patents Act 1988 as a person having the right (whether under a licence agreement or otherwise) to use the program. Typically, a lawful user will be a person who has acquired a copy of a program under a licence agreement. However, the definition is potentially wider than this and would extend, for example, to employees and agents of a licensee and, probably, also to external auditors and persons lawfully executing search warrants.

Licence

A licence is a permission to perform an act that would otherwise infringe some legal right. For example, a licence might permit the copying or other controlled use of a computer program. The person who owns the right and grants the licence is called the licensor whilst the other person who obtains the permission under the licence is called the licensee. Computer software is commonly acquired under a licence agreement. Typically, a software licence will permit, for payment of a fee, the licensee to use the software for specified purposes, for example, for internal use only and to be used on not more than a certain number of computers (eg a ten user licence). A licence may be exclusive where the permission is given to one person only who can do the acts concerned even to the exclusion of the copyright owner. Alternatively, a licence may be non-exclusive so that the permission may be granted concurrently to a number of different persons.

Royalty

A royalty is a payment normally calculated on a percentage of the income derived from sales of works. This is a common method of paying for a licence to exploit a work subject to an intellectual property right. For example, the owner of the copyright subsisting in computer software might grant an exclusive licence to a software publisher so that he or she can make copies of the software and grant non-exclusive licences to others permitting them to use the software. The owner may be paid a royalty of, say, 10 per cent of the income derived on the 'sale' of the software.

Selected bibliography

BOOKS

Bainbridge, D I *Intellectual Property* (London: FT Pitman Publishing, 4th edn, 1999)

Bainbridge, D I *Introduction to Computer Law* (London: FT Pitman Publishing, 4th edn, 1999)

Bainbridge, D I *Software Licensing* (Birmingham: Central Law Publishing, 2nd edn, 1999)

Coleman, A *The Legal Protection of Trade Secrets* (London: Sweet & Maxwell, 1992)

Cornish, W R *Intellectual Property: Patents, Copyright, Trade Marks and Allied Rights* (London: Sweet & Maxwell, 4th edn, 1999)

Dworkin, G & Taylor, R D *Blackstone's Guide to the Copyright, Designs and Patents Act 1988* (London: Blackstone, 1989)

Henry, M *Publishing and Multimedia Law* (London: Butterworths, 1994)

Laddie, H, Prescott, P and Vittoria, M *The Modern Law of Copyright* (London, Butterworths, 2nd edn, 1995)

Lehmann, M & Tapper, C (eds) *A Handbook of European Software Law* (Oxford: Clarendon Press, 1993)

Lloyd, I *Information Technology Law* (London: Butterworths, 2nd edn, 1997)

Merkin, R *Copyright, Designs and Patents: The New Law* (London: Longman, 1989)

Morgan, R & Steadman, G *Computer Contracts* (London: FT Law & Tax, 5th edn, 1995)

Pearson, H E and Miller, C G *Commercial Exploitation of Intellectual Property* (London: Blackstone, 1990)

Phillips, J (ed) *Butterworths Intellectual Property Law Handbook* (London: Butterworths, 3rd edn, 1997)

Phillips, J & Firth, A *Introduction to Intellectual Property Law* (London: Butterworths, 3rd edn, 1995)

Phillips, J, Durie, R & Karet, I *Whale on Copyright* (London: Sweet & Maxwell, 4th edn, 1993)

Prime, T *The Law of Copyright* (London: Fourmat, 1992)

Reed, C (ed) *Computer Law* (London: Blackstone, 3rd edn, 1996)

Reid, B C *Confidentiality and the Law* (London: Waterlow, 1986)

Stewart, S M *International Copyright and Neighbouring Rights* (London: Butterworths, 2nd edn, 1989)

Tapper, C *Computer Law* (London: Longman, 4th edn, 1989)

REPORTS

The Whitford Committee *Copyright - Copyright and Design Law* Cmnd 6732 (London: HMSO, 1977)

The Law Commission, Law Comm No 110 *Breach of Confidence* Cmnd 8388 (London: HMSO, 1981)

Intellectual Property and Innovation Cmnd 9712 (London: HMSO, 1986)

Intellectual Property Rights and Innovation Cmnd 9117 (London: HMSO, 1983)

Reform of the Law Relating to Copyright, Designs and Performers' Protection Cmnd 8302 (London: HMSO, 1981)

JOURNAL ARTICLES

Anon 'Appellate Court gives Green Light to Reverse Engineering' (1991) 2 *Intellectual Property in Business Briefing* 3

Archer, Q 'Transatlantic Co-operation and the Microsoft Case' [1996] 12 *Computer Law and Security Report* 101

Bainbridge, D I 'Computer Programs and Copyright: More Exceptions to Infringement' [1993] 56 *Modern Law Review* 591

Bainbridge, D I 'The Copyright Act: a legal red herring' (1989) 1(8) *Computer Bulletin* 21

Bender, D 'Computer Programs: Should They Be Patentable?' (1968) 68 *Columbia Law Review* 241

Benson, J R 'Copyright Protection for Computer Screen Displays' (1988) 72 *Minnesota Law Review* 1123

Cameron, J 'Approaches to the Problems of Multimedia' [1996] 3 *European Intellectual Property Review* 115

Chalton, S 'Implementation of the Software Directive in the United Kingdom: The Effects of the Copyright (Computer Programs) Regulations 1992' [1993] 9 *Computer Law and Security Report* 115

Chalton, S 'The Amended Database Directive Proposal: A Commentary and Synopsis' [1994] 3 *European Intellectual Property Review* 94

Cornish, W R 'Interoperable Systems and Copyright' [1989] 11 *European Intellectual Property Review* 391

Davidson, D M 'Protecting Computer Software: A Comprehensive Analysis' (1983) 23(4) *Jurimetrics Journal* 337

Goldblatt, M 'Copyright Protection for Computer Programs in Australia: the Law since Autodesk' [1990] 5 *European Intellectual Property Review* 170

Grewal, M 'Copyright Protection of Computer Software' [1996] 8 *European Intellectual Property Review* 454

Hart, R J 'Applications of Patents to Computer Technology - UK and the EPO Harmonisation?' [1989] 2 *European Intellectual Property Review* 42

Hayes, D 'Software Copyright' (in parts) [1996] 12 *Computer Law and Security Report* 14, 66, 134, 214 and 270

Hoffman, G, Grossman, J, Keane, P and Westby, J 'Protection for Computer Software: An International Overview: Part 2' [1989] 1 *European Intellectual Property Review* 7

Kelman, A 'Certainty of Rights in the Information Society' [1996] 12 *Computer Law and Security Report* 294

Kurtz, L A 'Copyright and the National Information Infrastructure in the United States' [1996] 3 *European Intellectual Property Review* 120

Lea, G 'Database Law - Solutions beyond Copyright' [1993] 9 *Computer Law and Security Report* 127

Lea, G 'Passing Off and the Protection of Program Look and Feel' [1994] 10 *Computer Law and Security Report* 82

Monotti, A 'The Extent of Copyright Protection for Compilations of Artistic Works' [1993] 5 *European Intellectual Property Review* 156

Pearson, H 'Information in a Digital Age - the Challenge to Copyright' [1996] 12 *Computer Law and Security Report* 90

Rumphorst, W 'Fine-tuning Copyright for the Information Society' [1996] 2 *European Intellectual Property Review* 79

Taylor, W D 'Copyright Protection for Computer Software after *Whelan Associates v Jaslow Dental Laboratory*' (1989) 54 *Missouri Law Review* 121

Worthy, J 'Reverse Engineering and Clean Room Procedures – A Way of Avoiding Infringement' [1994] 10 *Computer Law and Security Report* 123

Worthy, J & Weightman, E 'Exploiting Commercial Information: A Legal Status Report' [1996] 12 *Computer Law and Security Report* 95

Index